PRAYERS
THAT HEAL THE
Heart

—— REVISED & EXPANDED ——

— REVISED & EXPANDED —

MARK & PATTI VIRKLER

Newberry, FL 32669

Bridge-Logos
Newberry, FL 32669

**Prayers That Heal the Heart, Revised and Expanded:
Prayer Counseling That Breaks Every Yoke**
by Mark & Patti Virkler

Copyright ©1999 by Mark and Patti Virkler

Revised Edition Copyright © 2021 by Mark and Patti Virkler

All rights reserved. Under International Copyright Law, no part of this publication may be reproduced, stored, or transmitted by any means—electronic, mechanical, photographic (photocopy), recording, or otherwise—without written permission from the publisher.

Printed in the United States of America.

Library of Congress Control Number: 2020949844

International Standard Book Number: 978-1-61036-258-0

Editing services by ChristianEditingServices.com

Cover/Interior design by Kent Jensen | knail.com

Scripture quotations are taken from the King James Version of the Bible.

Scripture quotations are also taken from the New American Standard Version of the Bible. Copyright © 1960, 1962, 1963, 1968, 1971, 1972, 1973, 1975, 1977 by the Lockman Foundation. Used by permission.

Scripture quotations marked NLT are taken from the Holy Bible, New Living Translation, copyright ©1996, 2004, 2007, 2013, 2015 by Tyndale House Foundation. Used by permission of Tyndale House Publishers, Inc., Carol Stream, Illinois 60188. All rights reserved.

Scripture quotations marked NKJV are taken from the New King James Version. Copyright © 1994 by Harper Collins. Used by permission. All rights reserved.

DEDICATION

This book is dedicated to those presenting various healing models each incorporating divine encounter. The group below was drawn together by Cathy Little and Melinda Wilson of Face to Face Ministries.

- Restoring the Foundations—restoringthefoundations.org
- Elijah House Ministries—elijahouseministries.org
- Bethel Sozo—bethelsozo.com
- Rita Bennett Ministries—emotionallyfree.org
- Face to Face Ministries—facetofaceministries.org
- Christian Healing Ministries—christianhealingmin.org
- Immanuel Approach—immanuelapproach.com
- Jim and Pat Banks Ministries—jimandpatbanks.com
- Communion With God Ministries—cwgministries.org
- Shiloh Place Ministries—shilohplace.org
- HeartSync Ministries—heartsyncministries.org
- Ellel Ministries—ellel.org/uk/about/ellel-grange

FOREWORD

In 2003 I had just embarked upon my journey of inner healing. A Christian for twenty-seven years at the time, I had already experienced a level of emotional healing. Still, now the Lord was taking me on a further journey. A friend had given me the book, *Prayers That Heal the Heart*. I read it with great enthusiasm and was eager to learn how to apply its principles, but I have to admit that I wasn't entirely sure how it worked. When I heard that the author would be teaching the material in a live seminar, I jumped at the chance to go.

As Mark presented the need to hear God's voice and use the eyes of our heart, everything I had read in the book fell into place, and I was able to experience the power and efficacy of the seven prayers.

I didn't know that this would ignite a flame in my heart to see others receive healing the way I had that would burn brightly for years to come. I only knew then that *Prayers That Heal the Heart* had led me through the process of getting set free from shame. My book, *Leaving Home—Finding Home: My Journey From Shame to Sonship Through Journaling*, chronicled that healing and the integral part that *Prayers That Heal the Heart* played in it.

Since then, it has been my privilege to count Mark as a spiritual advisor and friend. I was all too happy to help when

FOREWORD

he invited me to give feedback on this revision to *Prayers That Heal the Heart*. What he and Patti have produced is an even more powerful tool for healing.

In the first chapter, the authors lay out the foundation for healing: connecting deeply with the Father and experiencing His love through hearing His voice. Each subsequent chapter will take you deeper into a solid Biblical understanding of the wounded heart and God's provision for healing. A few new sections have been added, notably, chapters on physical healing and trauma.

Among other things, you will learn the language of the heart, the necessity for confession, repentance and forgiveness, and the graciousness of God to replace ashes with beauty.

The journaling exercises and prayer assignments will provide practical applications of what you are reading and deepen your understanding of what is going on in your heart.

This book is full of scriptural principles and definitions that will inform your journey to healing and wholeness and is presented in simple terms for the layman and the practitioner alike.

Today I am a prayer counselor with my own ministry. *Prayers That Heal the Heart* is an invaluable tool that I regularly use to help clients get set free to be and do all that God has called them to be and do. I see amazing results as we pray through generational sins and curses, ungodly soul ties, negative beliefs and inner vows, word curses, traumatic memories and demonic oppression.

Over the years, I have used the principles and teachings of this book to pray through my own heart issues as the Holy Spirit has led.

Whether you are new to inner healing as I was in 2003 or have gone through much healing, this way of praying WILL revolutionize your life. One student told me that after 20+ years of her healing journey, she experienced what she called a "great spiritual tidying up" due to *Prayers That Heal the Heart*.

I encourage you to take a deep dive into this new and enhanced edition. I am confident that it will be a well-worn resource in your library.

—Jessie Mejias
Sunodía Prayer Counseling
sunodia.org

ACKNOWLEDGEMENTS

Special thanks to our contributing writers which include: Jim Banks from Jim and Pat Banks Ministries, Dawna De Silva from Bethel Sozo Ministries, Rochelle Holben from Elijah House Ministries, Karl Lehman and Kent Larson from Immanuel Approach.

Special thanks to Steve and Kay Cox, Bill and Sue Banks, Dennis and Rita Bennett—founders of Christian Renewal Association, Peter Horrobin—founder of Ellel Ministries, Chester and Betsy Kylstra—founders of Restoring the Foundations, John and Paula Sandford—founders of Elijah House and Francis and Judith MacNutt—founders of Christian Healing Ministry. Each of these ministries has provided a stimulus in the writing of this book.

Special thanks to Gale Chapple and her counselees who allowed us to test out these principles in their counseling sessions. Special thanks to those who helped critique this book. This includes Paul Stanton, Patty Sadallah and Jessie Mejias, and to Michael Sullivant who helped widen my understanding.

Thank you all for your friendship and your amazing contributions to the body of Christ. To any others whom I may have forgotten to mention, special thanks to you as well.

Experience salvation, God's greatest gift—
www.bornofthespirit.today

ENDORSEMENTS

"In their book, *Prayers That Heal the Heart*, Mark and Patti Virkler give us valuable practical tools for applying the teachings so many of us have pioneered in inner healing and deliverance. Much has been discovered. What has been lacking is how the common man can apply inner healing revelations to his own life. Some have wanted healing to happen sovereignly, by God's intervention, or through the prayers of others (requiring little personal effort), and sometimes it does occur those ways. But we who are in the inner healing ministry have long wanted tools to help those who know that healing often requires diligent personally disciplined efforts. Mark and Patti's book goes a long way towards filling that 'how-to' gap. Their book is really a workbook, an invaluable hand-out for counselors to assign to their counselees. Much healing and transformation can result from its use."

—JOHN SANDFORD, Co-founder of Elijah House

"A person who is sick and doesn't know it will never go to a doctor. A Christian who is crippled on the inside but who thinks his life is normal will never ask for help! Many Christians struggle with major issues in their life but are ignorant of the fact that the victory Jesus won for them on the cross does not only assure them of eternal salvation, but also provides the keys to healing.

ENDORSEMENTS

"Mark Virkler's new book is a very practical guide to how the keys to healing that are contained within Scripture can be applied with great effect in the life of a believer. His own testimony illustrates how God brought deep healing into his own life as he looked again at the consequences of things that had happened in earlier days and was willing to let God have His way.

The road to healing is not, however, a road without choices. Some of the choices are like cross-roads with different ways to go—do I go this way or that way? Am I willing to forgive or not forgive? Am I willing to own mistakes I have made or am I going to sweep them under the carpet? Am I going to admit to the consequences of wrong relationships or pretend they never happened? Have I really understood that in life there is a law of sowing and reaping? These and many other issues are tackled with sensitivity and genuine insight and in such a practical way that the teaching can be readily applied.

"An excellent book which will encourage pastors and people alike to begin a journey towards wholeness and realize that discipleship and healing are two facets of the same precious diamond of truth."

—PETER HORROBIN, International Director of Ellel Ministries
Ellel Grange, England

"Mark and Patti have creatively and concisely expressed the Lord's revelations to them, to us, and to others. We are delighted that the revelation, understanding, and necessity for the Integrated Approach to Ministry will be shared even more broadly throughout the Body of Christ. The Virklers have expressed these revelations in a very user-friendly and practical way. With the exercises and worksheets, anyone that desires can use these tools to receive more healing and freedom from the Lord. This is His Heart, that our hearts be healed."

—CHESTER AND BETSY KYLSTRA, Founders and Overseers of Proclaiming His Word Ministries

This book, *Prayers That Heal the Heart*, is another confirmation that experience is indeed the best teacher. Mark's personal experience has provided needed insight and has paved a very practical way for people to become healed from the wounds, bondages and mindsets that accompany the ups and downs of life. I am particularly thankful for the worksheets and exercises provided that help individuals thoroughly process their way through each element of the healing process. Well done!

—JIM BANKS, Founder of Jim and Pat Banks Ministries

For those who have not been trained to hear God's voice, this book is a must buy! In it you will find 7 interlocking prayers to experience thorough healing of the heart and practical worksheets making each step easy to follow and apply. Once you understand God is interested in connecting with you, you will be able to allow the Holy Spirit to lead you into freedom!

—DAWNA DE SILVA, Founder and Co-Leader of Bethel Sozo betheltransformationcenter.com, Author of *Sozo: Saved, Healed, Delivered, Shifting Atmospheres, Overcoming Fear, 90 Day Declarations,* and *Warring With Wisdom*

ENDORSEMENTS

Mark Virkler's book is a foundational healing resource which I heartily recommend. As a veteran of inner healing, as a recipient, a student, a teacher and now a trainer of prayer ministers, one of the most important concepts in heart healing is that healing doesn't happen outside of relationship. This book makes that clear. Learning to receive and experience God's love as a right hemisphere brain experience is not only necessary, but vital for true healing to occur. Dr. Virkler lays out simple but powerful tools which guide people into transformational encounters with the tangible love of God. When done in partnership with a praying friend or guide, the process carries even greater effectiveness. I appreciate this book and highly recommend it to anyone desiring to receive healing for themselves or help others.

—MELINDA WILSON, Co-Founder and Director
Face to Face Ministries, facetofaceministries.org

Dr. Mark Virkler is one of the most gifted authors and teachers of our day with a powerful anointing to brilliantly boil down big concepts of the Christian life into simple and accessible bites. In *Prayers That Heal the Heart*, he beautifully lays out proven tools for the reader to experience greater emotional freedom—prayers that will move you from places of fear, doubt, anger, and unbelief into true joy, peace, love, and gratitude. This book is a beautiful companion for your healing journey.

—CATHY LITTLE, Co-Director, Face to Face Ministries

TABLE OF CONTENTS

Dedication v
Foreword vi
Acknowledgements ix
Endorsements x
Prologue xvi

PART ONE

Healing Begins by Experiencing the Father's Love 1
How Do I Minister Effectively to a Wounded Heart? 15
Breaking Generational Sins and Curses 33
Severing Ungodly Soul Ties 51
Renouncing Unbiblical Beliefs and Inner Vows 64
Replacing Ungodly Beliefs with Godly Beliefs 84
Replacing Word Curses with Blessings 97
Traumatic Pictures Healed Through Inner Healing 111
Delivered From Demons 124
Maintaining the Victory by Staying Filled
   with the Holy Spirit 139
Clearing Cellular Memories 154
The "Trauma Prayer" 165

The Kingdom Lifestyle 185
Pray for One Another 201
Tips for the Prayer Minister 216

PART TWO

Additional Ways God Heals by Kay Cox 232
Available Training Packages for Prayers That Heal the Heart 244
Bible Meditation on Judging 247
Bible Meditation on Sex 259
Common Demon Groupings 265
Contributions from John Sandford and
   Elijah House Ministries 270
Extended Journaling Quickens the Healing Process 273
Freedom in Sozo by Dawna De Silva 276
How Often Did Jesus Minister Deliverance? 285
How to Hear God's Voice 290
Immanuel Approach to Heart Healing by Kent Larson 292
Immanuel Journaling to Heal Painful
   Feelings/Memories by Kent Larson 297
Impassioned Repentance Removes Blockages 301
Impassioned Repentance Worksheet on Lust 304
Inner Healing for an Organ Prayer Worksheet 316
Inner Healing for Hellish Situations 321
Ungodly Beliefs Worksheet–Completed Sample 324
Ungodly Beliefs Worksheet–To Complete 326
What If I Get Stuck? 328

PROLOGUE—MY HEALING IN AUSTRALIA

TOUCHDOWN

Our plane landed at 6:00 A.M. in Sydney, Australia. It was the last day of August and the weather was still warm. The entire city was under construction, as in just twelve months the 2000 Olympics would be held here. My wife Patti and I spent the day sightseeing, taking in a bus tour of the city and a two-and-a-half hour boat tour of the beautiful Sydney Harbor. We hoped that if we stayed up all day we would be able to sleep in the evening and get our body clocks readjusted from Buffalo, NY time, which was a full 14 hours different than Sydney time.

It worked. We slept the entire night and were ready the next day for a two-hour drive to Newcastle, where I would begin the first of five ten-hour Hearing God's Voice training seminars in five different cities in Australia.

This was my fifth trip to Australia in twelve years. Peacemakers Ministries had published our book Communion with God as well as other titles in Australia, and had been responsible for scheduling four of the five tours in Australia, including this one.

As I prepared for the first seminar at Church at the Bay, I was aware of the inner tension in my heart, which had seemed to grow stronger in recent years. I struggled with fear and doubt and anger when I prepared to speak. I fought against them and sought to prepare my heart so I could speak and teach in the anointing of the Holy Spirit.

I could teach in the anointing of the Holy Spirit—that is what everyone always said. They would tell me that the teaching was so life-giving and so transforming that everyone came out of the seminars hearing God's voice and journaling and seeing vision. They were such exciting times, watching the transformation take place in people's lives. I loved it. And I loved the fact that God had allowed me the privilege of committing my life's ministry to seeing this happen over and over with audiences around the world. What a wonderful opportunity to minister unto God in such a marvelous way! I truly felt I was blessed to be called by God to carry such a message to the world as communion with Him.

However, I was increasingly disturbed by the fact that it took longer and longer to fight through the issues in my heart so that I would be ready to minister. Over the last year especially, I had struggled with a fear that people would reject the message I generally spoke on Sunday mornings entitled "Experiencing Covenant Blessings." During the worship time before I preached, I would battle with this fear of rejection and bind it and command it to go. Eventually faith would triumph and, sure enough, as soon as I began to preach, I was fine. The message was anointed, people were challenged and transformed by it, and everything was okay.

However, it was not okay with me that the battle seemed to have become more and more intense within my heart as I prepared to preach this message. Somehow I knew I did not have the faith and confidence that I had had in my younger years, when I was in my twenties—not that I was old then or anything like that! I was *only* 47, you see.

In my twenties, I would attack and battle anything with no fear—probably because I had no common sense! Now that I had "matured," I had learned that there were things to fear. "Things to be cautious about," was the way I put it. My caution, however, was actually a constant inner battle against fear and anger and rejection.

It seemed like everything made me angry. When things didn't go right, I felt anger. When I "goofed up," I felt anger. When I heard about the antics of the government, I felt anger. When I viewed the phariseeism in the Church, I felt extreme anger. The fear of the New Age Movement (and anything and everything else) that the Church manifests made me angry. Was the Church called to live in fear or in faith? Faith, obviously, and so I stormed against their fear as I preached in city after city.

I was not too happy, however, with the inner anguish I was experiencing. I sensed I was "damaged goods," that life had dealt me some fairly heavy blows and my heart was not open and free as it had been in my younger years. Well, perhaps that was just the way life was. Perhaps as you grew older and wiser, you realized that life was not the utopia you had hoped it would be when you were young. Perhaps maturity was acknowledging the pain and the disappointments, and learning to live in an imperfect world, holding on as best you could. Perhaps I was just finally growing up.

Well, perhaps, but perhaps not, for you see the Lord was preparing me for big change. Just before leaving for Australia, I had finished writing a book that capsulized the lessons God had taught me during my 32 years as a Christian. One of the things I had reviewed in Chapter Four of this book, *Wading Deeper In The River Of God*, was the ways God heals the heart. I had reviewed what I had learned over the years concerning inner healing, deliverance, renouncing negative expectations and inner vows, and breaking generational sins and curses. In addition, just a week before leaving for Australia, I had discovered from my mom that her father, my grandfather, was a Mason.

I was coming to the conclusion that perhaps I needed prayer ministry to heal some of these things in my heart. God's grace and leading always astound and amaze me! Not only was there a brand new book on Peacemakers' book table detailing how to become free from the generational power of Freemasonry, but at the first church I preached at in Australia, I met a surgeon, Stephen Cox, who told me how he and his wife work together in ministering to his patients. His wife, Kay, is extremely skilled in ministering inner healing, deliverance, and the breaking of generational sins and curses. He told me of one of his patients who had gone through two or three surgeries for abdominal pain, yet no one had been able to find the root cause. He asked this patient if she would like Kay to pray with her. She agreed, so Kay asked her, "When did the pain begin?" She answered, "About five years ago." Kay's next question was, "What did you do five years ago?" She replied, "I had my tarot cards read." A quick renunciation and prayer of deliverance brought this patient to health and canceled her need for future surgery.

Stephen joked that he is careful not to give all his patients to his wife for prayer ministry or he wouldn't have a job anymore!

That was enough for me. With my inner battle against

anger, fear, and doubt, and eighteen days of constant teaching set before me, I asked what I should have asked for a few years earlier: "Is there any chance you and your wife could get together and pray for me?" The answer was immediate and affirmative. I was thrilled. The following day, Sunday afternoon after I had preached, we got together and Steve and Kay prayed for two-and-a-half hours with me.

Kay was the most anointed, effective, Spirit-led minister from whom I have ever had the privilege of receiving ministry. With an adeptness and skill that took my breath away, she identified various demons, negative expectations, and inner vows, along with generational sins, which we broke and of which I repented.

That day I was set free from various generational sins and curses, several inner vows and negative expectations, and about half a dozen demons. The change was powerful and instantaneous. I preached that night with a new freedom, a freedom I had never had in my entire 30 years of ministry, since some of these inner spiritual forces had been with me since birth. And some, of course, I had picked up in more recent years.

My new-found freedom lasted the entire 18-day ministry tour in Australia, and continues today. I was astounded! I am astounded—over several things. One is that I have experienced such a wonderful new freedom in my heart in the areas in which I received deliverance. These were problems I had battled for years and just assumed they were a part of who I was. I figured they were a part of the battle of life. And now I found that they were negative spiritual forces operating within me and seeking to bring me down.

PROLOGUE

How could I, as a Spirit-filled pastor and teacher in the body of Christ, make such a horrific mistake? How could I assume that these things were *me*, when in actuality they were demons within me? How could I be so unaware of the reality of spiritual forces within me, especially since I had ministered deliverance and inner healing to hundreds, if not thousands, myself? How could I have battled these things, using ineffective prayers that did not solve the problems but only put a Band-Aid on them for a short time? How could I have been so blind?

I was elated over my healing, but aghast at the spiritual blindness which had allowed me to walk for so many years under the influence of negative spiritual energies within my heart and my soul. I knew I must search out and discover what I had failed to see. I realized I needed to experience an even deeper revelation of a truth I had written about years earlier, the truth that I am a vessel who contains another. Most of what goes on inside me is not me but the one I contain. The negative energies within me are driven by the sin energies of the curse and/or demons. The positive energies are empowered by the blessing and Holy Spirit of God.[1]

Since I am a teacher, I wanted to share with others the story of my healing and my new understandings so they would not need to walk in bondage as I had.

I began by rereading the books on my shelves on inner healing, deliverance, breaking generational sins, and renouncing inner vows and negative expectations, for I was sure these all worked together to destroy a life, and that the counselor who would heal must use them all together in order to be mightily effective.

I re-read *The Transformation of the Inner Man* by John and Paula Sandford, *Restoring the Foundations* by Chester and Betsy Kylstra, *Healing Through Deliverance* by Peter Horrobin, *Healing From the Inside Out* by Tom Marshall, and others.

I meditated and prayed, dialogued with these authors, and then wrote my story of what God was showing me so I would not be easily caught in this trap again, and so I could help others who were likewise in bondage to find the release and healing I had found. That is what this book is about. It is what I have discovered about how to determine one's need for such prayer ministries, what these ministries are, and how to progress through them. The design is practical, and has examples to help you throughout the material. As I come to the sections that discuss the different kinds of healing prayer, I will describe in more detail my own personal healing as it relates to the area being discussed.

I will try to be extremely practical, so an individual or a small group can pray through these different kinds of prayers and receive ministry themselves. Obviously, if one can receive ministry from a skilled counselor who knows all these types of prayer ministries and can minister them under the anointing and guidance of the Holy Spirit, that is by far the best. However, if that kind of person cannot be accessed for one reason or another, then this book becomes a place to start in praying these prayers for yourself and for others in your small group.

We have extended teaching articles on our website for those who want to go deeper on certain subjects and often refer the interested reader to those specific blogs.

PRIDE AND RECEIVING MINISTRY FROM A STRANGER

Was it easier for me to receive ministry from a complete stranger in Australia than it was from someone I know? Perhaps. I suppose we always like to think we have it all together and to project that image. To admit that we are not seems hard for some reason. Perhaps we want to be able to say we have reached some outstanding spiritual level in our Christian walk, and to admit that we still have such negative energies harassing us just seems to be unspiritual.

Well, I have decided that it is best if I simply accept the fact that I am a saint who still sometimes sins. Without a daily dose of God's almighty grace to sustain me, I am nothing. I am content with that. If you need me to be more than that, then I will have to disappoint you. If I need me to be more than that, then I will just have to disappoint myself. Perhaps, however, being a vessel filled and sustained daily with the grace of God is a sufficient function for people. Perhaps I should be more than content that this miracle can happen on a daily basis. Perhaps I should be glad to simply celebrate this wonderful miracle and let it go at that.

HEALING PRAYERS WE WILL LEARN ABOUT IN FUTURE CHAPTERS

1. Breaking generational sins and curses by putting the cross of Jesus between the generations (Ex. 20:4-6).
2. Identifying and renouncing ungodly soul ties.
3. Identifying and renouncing negative expectations and replacing them with godly expectations.
4. Identifying and renouncing inner vows (underlying promises

you have made because of the hurts you have experienced). Replacing these with godly purposes.
5. Experiencing inner healing, allowing Jesus to walk through the art gallery of your heart, removing pictures which do not have Him in them and replacing them with pictures which do have Him in them.
6. Replacing word curses by speaking blessing.
7. Experiencing deliverance, becoming free of demons in the name of Jesus Christ. Once the demons' home is dismantled by the preceding six steps, demons come out quite easily.

PERSONAL JOURNALING APPLICATION

1. Are there any areas of your heart or mind that are under constant attack by the enemy? Do you fight with negatives in any area of your life? Is this a continual battle? If so, it is likely an area that could be helped with some prayer ministry.
2. Have you ever experienced inner healing, deliverance, or any of the other prayer ministries mentioned in this chapter? If so, can you recall and describe the situation and the release it brought to your life?
3. Are there any areas in your life today that might be improved if you experienced more prayer ministry?

GROUP APPLICATION

1. Invite people to share their answers to the above questions as they feel comfortable doing so. Do not force anyone to share what they do not feel ready to.
2. Pray at least a general prayer for God's sustaining grace to minister to the needs of those who share. If you have

someone skilled in the prayer ministries discussed in this book, that person may feel led to pray more specifically for an individual in the group. If there is an individual in the group who desires such prayer ministry even this first week, invite him or her to volunteer and, as long as you have one in the group trained in at least one of these prayer approaches, that one, along with the group, may minister to the volunteer.
3. Close in worship for what God has done.

ENDNOTE

1. See *Naturally Supernatural* by the same author.

PART One

Chapter One

HEALING BEGINS BY EXPERIENCING THE FATHER'S LOVE

Jesus is the "Wonderful Counselor."

His name will be called Wonderful Counselor, Mighty God, Eternal Father, Prince of Peace. (Isaiah 9:6)

Hearing the voice of my Wonderful Counselor was for me, and many others, the key to experiencing the Father's love. For the first ten years of my Christian life, I was not able to identify God's voice within me, even though He was speaking to me. So to me, God was distant and harsh and legalistic. I discovered so many laws in the Bible and I just couldn't keep them all, even though I utilized all the strength my flesh could muster (Rom. 7:5). I was failing and I felt condemned. The verse, "there is no condemnation to those who are in Christ Jesus" just was not working for me (Rom. 8:1).

That all changed the day I learned to hear His voice. It was so exciting that I spent five hours that day writing out what the Lord was speaking to me. My biggest discovery was how much He loved me. It was the first time I had touched unconditional, incomprehensible love (Rom. 5:5; Eph. 3:17-19). It blew me away.

My heavenly Father's love for me was so much stronger and more compassionate than my love for myself. He actually taught me how to love myself and, as a result, how to love others. He told me to observe how tenderly He loved me. I did, and it was astounding. When I was beating on myself for failing, He wasn't. He said to me, "It's just a learning curve mistake. No big deal. Let's press on." I was experiencing the Father's love! You will, too, as you learn how to hear His voice and do two-way journaling. So let's dig right in to the four keys God taught me that day. Two-way journaling transformed me, my marriage, my relationship with others, my preaching, and everything I did.

Hearing from Him is key to healing our hearts. In this chapter we will teach you four very simple keys that will allow you to enter into a two-way journaling dialogue with Jesus, where He provides wonderful counsel. **The four keys are: stop, look, listen and write.**

WHEN I LEARNED TO HEAR HIS VOICE

During the years we had a ministering household my wife simply couldn't handle all the work on her own. Our ministering household included remnants of three struggling families plus our own toddler and newborn. Everyone had to pull their own weight. At fourteen, Rachel and her younger brother were living with us while her parents tried to overcome lifestyle patterns that had resulted in the children running away to escape the dysfunction. I felt sorry for Rachel, but, honestly my wife was my greatest concern.

When Rachel once again ignored her chores to spend time with her friends, I decided it was time to lay down the law and make it very clear that if she was going to live under my roof, she would obey my rules.

But…she wasn't home yet. And I had recently been learning to hear God's voice more clearly. Maybe I should try to see if I could hear anything from Him about the situation. Maybe He could give me a way to get her to do what she was supposed to (i.e. what I wanted her to do). So I went to my office and reviewed what the Lord had been teaching me from Habakkuk 2:1,2: "I will stand on my guard post and station myself on the rampart; And I will keep watch to see what He will speak to me…Then the Lord answered me and said, 'Record the vision….'"

A KEY—STILLNESS

Habakkuk said, "I will stand on my guard post…" (Hab. 2:1). **The first key to hearing God's voice is to go to a quiet place and still our own thoughts and emotions.** Psalm 46:10 encourages us to be still, let go, cease striving, and know that He is God. In Psalm 37:7 we are called to "be still before the Lord and wait patiently for Him." There is a deep inner knowing in our spirits that each of us can experience when we quiet our flesh and our minds. Practicing the art of biblical meditation helps silence the outer noise and distractions clamoring for our attention.

I didn't have a guard post but I did have an office, so I went there to quiet my temper and my mind. If you don't have an office or a room you can go to which is private, you may find it necessary to drive to a quiet place without your telephone, so it is just you and God.

Loving God through a quiet worship song is one very effective way to become still. In 2 Kings 3, Elisha needed a word from the Lord so he said, "Bring me a minstrel," and as the minstrel played, the Lord spoke. I have found that playing a worship song on my autoharp is the quickest way for me to come to stillness. I need to choose my song carefully; boisterous songs of praise do not bring me to stillness, but rather gentle songs that express my love and worship. And it isn't enough just to sing into the cosmos—I come into the Lord's presence most quickly and easily when I use my godly imagination to see the truth that He is right here with me and I sing my songs to Him, personally.

Along with quieting through soothing worship songs, it's also important to begin with gratitude. Psalm 100:4 instructs us to, "Enter His gates with thanksgiving and His courts with praise. Give thanks to Him, bless His name." Practicing gratitude daily will get us in touch with God's goodness towards us, and according to Dr. Karl Lehman, "We have circuits in our brains that serve as the neurological hardware for running relationships, and we can connect with each other and with God much more easily when these relational circuits are online and strongly active. Furthermore, we can predictably, reliably, consistently get these relational circuits online and strongly active by recalling and connecting with positive memories, and then deliberately generating, or stirring up, strong appreciation. Therefore, deliberately stirring up gratitude will activate our brain/mind/spirit system and the relational parts of our brains so we can hear and receive more easily from God." As we enter into His presence with quieting and gratitude, we are ready for the second key to hearing His voice.

A KEY—FIXING MY EYES ON JESUS

"I will keep watch to see," said the prophet. To receive the pure word of God, it is very important that my heart be properly focused as I become still, because my focus is the source of the intuitive flow. If I fix my eyes upon Jesus (Heb. 12:2), the intuitive flow comes from Jesus. But if I fix my gaze upon some desire of my heart, the intuitive flow comes out of that desire. To have a pure flow I must become still and carefully fix my eyes upon Jesus. Quietly worshiping the King and receiving out of the stillness that follows quite easily accomplishes this.

So I used **the second key to hearing God's voice: As you pray, fix the eyes of your heart upon Jesus, seeing in the Spirit the dreams and visions of Almighty God.** Habakkuk was actually looking for vision as he prayed. He opened the eyes of his heart, and looked into the spirit world to see what God wanted to show him.

God has always spoken through dreams and visions, and He specifically said that they would come to those upon whom the Holy Spirit is poured out (Acts 2:1-4, 17).

Being a logical, rational person, observable facts that could be verified by my physical senses were the foundations of my life, including my spiritual life. I had never thought of opening the eyes of my heart and looking for vision. However, I have come to believe that this is exactly what God wants me to do. He gave me eyes in my heart to see in the spirit the vision and movement of Almighty God. There is an active spirit world all around us, full of angels, demons, the Holy Spirit, the omnipresent Father, and His omnipresent Son, Jesus. The only reasons for me not to see this reality are unbelief or lack of knowledge.

In his sermon in Acts 2:25, Peter refers to King David's statement: "I saw the Lord always in my presence; for He is at my right hand, so that I will not be shaken." The original psalm makes it clear that this was a decision of David's, not a constant supernatural visitation: "I have set (literally, I have placed) the Lord continually before me; because He is at my right hand, I will not be shaken" (Ps.16:8). Because David knew that the Lord was always with him, he determined in his spirit to see that truth with the eyes of his heart as he went through life, knowing that this would keep his faith strong.

In order to see, we must look. Daniel saw a vision in his mind and said, "I was looking...I kept looking...I kept looking" (Dan. 7:2, 9, 13). As I pray, I look for Jesus, and I watch as He speaks to me, doing and saying the things that are on His heart. Many Christians will find that if they will only look, they will see. Jesus is Emmanuel, God with us (Matt. 1:23). It is as simple as that. You can see Christ present with you because Christ *is* present with you. In fact, the vision may come so easily that you will be tempted to reject it, thinking that it is just you. But if you persist in recording these visions, your doubt will soon be overcome by faith as you recognize that the content of them could only be birthed in Almighty God.

Jesus demonstrated the ability of living out of constant contact with God, declaring that He did nothing on His own initiative, but only what He saw the Father doing, and heard the Father saying (Jn. 5:19,20,30). What an incredible way to live!

Is it possible for us to live out of divine initiative as Jesus did? Yes! We must simply fix our eyes upon Jesus. The veil has been torn, giving access into the immediate presence of God, and He calls us to draw near (Lk. 23:45; Heb. 10:19-22). "I pray that the eyes of your heart will be enlightened…."

When I had quieted my heart enough that I was able to picture Jesus without the distractions of my own ideas and plans, I was able to "keep watch to see what He will speak to me." I wrote down my question: "Lord, what should I do about Rachel?"

A KEY—TUNE TO FLOWING THOUGHTS

Immediately the thought came to me, "She is insecure." Well, that certainly wasn't my thought! Her behavior looked like rebellion to me, not insecurity.

But like Habakkuk, I was coming to know the sound of God speaking to me (Hab. 2:2). Elijah described it as a still, small voice (I Kings 19:12). I had previously listened for an inner audible voice, and God does speak that way at times. However, I have found that usually, God's voice comes as spontaneous thoughts, visions, feelings, or impressions.

For example, haven't you been driving down the road and had a thought come to you to pray for a certain person? Didn't you believe it was God telling you to pray? What did God's voice sound like? Was it an audible voice, or was it a spontaneous thought that dropped into your mind?

Experience indicates that we perceive spirit-level communication as spontaneous thoughts, impressions and visions, and Scripture confirms this in many ways. For example, one definition of *paga*, a Hebrew word for intercession, is "a chance encounter or an accidental intersecting." When God lays people on our hearts, He does it through paga, a chance-encounter thought "accidentally" intersecting our minds.

So **the third key to hearing God's voice is recognizing that God's voice in your heart often sounds like a flow of spontaneous thoughts.** Therefore, when I want to hear from God, I tune to chance-encounter or spontaneous thoughts.

A KEY—TWO-WAY JOURNALING

Finally, God told Habakkuk to record the vision (Hab. 2:2). This was not an isolated command. The Scriptures record many examples of individual's prayers and God's replies, such as the Psalms, many of the prophets, and Revelation. I have found that obeying this final principle amplified my confidence in my ability to hear God's voice so that I could finally make living out of His initiatives a way of life. The **fourth key, two-way journaling, or the writing out of your prayers and God's answers, brings great freedom in hearing God's voice.**

I have found two-way journaling to be a fabulous catalyst for clearly discerning God's inner, spontaneous flow, because as I journal I am able to write in faith for long periods of time, simply believing it is God. What I believe I have received from God must be tested. However, testing involves doubt and doubt blocks divine communication, so I do not want to test while I am trying to receive. (See James 1:5-8.) With journaling, I can receive in faith, knowing that when the flow has ended I can test and examine it carefully.

So I wrote down what I believed He had said: "She is insecure."

But the Lord wasn't done. I continued to write the spontaneous thoughts that came to me: "Love her unconditionally. She is flesh of your flesh and bone of your bone."

My mind immediately objected: She is not flesh of my flesh. She is not related to me at all—she is a foster child, just living in my home temporarily. It was definitely time to test this "word from the Lord"!

There are three possible sources of thoughts in our minds: ourselves, satan and the Holy Spirit. It was obvious that the words in my journal did not come from my own mind—I certainly didn't see her as insecure or flesh of my flesh. And I sincerely doubted that satan would encourage me to love anyone unconditionally!

Okay, it was starting to look like I might have actually received counsel from the Lord. It was consistent with the names and character of God as revealed in the Scripture, and totally contrary to the names and character of the enemy. So that meant that I was hearing from the Lord, and He wanted me to see the situation in a different light. Rachel was my daughter—part of my family not by blood but by the hand of God Himself. The chaos of her birth home had created deep insecurity about her worthiness to be loved by anyone, including me and including God. Only the unconditional love of the Lord expressed through an imperfect human would reach her heart.

But there was still one more test I needed to perform before I would have absolute confidence that this was truly God's word to me: I needed confirmation from someone else whose spiritual discernment I trusted. So I went to my wife and shared what I had received. I knew if I could get her validation, especially since she was the one most wronged in the situation, then I could say, at least to myself, "Thus sayeth the Lord."

Needless to say, Patti immediately and without question confirmed that the Lord had spoken to me. My entire planned lecture was forgotten. I returned to my office anxious to hear more. As the Lord planted a new, supernatural love for Rachel within me, He showed me what to say and how to say it to not only address the current issue of household responsibility, but the deeper issues of love and acceptance and worthiness.

Rachel and her brother remained as part of our family for another two years, giving us many opportunities to demonstrate and teach about the Father's love, planting spiritual seeds in thirsty soil. We weren't perfect and we didn't solve all of her issues, but because I had learned to listen to the Lord, we were able to avoid creating more brokenness and separation.

The four simple keys that the Lord showed me from Habakkuk have been used by people of all ages, from four to a hundred and four, from every continent, culture and denomination, to break through into intimate two-way conversations with their loving Father and dearest Friend. Omitting any one of the keys will prevent you from receiving all He wants to say to you. The order of the keys is not important, just that you *use them all.* Embracing all four, by faith, can change your life. Simply quiet yourself down, tune to spontaneity, look for vision, and journal. He is waiting to meet you there.

You will be amazed when you journal! Doubt may hinder you at first, but throw it off, reminding yourself that it is a biblical concept, and that God is present, speaking to His children. Relax. When we cease our labors and enter His rest, God is free to flow (Heb. 4:10).

Why not try it for yourself, right now? Sit back comfortably, take out your pen and paper, and smile. Turn your attention toward the Lord in praise and worship, seeking His face. Many people have found the music and visionary prayer called "A Stroll Along the Sea of Galilee" helpful in getting them started. You can listen to it and download it free at CWGMinistries.org/Galilee.

After you write your question to Him, become still, fixing your gaze on Jesus. You will suddenly have a very good thought. Don't doubt it; simply write it down. Later, as you read your journaling, you, too, will be blessed to discover that you are indeed dialoguing with God. If you wonder if it is really the Lord speaking to you, share it with your spouse or a friend. Their input will encourage your faith and strengthen your commitment to spend time getting to know the Lover of your soul more intimately than you ever dreamed possible.

IS IT REALLY GOD?

Five ways to be sure what you're hearing is from Him:

1. Test the Origin (1 Jn. 4:1)

Thoughts from our own minds are constructed analytically, with one thought leading to the next, however tangentially. Thoughts from the spirit world are spontaneous. The Hebrew word for true prophecy is *naba*, which literally means to bubble up, whereas false prophecy is *ziyd* meaning to boil up. True words from the Lord will bubble up from our innermost being; we don't need to cook them up ourselves.

2. Compare It to Biblical Principles

God will never say something to you personally which is contrary to His universal revelation as expressed in the Scriptures. If the Bible clearly states that something is a sin, no amount of journaling can make it right. Much of what you journal about will not be specifically addressed in the Bible, however, so an understanding of biblical principles is also needed.

3. Compare It to the Names and Character of God as Revealed in the Bible

Anything God says to you will be in harmony with His essential nature. Journaling will help you get to *know* God personally, but knowing what the Bible says *about* Him will help you discern what words are from Him. Make sure the tenor of your journaling lines up with the character of God as described in the names of the Father, Son and Holy Spirit.

4. Test the Fruit (Matt. 7:15-20)

What effect does what you are hearing have on your soul and your spirit? Words from the Lord will quicken your faith and increase your love, peace and joy. They will stimulate a sense of humility within you as you become more aware of Who God is and who you are. On the other hand, any words you receive which cause you to fear or doubt, which bring you into confusion or anxiety, or which stroke your ego (especially if you hear something that is "just for you alone—no one else is worthy") must be immediately rebuked and rejected as lies of the enemy.

5. Share It with Your Two or Three Spiritual Counselors (Prov. 11:14)

We are members of a Body! A cord of three strands is not easily broken and God's intention has always been for us to grow together. Nothing will increase your faith in your ability to hear from God like having it confirmed by two or three other people. Share it with your spouse, your parents, your friends, your elder, your group leader, even your grown children can be your sounding board. They don't need to be perfect or super-spiritual; they just need to love you, be committed to being available to you and maintaining confidentiality, have a solid biblical orientation, and most importantly, they must also willingly and easily receive counsel. Avoid the authoritarian who insists that because of their standing in the church or with God, they no longer need to listen to others. Find two or three people and let them confirm that you are hearing from God.

THREE JOURNALING QUESTIONS FOR YOU TO COMPLETE

1. Write a two-way love letter, where in paragraph one you share a reason why you love Jesus. Then fix your eyes on Jesus and tune to flow, and in paragraph two, let Him tell you how much He loves you.
2. Lord, show me the ways my earthly father demonstrated his love toward me.
3. Lord, You are my heavenly Father. Would you speak a **Father's blessing over me?** What do You have in store for my life? What is the destiny You have planned for me?

I desire to hear Your blessing, Your purposes, and Your vision for my life. Thank You, Lord.

DIGGING DEEPER

How did your journaling time with Jesus go? Were you able to hear from Him in your heart? If you tried the four keys in this chapter and feel stuck in any area, don't give up. Please refer to Part Two of this book, "How to Hear God's Voice," and allow us to assist you in developing an intimate and conversational relationship with Jesus.

How can we receive counsel from our Wonderful Counselor if we cannot hear His voice? We see then how cultivating a two-way dialogue is absolutely *foundational* to receiving His counsel and His healing. We are convinced **heart healing occurs through divine encounter** and would love to share the journey to wholeness with you.

Chapter Two

HOW DO I MINISTER EFFECTIVELY TO A WOUNDED HEART?

IS THE HEART MORE THAN A PUMP THAT CIRCULATES MY BLOOD?

Absolutely! Science has proven this and the Bible clearly states it.[1] Yes, we know the heart pumps blood, but when the Bible declares that "out of the heart flow the springs of life," it is talking about something more than pumping blood (Prov. 4:23).

> *Watch over your heart with all diligence, for from it flow the springs of life.*

Years ago, my wife Patti and I looked up and analyzed all 1200 Scripture verses on heart and spirit. Patti then suggested this definition:

"The heart is underlying attitudes, motivations, and character traits."

I consider this the best and most biblical definition of the heart that I have ever heard. As we go through the verses below which delineate both a wounded heart and a healed heart, see if you don't agree that all of these words are descriptions of underlying attitudes, motivations and character traits.

BEFORE WE ATTEMPT TO HEAL THE HEART, WE NEED TO ANSWER SOME QUESTIONS

Have you ever issued a command to your heart saying, "Stop feeling that way!" and your heart completely ignored your order? Not only that, but your heart also ignored your list of reasons why it has no right to feel this way? How successful is your self-talk to stop being depressed because you're a Christian and have no reason to be down? Or to just get over your anger or to ignore the hurtful words?

Or have you ever confessed a scriptural truth, and your heart's emotions didn't feel at all in agreement? For instance, I can confess that "I am the righteousness of God in Christ Jesus," and yet I feel like a miserable sinner. What's up with that? Why isn't my confession working? Why won't my heart come into agreement? Why do I still feel so unrighteous? Why don't my well-reasoned commands make a difference?

Does the heart have its own language and is it different from the language of my mind? Does the language of my mind work for healing the heart? What does a wounded heart look like? What does a healed heart look like? Are there unique energy flows within my heart? If so, how can I change from a negative energy flow to a positive energy flow? This chapter will explore and answer each of these questions, equipping you to effectively restore your heart.

DEFINING THE LANGUAGE OF THE HEART

Will an eloquent Englishman be of much assistance to a French-speaking person seeking information? Why not? Just as English and French are two different languages, the heart speaks in a language that is different from that of the mind. The language of the mind is logical ideas. The language of the heart is pictures, emotions, flow and faith. The heart's healing occurs in the heart, not in the mind. To heal the heart *we must use the language of the heart.*

THE HEART SPEAKS USING A LANGUAGE THAT IS DIFFERENT FROM THAT OF THE MIND

Analytical reason is the language of the mind. Mental reasoning takes place when one reasons alone and does not merge reason with faith and revelation from the Holy Spirit. Examine the King James Version of the Bible for the references which follow and note Jesus' comments on the ineffectiveness of using man's unanointed reason: Matthew 16:5-12; Mark 2:5-12; Mark 8:15-18; Luke 5:21-22. The result of using man's reasoning **without revelation** is vanity or meaninglessness (Eccl. 12:8).

In today's society, man's analytical reason would be considered the language of the mind. From the above KJV references, it is clear that man's analytical reason is **not an effective language** of the heart.

WHY ISSUING A COMMAND TO MY HEART TO "SHAPE UP" JUST DOESN'T WORK

Commanding my heart to "stop feeling that way" is usually ineffective in healing emotional trauma because the heart has its own language. The language of the heart is different from the language of the mind. The primary language of the mind is "logic and reason." I reason things through and then make decisions. I remember telling my heart, "You have no reason to feel this way, so just stop it!" My heart simply did not respond to my well-reasoned thoughts as to why I should be experiencing joy and not sorrow. Hmm, I wonder why not? I had issued a command, "Stop feeling that way," and my heart simply ignored my order and went right on feeling sadness and sorrow and pain. So the answer is…

I MUST USE THE LANGUAGE OF THE HEART TO HEAL THE HEART

Briefly summarized, the language of the heart is:

1. **Flow**—"out of his heart will flow" (Jn. 7:38 NKJV)
2. **Imagination**—"keep this forever in the imagination of the thoughts of the heart" (1 Chron. 29:18 KJV)
3. **Emotions**—"He was grieved in His heart" (Gen. 6:6)
4. **Meditation**—"I will meditate with my heart" (Ps. 77:6)

Now let's consider each of these four elements in a bit more depth.

EXPLORING FLOW, ONE ELEMENT OF THE LANGUAGE OF THE HEART

"From his innermost being shall FLOW rivers of living water, but this He spoke of the Spirit." (Jn. 7:38-39)

Did you ever try to remember something but you just couldn't? Then later you were relaxed and the answer simply popped (flowed) into your mind? This is because the mind can only command the recall of 10% of what we know while the flow of our hearts can recall everything we know, plus receive words of knowledge and words of wisdom from the Holy Spirit (1 Cor. 12:8). The heart responds with "flowing" ideas, pictures and emotions.

In healing the heart, I tune away from command and analytical thoughts. Instead, I still myself and tune to flow (Ps. 46:10, Jn. 7:38). For the Christian this involves the river of the Holy Spirit Who flows from his innermost being.

Living from the river within is a much deeper, more satisfying and more creative place from which to live. We have all experienced "flow." For example a creative idea just "lights upon us" or a person's name just "comes to us" and we know we are to pray for them. These are coming from the Holy Spirit.

On the other hand, we have all experienced evil pictures and thoughts light upon us, even while in prayer or worship. These spontaneous flowing thoughts are also coming from the spirit world—from evil spirits rather than the Holy Spirit.

To heal the heart we must become aware of all these flowing thoughts. So once I choose to tune from my mind to my heart, from reasoned thoughts to flowing thoughts, I then need to take every thought captive. Any flowing thought coming from an evil spirit (i.e., in alignment with a name of satan—accuser, liar, thief, adversary), I renounce in Jesus' name, and ask the Holy Spirit to replace it with His flowing thoughts which line up with His names (Comforter, Healer, Deliverer, Giver of Life).

When ministering to the heart, both the counselor and the counselee tune to flow and honor flow, which allows us to follow the direction the Holy Spirit. That is why we ask the question, "What is in my heart?" If we still ourselves and tune to flow, the heart will send up a response (i.e., a spontaneous thought, picture or emotion) of the issue that needs to be dealt with **now**. The heart is communicating directly with us. Working with the language of the mind does not heal the heart. Working with the language of the heart heals the heart. Understand this, or all is lost in your attempts to heal the heart!

EXPLORING DREAM, VISION AND IMAGINATION, ANOTHER ELEMENT IN THE LANGUAGE OF THE HEART

We have eyes in our hearts which can see pictures.

> *I pray that the **eyes of your heart** may be enlightened.*
> (Eph. 1:18)

Pictures are powerful. We say a picture is worth a thousand words. The Bible confirms this in God's encounter with Abraham.

> *He took him outside and said, "Now **look** toward the heavens, and count the stars, if you are able to count them." And He said to him, "So shall your descendants be."* (Gen. 15:5)

What was the immediate result of gazing upon a picture placed in the heart by God?

> **Then he believed** in the LORD. (Gen. 15:6)

Heart faith erupted from this heavenly picture (Gen. 15:1-6). Heart faith is surely one aspect of a healed heart. So I seek pictures from God which I can gaze upon, and I lead my clients into seeing Jesus and what He is doing. This will inspire faith.

I recall being told that I was to confess that "I am the righteousness of God in Christ Jesus" (Phil. 3:9). I did so, probably a hundred times, and yet I was **picturing** myself as a miserable sinner. The picture won. When God changed the picture and I began seeing myself robed in His garment of righteousness, radiating His divine glory, my heart was healed of the feeling that I was a miserable sinner (Gal. 3:27; Isa. 61:10; Zech. 3:4).

My heart, my emotions and my life are very powerfully influenced by the pictures I am gazing upon.

PICTURES CAN CONSIST OF EVIL IMAGINATION, GODLY IMAGINATION, DREAM OR VISION

Dreams, visions, pictures and imagination are all outworkings of the visionary capacity which the Bible says is located on the level of the heart.

- **Imagination** is spoken of as being a function of the heart (KJV: 1 Chron. 29:18; Gen. 8:21; Ps. 140:2; Prov. 6:18; Jer. 7:24; 23:16).
- **"Godly imagination"** is something we are commanded to do, and it is defined as picturing things God says are

true (1 Chron. 29:18 KJV). We are transformed and move **forward** while we look at what Jesus is doing (2 Cor. 3:18; 4:18; Heb. 12:1-2)

- **"Evil imagination"** is defined as picturing things contrary to Scripture (Gen. 8:21 KJV). We go **backward** when we gaze upon evil pictures (Jer. 7:24).
- **"A dream or a vision"** is when God fills man's visual capacity (Num. 12:6, Acts 2:17). One-third of the Bible is composed of the stories of dreams and visions God gave and the actions which resulted. So obviously this is a primary way God communicates with us.

Jesus, as our perfect example, saw vision **constantly** (Jn. 5:19-20, 30; 8:26, 38). Since He was ministering to people's hearts, He spoke in word pictures **continuously** (Matt. 13:34). The Bible itself is most largely a picture book filled with stories of people's lives.

However, since the western world has focused on the mind instead of the heart, pictures, dreams and visions have been lost in the shuffle. Join me in turning from the world's opinion to biblical truth: "Lord, I repent for allowing myself to be captured by rationalism and living in the logic and reason of my mind rather than the pictures in my heart. Heal me, I pray. Restore the eyes of my heart. I pray that the eyes of my heart would be enlightened (Eph. 1:18). Let me live as Jesus lived. Let me learn to reason as You have commanded me to reason, which is together with You, Lord, and grant me a revelation that such reasoning uses pictures (Isa. 1:18)."

HOW DO I MINISTER EFFECTIVELY TO A WOUNDED HEART?

*"Come now, and let us **reason together**," says the LORD, "Though your sins are as scarlet, They will be as white as snow; Though they are red like crimson, They will be like wool."* (Isa. 1:18)

WHAT TO DO IF THE COUNSELEE CANNOT SEE VISION

If the counselee's ability to see pictures has been stunted by western rationalism, several options are available to the counselor: 1) The counselor can look for vision himself and describe what they are seeing; or 2) they can let the counselee follow the emotion in his heart back to the initial hurt, then invite Jesus to speak into that pain, hearing Jesus' words of life; and/or 3) the counselor can have the counselee follow appropriate prayer approaches to heal his spiritual blindness and pray for God to restore the eyes of his heart.

Appropriate prayer approaches for restoring vision to one who is spiritually blind would include all seven basic prayers taught in this book: 1) breaking generational curses (previous generations who scorned seers) ; 2) cutting off negative soul ties (from parents, pastors and teachers who do not believe that dreams and visions are for today); 3) replacing negative expectations ("God doesn't give vision anymore today."); 4) renouncing inner vows ("I cannot or will not see vision."); 5) healing traumatic pictures ("I never want to see again because of the horrible flashbacks I used to have from a terrible tragedy in my life."); 6) breaking off word curses ("Visions are for emotionally unstable people.") 7) casting out demons (e.g. demon of blindness).

Then, using vision, see Jesus lay His hands on the counselee's blind eyes, and lay your own hands upon his physical eyes (seeing them as the hands of Christ), praying for Jesus to touch and heal. Vision should now begin to come alive in his life.

Practicing using your visionary capacity will increase your skill in this area. Practice by picturing: 1) Bible stories as you read them, 2) Bible promises to you, 3) Jesus at your right hand (Acts 2:25; Ps. 16:8), and 4) entering into throne room worship (Rev. 4).[2] If you do these things intentionally and daily for six weeks, your visionary capacity will greatly improve.

If the person has dreams but yet when awake cannot picture his living room couch, then he has made a vow not to see pictures. The result of this vow is that when his conscious mind is in control, he doesn't see, but when he goes to sleep and his unconscious comes to the forefront, he can see. Thus, it was a vow made at some time in his life. However, he may not be consciously aware he made this vow until he reflects back on his life in prayer and God shows him when he made it. He will need to repent of the vow and ask God to restore vision to him. If he cannot determine when he made the vow, then repent for making the vow at whatever point in his life he made it. Since the fruit of blindness is there, the root of a vow is also there.

Generally, at my seminars, two people in a hundred cannot picture their living room couch (meaning the eyes of their hearts have been blinded). The two basic reasons people make such vows are to either stop the constant replay of a traumatic scene or to overcome the sin of lust. For the person who says they can't see pictures, you can always ask them if they can lust, for if they can, then they can see pictures.[3]

EXPLORING EMOTION, ANOTHER ELEMENT IN THE LANGUAGE OF THE HEART

"A joyful heart makes a cheerful face but in sadness of heart the spirit is broken" (Prov. 15:13). "Let the peace of Christ rule in your hearts" (Col. 3:15). "The love of God has been poured out within our hearts through the Holy Spirit who was given to us" (Rom. 5:5). "I went embittered in the rage of my spirit" (Ezek. 3:14). "I will speak in the anguish of my spirit" (Job 7:11). Clearly the Bible teaches that deep emotions, both positive and negative, are in the heart. HeartMath.org also has much research which agrees that emotions are located in the heart.

EMOTIONS ARE *BY-PRODUCTS* OF THE PICTURES WE GAZE UPON

If I am picturing the end of the world with the antichrist ruling and me hiding in a cave, I will have emotions of fear.

If I am picturing "of the increase of His government there shall be no end" (Isa. 9:7), I will have emotions of excitement, joy and peace as I see righteousness expanding and wickedness declining.

If I picture that my spouse has been in an accident, imagining a smashed car and an ambulance and police, I will likely have emotions of fear and distress.

If I see a picture of an angel sitting on the hood of the car while my spouse is stuck in a traffic jam, I would likely have emotions of peace.

This is why issuing a command to "stop feeling this way" doesn't work. What I need to do instead is ask God to replace the pictures in my mind, showing me His picture concerning the situation I am gazing at. After asking, I tune to flow, and a picture pops into my mind. This picture is His vision which, *if I gaze upon it*, will heal the emotions of my heart.

Each of us must be always aware of what we are picturing. Clean, faith-filled, godly pictures produce vibrant life. The Lord spoke this truth in my journal, and it has transformed my life: Whatever you gaze upon grows within you, and whatever grows within you, you become.

EXPLORING MEDITATION/PONDERING, ANOTHER ELEMENT IN THE LANGUAGE OF THE HEART

Let the words of my mouth and the meditation of my heart be acceptable in Your sight (Ps. 19:14).

Thinking is an activity of the mind. Meditation involves both the mind and the heart. Meditation is when I am "lost in thought." Meditation involves prayer, reflection and revelation. The Hebrew word translated meditate includes "imagine" as part of its definition (Josh. 1:8). The *Strong's* numbers for Old Testament words translated meditate and meditation include 1897, 1900, 1901, 1902, 7878, 7879, and 7881. New Testament words include 3191 and 4304.[4]

"Pondering" is considered the language of the heart (Ps. 77:6). When God fills our ability to ponder, it becomes "anointed reason" (Isa. 1:18; Lk. 1:1-3) in which the Holy Spirit's "flow" (Jn. 7:37-39) guides the reasoning process, turning it into godly meditation (Ps. 19:14). This results in perception (Ps. 73:16-17), illumination, and revelation (Eph. 1:17-18).

DEFINING A HEALED HEART

A healed heart is one that is permeated with faith, hope and love (1 Cor. 13:13). Faith, hope and love are also the spiritual attitudes which protect the heart and the mind (1 Thess. 5:8). These same three spiritual attitudes, true heart (love), faith, clear conscience (i.e., which results in hope) are what grant us access into the throne room (Heb. 10:22). These same three attitudes are the goal of our instruction: faith, love, good conscience (i.e., hope—1 Tim. 1:5). Paul commended believers for having these three key attitudes: faith, hope, and love (Eph. 1:12, 15; Col. 1:4-5).

IS MY HEART HEALED AND MANIFESTING KINGDOM EMOTIONS?

Are there any areas of life which disturb or remove my faith, hope, and love when I think about them? Are there any situations I cannot face with a heart full of faith, hope and love? If so, these need healing. When God fills the emotions of the heart, I experience His kingdom emotions of...

> Faith, hope, love, peace, laughter, joy unspeakable, mercy, forgiveness, honor, gratitude, praise, belief, worship, thankfulness, gentleness, kindness

Supporting Scriptures: 1 Cor. 13:13; Rom. 14:17; Gal. 5:22-25; Eph. 5:20; 1 Thess. 5:18; Heb. 12:28.

DOES MY HEART HARBOR ANY OF THESE WOUNDS?

Troubled, sorrowful, oppressed, angry, discouraged, forsaken, grieved, enraged, distressed, hardened, doubting, fearful, haughty, defiled, lonely, rejected

Supporting Scriptures: Gen. 41:7b, 8; Dan. 2:1, 3; Jn. 13:21; 1 Sam. 1:15; Eccl. 10:4; Isa. 19:3; Isa. 54:6; Ezek. 3:14; Dan. 7:15; Deut. 2:30; Mk. 11:23; Lk. 24:25; Deut. 2:30; Prov. 16:18; 2 Cor. 7:1.

SUMMARY

So now we have a sense of what a wounded and a healed heart look like. When I am full of peace and joy, I am filled with God's Kingdom emotions and my heart is healed. When I am downtrodden with sin and brooding in the emotions of fear, anger, discouragement or abandonment, then I need healing prayer.

I once lived with ongoing anger, hostility, judgment, fear, doubt, unbelief and lust. Now I live in laughter, joy, peace, faith, hope and love. Yes, it's quite an amazing testimony of the healing power of our Lord and Savior Jesus Christ! This book will guide you through taking the same steps God took me through to experience healing. We are going to present to you a simple series of seven prayers which work together. They build one upon another. They have as a foundation hearing God's voice and seeing God's visions. This allows the Wonderful Counselor to counsel us (Isa. 9:6). Once healed, we experience freedom and fun.

EFFECTIVE HEART PRAYER AVAILS MUCH

The effective prayer of a righteous man can accomplish much
(Jas. 5:16).

This means prayer can be more or less effective depending on how I go about it. What are the two keys to effective prayer discovered in the following verses?

> *"Truly I say to you, whoever says to this mountain, 'Be taken up and cast into the sea,' and **does not doubt in his heart**, but believes that what he says is going to happen, it will be granted him. Therefore I say to you, all things for which you pray and ask, **believe** that you have received them, and they will be granted you. Whenever you stand praying, **forgive**, if you have anything against anyone, so that your Father who is in heaven will also forgive you your transgressions. [But if you do not forgive, neither will your Father who is in heaven forgive your transgressions.]"*
>
> (Mk. 11:23-26)

Heart faith and **forgiveness** are two of the foundational keys to effective prayer.

Forgiveness replaces our tendency toward judging and condemning. Jesus walked in mercy, forgiveness and compassion. Jesus healed as He was moved by compassion (Matt. 14:14). The power to heal rides on the wave of compassion, not the wave of judgment. What we judge comes back to capture and enslave us with negative spiritual forces. *"In the way you judge, you will be judged"* (Matt. 7:1-5).

Belief—Abraham, the father of all who believed, received a spoken word (Gen. 12:1-3) and a vision (Gen. 15: 1-5) from God. Genesis 15:6 says THEN Abraham believed. Belief on a heart level is born by the spoken words of God to our hearts and the divine pictures God gives to us.

So in all these seven healing prayers we want and need to hear God's voice and receive His vision. Prayer counselors can help lead us into these encounters through excellent coaching. Hearing God's voice (*rhema*) and seeing the pictures He has concerning each situation is essential to experiencing healing of our hearts!

BUT I'VE TRIED TO PUSH THE DARKNESS OF EVIL AND SIN OUT OF MY LIFE AND IT DOESN'T WORK!

You cannot push darkness out of a room. You MUST turn on the light. The Bible says: "**Turn** from **darkness to light** and from the dominion of satan to God" (Act 26:18). Jesus is the Light of the world, so we invite HIM into these dark scenes. Healing requires replacement of darkness with light.

I never try to push negative energy out of my heart. Instead I turn on the light by inviting Jesus to be present and speak truth and life to me. I receive the words He speaks. Then I repent from being in agreement with demons, and I command, "In Jesus' name I bind these demons manifesting within me and command you to be still and leave NOW, in Jesus' name!" I breathe out heavily a couple of times and feel the pressure lift off from me.

SEVEN INITIAL CLUES THAT INDICATE THERE IS A HEART WOUND

1. Pressures within that are held at abeyance but are never truly gone.
2. Issues which come back regularly.
3. Any habitual or stubborn sin pattern.

4. Habitual weaknesses—mental, emotional, spiritual, physical.
5. Anything within that is contrary to peace, faith, hope and love.
6. Anything within that lines up with any activity of satan.
7. Addictions or out-of-control areas.

PERSONAL JOURNALING APPLICATION—LORD, WHAT IS THE MAJOR HEART WOUND YOU WANT TO HEAL TODAY?

Generally a combination of 3-5 words describes a heart wound. Common heart wounds are:

1. Fear, doubt, unbelief
2. Anger, hatred, rage, bitterness
3. Rejection, abandonment, loneliness
4. Financial lack, poverty, failure
5. Sensuality, lust, pornography
6. Depression, hopelessness, despair
7. Grief, loss, sorrow
8. Shame, guilt, condemnation

Select and write down 3-5 words from the list above which the Spirit highlights to you as the heart wound for you to process now. You do not have to use the exact three words in any of the eight suggestions above. They are only suggestions. Let your heart select the right three or so words for the heart wound God wants you to work with now. You may find you come back and repeat the entire healing process a second and third time if you discover you have more than one heart wound. However, deal with one heart wound at a time.

GO DEEPER

- For a detailed exploration of heart, mind, flow, and spirit, please see the training resources on *How to Walk by the Spirit* by the same authors. Available at: cwgministries.org

---

ENDNOTES

1. heartmath.org/research/science-of-the-heart
2. See article: cwgministries.org/throne.
3. For a powerful testimony of vision being restored as a vow is repented of see: cwgministries.org/BlindSee.
4. I discuss meditation in depth in Chapter Ten of this book and in this article: cwgministries.org/meditation.

Chapter Three

BREAKING GENERATIONAL SINS AND CURSES

THE FOUNDATION OF HEALING—HEARING THE VOICE OF OUR WONDERFUL COUNSELOR

In Chapter One we taught the four keys to hearing God's voice: stillness, vision, spontaneity and journaling. Make this a daily practice. Through two-way journaling, you bask in the Father's love. God's wisdom, strength, enlightenment and wonderful counsel pour into you, driving out the darkness and replacing it with light.

NEXT—REMOVE THE ROOTS OF SEVEN SIN ENERGIES WHICH FUEL HEART WOUNDS

1. **Generational sins and curses**—negative energy coming down through the family line
2. **Ungodly soul ties**—negative energy coming from close, bonded relationships
3. **Negative expectations**—negative energy coming from unbiblical beliefs
4. **Inner vows**—negative energy coming from the strivings of my flesh
5. **Word curses**—negative energy coming from unbiblical spoken words
6. **Traumatic pictures**—negative energy coming from unbiblical pictures
7. **Demonic oppression**—negative energy coming from evil spirits

AFTER DELIVERANCE—WE SEAL OUR VICTORY WITH…

- Bible meditations
- Prayer for the cleansing of cellular memories

A HOUSE FIT FOR A DEMON

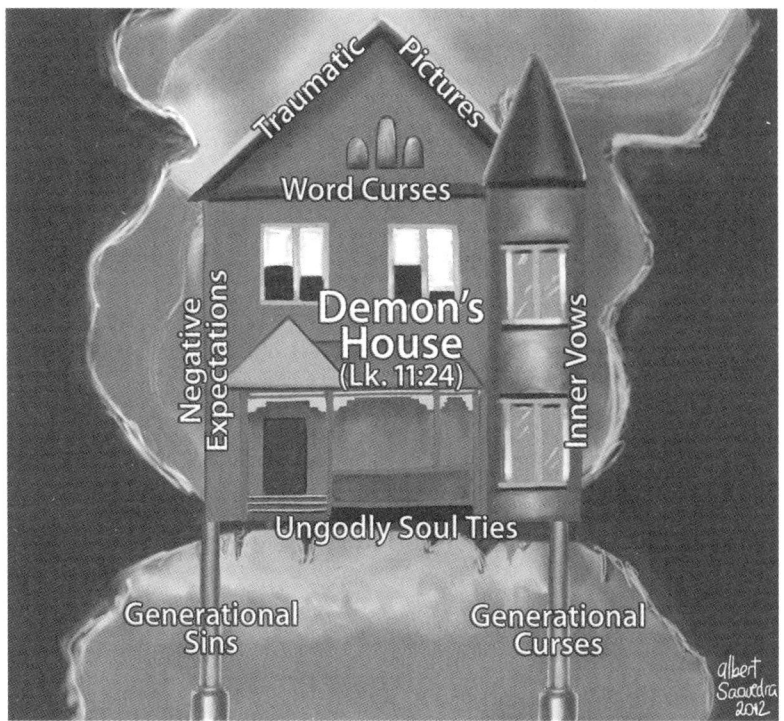

DO I GET MORE THAN MY PHYSICAL FEATURES FROM MY PARENTS?

Of course I do. We may say that a child has her mother's face or his father's build. We are quick to see physical features which are passed from parents to their children. However, much more than that is passed down. The anointings, gifts and passions within us also come from our parents.

Where did I get my passion to be a minister? Well, for several generations before me, my ancestors were active in ministry. So I have been in ministry all my life, as are my children and now my grandchildren. The same runs true for thieves and lawbreakers.

Their problems just continue running down through the family line. What does the Bible say about all this?

GENERATIONAL CURSES AND BLESSINGS PASS SIN ENERGY DOWN THROUGH THE FAMILY LINE

- *I, the LORD your God, am a jealous God, visiting the iniquity of the fathers on the children, on the **third** and the **fourth** generations of those who hate Me* (Ex. 20:5).
- *God, who keeps His covenant and His lovingkindness to a **thousand** generations with those who love Him and keep His commandments* (Deut. 7:9).

We see from the above verses that the power of sin and the power of blessing are passed from generation to generation.

THE RESULTS OF 150 YEARS OF BLESSING OR CURSE COMING DOWN THROUGH THE FAMILY LINE

Al Sanders, in his book *Crisis in Morality*, compares the descendants of two men who lived in the United States about 150 years ago. Max Jukes was an atheist. He did not believe in Christ or in Christian training. He married an ungodly girl and refused to take his children to church, even when they asked to go. At the time of this research, there were approximately 1200 descendants from this union. Of these, 310 died as paupers, at least 150 were criminals, 7 were murderers, 100 were drunkards, and more than half of the women were prostitutes.

Jonathan Edwards lived at the same time as Max Jukes, but he married a godly woman. He loved the Lord and saw that his children were in church every Sunday as he served the Lord to the best of his ability. An investigation was made of 1,394 of his known descendants. Thirteen of his offspring became college presidents, 65 became college professors, 100 lawyers, 30 judges, 60 physicians, 76 army and navy officers, 100 preachers and missionaries, 60 authors of prominence, 3 United States Senators, one Vice President of the United States, 80 public officials in other capacities, and 295 college graduates, among whom were governors of states and ministers to foreign countries.

WHAT IS NOT PASSED DOWN THROUGH THE FAMILY LINE?

- The **guilt** of ancestors is not heaped on the head of their descendants
- *Behold, all souls are Mine; the soul of the father as well as the soul of the son is Mine. The soul **who sins will die*** (Ezek. 18:2-4).

So I will not suffer spiritual guilt or death because of the sins of my father. However, if I continue the same pattern of sin, then I have the guilt of my own sin which will bring about a death process within me.

WHAT CAN BE PASSED THROUGH THE FAMILY LINE?

- Alcoholism and all other kinds of addictions; all kinds of physical ailments and sicknesses; all kinds of emotional and mental problems; besetting sins, bullying, sexual sins, child abuse, anything

- All types of spiritual blessings, anointings, giftings and passions

The signs of a wounded heart need to be examined to determine the root causes of this heart wound. This can be a momentary painful exercise but the ultimate healing is worth the pain, and if the Wonderful Counselor is guiding the healing process, the pain is minimized.

DIDN'T CHRIST REDEEM US FROM THE CURSE OF THE LAW AND POUR BLESSINGS INTO OUR LIVES?

Christ redeemed us from the curse of the Law, having become a curse for us—for it is written, "CURSED IS EVERYONE WHO HANGS ON A TREE"—in order that in Christ Jesus the blessing of Abraham might come to the Gentiles, so that we would receive the promise of the Spirit through faith (Gal. 3:13-14).

YES—BUT WE NEED TO PERSONALLY APPLY WHAT CHRIST PROVIDED AT CALVARY

Jesus' death on the cross paid the penalty and broke the power of sin for every member of the human race from Adam to the last man standing at the end of the age. Every single person was provided salvation by Jesus' death (1 Tim. 2:4). Yet that salvation, that forgiveness of sin and deliverance from its power, was not effective in our lives, was not applied to us, was not accounted to our behalf, **until we personally accepted it by faith and appropriated it in our own lives.** We must individually receive the benefits of the cross for them to be effectual for us. And *only* *the benefits that we personally receive by faith are effectual for us.* There are at least 12 things Christ provided for us at Calvary. We must believe for and apply each one in order to walk in them.[1]

For many years I was not aware of these twelve exchanges. For example, I did not know that I was healed by His stripes (Isa. 53:5). I did not believe for healing and I did not receive the benefit of healing. Now I know what Jesus accomplished for me in these exchanges. I believe for them, apply them to my life and walk in them. We have not because we ask not (Jas. 4:2). So in this chapter we are **asking specifically** that the power of the cross be placed between us and our ancestors and that all generational sins and curses be halted at the foot of the cross.

We will personally appropriate this cessation of generational sins and curses coming down through the family tree by praying and placing the cross of Christ between us and our ancestors. We command the curse to stop at the cross, and the blessings of Calvary to flow down upon us and our descendants.

When we personally take the cross of Jesus Christ and place it by faith between us and our ancestors, immediately all those generational sins and curses that have been pouring down upon us and our children come to an abrupt and absolute end. They are absorbed into the cross, for Jesus has already paid the price and suffered the penalty. Their power over us is broken because of our faith in the work of Jesus on the cross.

A note of caution: We don't dig around trying to think up possible generational sins and curses. If there is any digging around to do, we allow the Holy Spirit to do it by asking our hearts and the Holy Spirit in our hearts to remind us of things and to show us truth. Thus, if the Holy Spirit brings something forth, it wasn't my own reasoning; it was the Holy Spirit revealing. It came to me through flow and not through analytical thinking. The Holy Spirit may reveal what He wants, when He wants. This is healing which is being guided by the anointing of the Holy Spirit.

ENERGY FLOWS WITHIN OUR HEARTS

When we worship in spirit (Phil. 3:3), God's manifest presence shows up and we feel an energizing in our spirits. Heaviness lifts as divine light and energy flow in. I love this experience! What exactly am I feeling?

There are three primary New Testament words which are used to describe the power and energy released to me from God:

- **Exousia** (108 times) which means "right or prerogative"
- **Dunamis** (108 times) which means "might, power, force"
- **Energeia** (and its forms—31 times) which means "active energy" (*Kittel's Theological Dictionary of the New Testament*)

Have you at times felt a negative energy sweep over you which pulls you down into depression and heaviness? This is the energy of evil spirits! Ephesians 2:2 speaks of living according to the prince of the power of the air, the spirit that is now **"working"** within the children of disobedience. "Working" is "*energeō,*" (a form of *energeia*) which means that this indwelling evil spirit is at this point "energizing" the individual. If I bind the demon and command it to leave in Jesus' name and I go back to worshiping in spirit, the negative energy lifts and the positive energy of the Holy Spirit descends upon me.

The seven streams of negative energy (sin energy) which are flowing into the heart wound are like various tentacles of an octopus which has ensnared its prey, and they all can and will be removed through the seven prayers which we cover in the next seven chapters. Each prayer removes one stream of negative energy, replacing it with a stream of positive energy from the Holy Spirit. As each "tentacle" is cut off, the person is freer to be who God has destined them to be. This victory is sealed with a Bible meditation which helps in building up a wall of defense so you never again fall prey to this darkness. Cleansing cellular memories removes all remaining remnants of our previous hurtful past.

Each prayer brings a level of release, so we don't quit after one or two prayers. Getting half healed does not interest us. We desire the full healing God has made available to us in Christ Jesus.

BECOMING AWARE OF THE POWER/ENERGY OF GOD AND SATAN WITHIN THE HEART

As far as we have been able to determine from our study of Scripture, "heart" and "spirit" refer to the same part of man and are used somewhat interchangeably. For the Christian, his spirit has been joined to the Holy Spirit, so in reality, his innermost being is joined to Almighty God through a wonderful miracle of grace.

But the one who joins himself to the Lord is one spirit with Him.
(1 Cor. 6:17)

And for this purpose also I labor, striving according to His power, which mightily works within me. (Col. 1:29)

The power of God's Spirit begins working within the heart of the individual at the point of salvation. As one works out his salvation, this power from the Holy Spirit permeates more and more of his heart and soul, and even his body (Phil. 2:12). As the light of God fills more of an individual, satan's darkness is progressively driven out. This process of sanctification is ongoing, probably until the day we die. So even though we deal with an issue on one level, years later we may come back and deal with it on an even deeper level. We are healed in layers.

The power of the Holy Spirit ministers the abiding realities of God into our beings, things like faith, hope, love, joy, peace, power, purpose, dream, vision, anointing, and everything else that God is. This is driving out demonic forces from the person, forces which are best characterized by satan's names and activities. These negative sin energies (pressures) include doubt, fear, anger, guilt, depression, madness, death, and anything that lines up with a name of satan. His names include the accuser (Rev. 12:10); the father of lies (Jn. 8:44); the adversary (1 Pet. 5:8); the condemner (Rom. 8:1—implied); and a thief who comes to steal, kill and destroy (Jn. 10:10).

Therefore, one can fairly easily take a barometric reading of his heart to see how well he is doing and if the presence of negative demonic energies is thriving or if godly positive power saturates his heart and mind.

THE WORDS "POWER" AND "SIN ENERGY"

I prefer using the expression "sin energy" rather than "power" for two reasons. First, "energy" is exactly what it feels like to me when these negative (or positive) influences are operating within and upon me, putting pressure on me to move in a particular direction. I love the energizing I feel in the manifest presence of the Holy Spirit and I renounce demons when I feel their negative energizing is present.

Secondly, one of the Greek words translated "power" in the New Testament is *energes,* and it literally means "active energy." *Strong's Concordance* defines *energes* (#1756) as "active, operative, effectual, powerful." *Strong's* goes on to define another form of *energes,* (energeia—#1753) as "efficiency, energy, operation, strong, effectual working."

Young's Concordance defines *energes* as "energetic, efficacious."

Colon-Brown defines *energes* as "adopted to accomplish a thing, to communicate energy, to come into activity, energetic in-working."

The Analytical Greek Lexicon by Zondervan defines *energes* as "active, energetic, effectual." It defines *energeia* as "energy, efficacy, power, active energy, operation." It defines *energew* as "to effect, to put into operation, to be active, to communicate energy and efficiency, to come into activity, to be an active power of principle instinct with activity, operative."

ENERGEIA CAN LEGITIMATELY BE TRANSLATED AS ENERGY WHEREVER IT OCCURS

Energeia is used in 2 Thessalonians 2:9 and 2:11 to describe the "working" of satan and the "working" of error or delusion.

The verb form of this word group, *energew,* is used in Romans 7:5 for the "impulses of sins that are, through the law, at work (*energew*) in our members to bear fruit leading to death" (this death is present in us inhibiting the life of Christ from flowing in us). Second Corinthians 4:12 also speaks of "death working (*energew*) in us."

In 2 Thessalonians 2:7, the "mystery of iniquity already works (*energew*)." Ephesians 2:2 speaks of living according to the prince of the power of the air, the spirit that is now "working" within the children of disobedience. "Working" is a form of the Greek word "*energes*," which means that this indwelling evil spirit is "energizing" the individual. So *energeia* and *energew* both demonstrate the Greek basis for the expression "negative energy."

These words are also used for God's positive energy. For example, it was the *energeo* of God that energized Peter to be an apostle to the Jews and Paul to be an apostle to the Gentiles (Gal. 2:7-8). And in Ephesians 3:20 we are told that God is able to do far more abundantly beyond all that we ask or think according to the power (*dunamis*) that works (*energeo*) within us.

In summary: the three primary words in the New Testament translated power are *exousia* (108 times) which means "right or prerogative," *dunamis* (108 times) which means "might, power, force," and *energes* (and its forms—31 times) which means "active energy, energetic in-working."[2]

"SIN ENERGY" AND THE "LAW OF SIN" IN ROMANS SEVEN

There are two words used in Romans 7 that help us understand this sin energy within us: "law" and "dwell."

The word "law" in Romans 7:23 ("the law of sin") has the meaning of a law or principle that cannot be evaded because of the presence, power, or force of that which energizes it and thus controls our conduct.

In Romans 7:17-18, 20, the word "dwell" is used. This word in the Greek is *sikew*, which has the meaning here "to be operative in one's being" (not merely passively "dwelling"). Here it is "sin" that "dwells" or is "operative in one's being." Being under sin's power is being controlled by the energy of sin that, in effect, enacts an actual "law" within us, which, Paul found, could not be overcome by mere willpower (Rom. 7:17-24).

Since willpower cannot overcome this sin energy, Paul declares that the solution is appropriating the power of the Holy Spirit. In Romans 8:2, Paul states that it is the law of the Spirit of life in Christ Jesus that sets us free from the law of sin and death. So the power (or energy) of the Holy Spirit, breaks the power (or energy) of sin in our lives.

ISN'T "ENERGY" A NEW AGE WORD?

Words take on different meanings at different times in various cultures. In other words, cultural context can change their connotation. Take the word "gay," which meant "happy" fifty years ago but means something entirely different today. It seems the same has happened with the word "energy," as lately it has been linked with the New Age. For the sake of all our readers, we will clarify our intent in using the word "energy" as follows.

The Church currently thinks of "power" as coming from God and "energy" as being more of a New Age concept. I think we would all agree that the New Ager is involved more in the demonic than in the power of God.

Since the junk in our hearts that we are trying to heal is essentially demonic garbage, perhaps "sin energy" and "demonic energy" are fully acceptable phrases to describe it. The Christian wants to replace this negative demonic sin energy, which pressures him toward acts of sin, with the power and anointing of the Spirit of Almighty God, which moves him toward acts of righteousness.

Thus, the Christian being delivered is being set free from "negative demonic sin energies" and becoming increasingly more filled with the power and anointing of Almighty God.

I do not think the New Age or any other group has the right to claim for themselves any word, such as meditation, or symbol, such as the rainbow. My personal feeling on the use of the word "energy" is as follows: I recommend that we not give the New Age anything. God created everything for Himself. It is all designed to bring glory to Him. So let's plan on maintaining the words "energy" and "energetic" for the Christian. "Energetic" is derived (via Latin and French intermediaries) from the Greek word "*energeia*." Even though the goal of this book is not to fight for the use of the word "energy," I resist any suggestion that these words be given to the New Age.

In an absolutely real sense, we are dealing with divine power and spiritual energies within our hearts, souls, minds and bodies. These energies respond to certain biblical laws and certain specific prayer approaches. Demonic sin energies are connected with the curse, satan, and the work of demons. Positive energies are connected to the anointing, blessing, and power of the Spirit of Almighty God.

GENERATIONAL SINS AND CURSES PASS SIN ENERGY DOWN THROUGH THE FAMILY LINE

So, returning to our original assertion at the beginning of this chapter, some sin energies and some godly anointings within you did not begin with you. They began in your ancestral line and have been passed down to you from previous generations. You were actually born with a sin energy or an anointing that is producing either a curse or a blessing in your life.

The Bible says that curses can be passed down to the third and fourth generations (Ex. 20:4-6). Sin energy from sexual sins has an effect to the tenth generation (Deut. 23:2). And the blessing of obedience to God is passed down a thousand generations (Deut. 7:9).

Therefore, praying to break generational sins and curses is always our first step when dealing with anything, for surely there are some roots to it in the family line. Practically speaking, I don't need to wonder if I should break generational sins and curses. I should.

It is wise to begin my healing by praying to break any specific generational sins and curses I am aware of, and then a general prayer for any and all remaining generational sins and curses to be cut off.

As I get into more detailed healing prayer later on and I am seeking to deal with a specific issue in my heart, I would again pray to break any generational sins and curses from the family line as they relate to that exact issue. I would rather be sure I don't miss anything than simply say, "Oh, I believe I dealt with that awhile back." Let's nail it down for certain.

REMEMBER THESE STEPS AS YOU PRAY

1. **Always use the language of the heart**—God's voice and vision as flowing thoughts, flowing pictures and flowing emotions. Picture everything you are praying. Continue to stay tuned to flowing pictures, flowing words and flowing emotions as this is the Holy Spirit leading.

2. **Extend love and forgiveness in all directions**—toward self, others, circumstances and God.
3. **Action**—Act/apply what God is revealing to you.
4. **NO Fishing!**—Remember that when any issue has been covered by His blood, Jesus puts up a "No Fishing" sign, which means you are not to go digging it up again. FAILURE to do this may result in having to go through the healing process again.

PRAYER APPLICATION EXERCISE

This is the **first of seven** prayer applications which you will be applying to the ONE heart wound of 3-5 words which God has told you to focus on at this time (i.e., the Application Exercise at the end of Chapter 2). The entire seven prayers (which follow in successive chapters) can be repeated for additional heart wounds *after* you have applied them to this first heart wound. That is, each of the prayers that follow in future chapters will be applied to this heart wound first. Record the heart wound in your journaling notebook or on our free downloadable **"Contributing Strands Worksheet"** which is available two ways—as a printout which you write in or as a file you can type in at cwgministries.org/prayers.

The following prayer deals with generational curses from your father's side of the family. Praying it **twice** deepens it.

1. **I confess** and repent of the sin of my ancestors, my parents, and my own sin of my anger and resentment against You, God, for allowing this to happen in my life.
2. **I forgive** and release my ancestors for passing on to me this curse of (be specific—list it). I ask You, God, to forgive

me, and I receive Your forgiveness. I forgive myself for participating in this sin.
3. **Action:** Picture yourself as a baby in your mother's womb. Picture the cross of Christ between your father and all generational sins and curses flowing toward that baby. "I command the generational sins and curses which are flowing from my father's side of the family and are contributing to (state the heart wound) to be halted at the cross of Jesus Christ. I command them to fall to the ground powerless at the foot of the cross. I release the blessings of Calvary to flow down upon that baby in the womb and to all descendants. I bless you with life. I bless you with life. I bless you with life. Come alive, Come alive, Come alive."

See what you are praying. Feel Christ's life flowing into you. Feel Christ's freedom descend upon you. Deepen this prayer by repeating it twice concerning generational curses from your **father's side** of the family. Then do the same for your mother's side of the family. If you are adopted and perhaps don't know who your biological parents are, pray this anyway. God knows.

If you have a problem seeing the curse halted at the cross, the best solution I have found is to forgive the parent so unforgiveness is not blocking your freedom and release.

GO DEEPER

Some prophetic counselors have estimated that 80% of the issues we struggle with come from the family line. You can ask God for a word of knowledge as to when this curse entered your family tree. A flowing thought and flowing picture will be the Holy Spirit answering. It may be 500 years ago in a cave (or whatever). So whatever you receive, pray for that person to be released, to see Jesus present with them so they can be delivered and be touched by Him, and then for the curse to be halted there for all generations which follow.

Remember, Jesus lives outside of time and is always I AM. So though you may be praying about an event that is in the past in your time, for Jesus, it is the eternal now. He IS in that place with that person in need. You can repeat this process numerous times and receive various words of knowledge which can be acted on by prayerfully releasing each person and each event. This can be follow-up prayer in the days to come. Prayer is never wasted time. Effective, Spirit-led prayer promotes freedom, blessing and abundant life. Keep praying until you sense full release.

During the healing/counseling process, sensitive issues may be revealed. Action is required whenever child abuse (either physically or mentally) is revealed.

TWO-WAY JOURNALING EXERCISE

Use the four keys to hearing God's voice taught in Chapter 1: stillness, vision, spontaneity and journaling. "Lord, what do You want to say to me concerning generational sins and curses?"

ENDNOTES

1. cwgministries.org/TwelveExchanges
2. See the article "All Uses of Energeo (and Its Various Forms)" at cwgministries.org/energeo.

Chapter Four

SEVERING UNGODLY SOUL TIES

Have you ever had a really close, committed relationship, like a bosom buddy or a soul mate? If so, a soul tie developed between the two of you and energy was passing back and forth from one to the other. Hopefully it was a righteous relationship and you passed Kingdom life back and forth; things such as faith, hope, joy, and peace, and not criticism, fear, doubt and negativity. Soul ties generally emerge naturally and are not consciously planned, and you may not even be aware that you have a soul tie.

I recall a soul tie I had with my Greek professor in college. He was a scorner of the charismatic movement and would often take time in class to ridicule charismatics. Since I was anti-charismatic at that time in my life, and I also had a sin problem of disdaining people I disagreed with, I loved his scorn and ridicule. It fed my contempt. We had a soul tie which passed death and not life back and forth.

Once I became a charismatic and began believing in the power of the Holy Spirit, I realized I needed to cut the ungodly soul tie between my Greek professor and me. I did so in prayer and was released from the negative energy which was flowing from him to me. I eventually realized I needed to sever ungodly soul ties with others and did so in an extended prayer session. Since our spirits stay awake all night and work on issues we present to them, as I was drifting off to sleep, I would offer up a simple prayer: "Lord, please remind me of any other individuals I have ungodly soul ties with, so I can sever the ties and be totally free. Thank You, Lord."

I would often wake up in the middle of the night or in the morning with the realization, "Here is another person whom I need to sever an ungodly soul tie with." I would guess there were 20-30 people total from whom I severed such relationships over a two to three week period. So even though you begin this process today, expect it to continue for a while until the Holy Spirit confirms in your heart that the job is done.

A BIBLICAL EXAMPLE OF A SOUL TIE—WHERE SOULS ARE KNIT TOGETHER

David and Jonathan had a soul tie:

> *Now it came about when he had finished speaking to Saul, that the soul of Jonathan was **knit** to the **soul** of **David**, and Jonathan loved him as himself* (1 Sam. 18:1).

Knit souls: what an interesting phrase. Tied together in some way. Energy and life flowing in some way.

I see a soul tie as a wire which connects two people. Energy flows along that wire from one to the other. The wire could be anything from a thin thread to a thick cable, depending on the depth and strength of the relationship. When you look with the eyes of your heart, God will show you this connection and how strong it is.

SOUL TIES CAN RELEASE LIFE OR DEATH

When we have a soul tie, we are passing energies back and forth from one to the other. I'm sure you have noticed that when you have a conversation, you often end up feeling lifted or depressed, depending on the relationship. Godly relationships and conversations release the energy of the Holy Spirit. Ungodly relationships and conversations release energy from evil spirits.

If I get together with people to grumble and share gossip and negativity, this constitutes ungodly soul ties. If I get together with people who share love and care and concern and minister grace to one another, then this constitutes a godly soul tie.

HOW SOUL TIES ARE FORMED

Soul ties are present in bosom buddies, close friendships, covenant relationships (1 Sam. 18:3), and sexual union (1 Cor. 6:16). All the following include soul ties: husband and wife; parent and child; pastor and parishioner; teacher and student; employer and employee; counselor and counselee. Grandparents can have wonderful godly soul ties with their grandchildren as they minister God's grace to them, love them and care for them.

What does the Bible say about our relationships?

> *Whoever walks with the wise becomes wise, but the companion of fools will suffer harm.* (Proverbs 13:20)
>
> *Leave the presence of a fool, for there you do not meet words of knowledge.* (Proverbs 14:7)
>
> *Make no friendship with a man given to anger, nor go with a wrathful man, lest you learn his ways and entangle yourself in a snare.* (Proverbs 22:24-25)
>
> *Do not be deceived: "Bad company ruins good morals."* (1 Corinthians 15:33)

Clearly, it is important to be wise when choosing who we will walk with in life.

SEXUAL UNION CONSTITUTES A SOUL TIE

Adultery, fornication, and sexual fantasy create ungodly soul ties which need to be severed. The Bible says that sexual union results in the two becoming one flesh (and creating a soul tie). This is true in marriage (Gen. 2:24) as well as in fornication or adultery.

> *Or do you not know that the one who joins himself to a prostitute is one body with her? For He says, "The two shall become one flesh."* (1 Corinthians 6:16)

In marriage, when one joins himself to his partner sexually, life and energies of the two individuals flow between them. Likewise, in adultery or fornication there is a joining of the life and energies of the two. And it is even more serious than that. If you unite yourself with someone who has already joined him or herself to other people, then logic dictates you become joined to those other people as well. The energies flowing through your sexual partner and their previous partners now have access to flow into you, causing all sorts of sins, sexual pressures, sicknesses and problems.

The solution to this horrible state of affairs is the breaking of all ungodly soul ties, and especially those between you and anyone with whom you had a sexual encounter outside of marriage. Even if the sexual encounter was not consummated, it is still wise to break off any soul ties. Jesus said that if you look at a woman to lust after her, you have committed adultery with her in your heart (Matthew 5:27-28). It is therefore important that the prayer for the breaking of soul ties be utilized to break all relationships that have been formed in lust, pornography, infatuation, sexual activity short of intercourse, and intercourse. If you do this, you will feel an amazing release and freedom from negative sexual energies that have been hounding you.

And I personally doubt that this joining is limited to the transmission of sexual energies one to another. The Bible doesn't indicate that the joining is only sexual; the Bible says the two have become one. So I suspect that any and all energies are passing from one to the other. The sin energy from multiple sexual partners, both physical and virtual, would be enough to do anyone in!

GREEK INSIGHTS CONCERNING FORNICATION AND SOUL TIES (DRAWN FROM A STUDY BY REV. MAURICE FULLER)

This section regards the specific results of soul ties in our body when one is joined to a harlot, or involved in any illegitimate sexual encounter, including the use of pornography. Here, I

Corinthians 6:18 is important: "Flee sexual immorality. Every sin that a man does is outside the body, but he who commits sexual immorality sins against his own body."

First, the word translated "sexual immorality" is *porneia*, from which the word pornography is derived. *Porneia* includes "every kind of unlawful sexual activity." "He who commits sexual immorality" is *ho porneuon* in the Greek, a present participle indicating one who chooses sexual immorality as a lifestyle and indulges in it on a relatively continuous basis.

The word translated "against" in the above verse more literally means "entry into." So Paul says that every sin which a man commits has its immediate effect outside of the body. (They could affect relationships and have many other consequences but all of which would be external to our inner being.) Sexual activity, on the other hand, affects a person internally, in the core of his being. So the idea of the deep spiritual effect of sexual activity of any sort has its solid basis in Scripture. (End of section by Maurice Fuller)

DOMINATION IS AN EXAMPLE OF AN UNGODLY SOUL TIE

Moreover, even soul ties formed in acceptable, legitimate relationships can become ungodly and release sin energies. Ungodly soul ties exist when one person seeks to **dominate, manipulate, or control** another. This is contrary to the Spirit of Christ. Jesus came as a servant to all, and laid down His life for all. Jesus emptied Himself, taking the form of a **bond-servant**, being made in the likeness of men (Phil. 2:7). Jesus gave His disciples the freedom to leave if they chose to without calling them rebellious or evil (Jn. 6:67).

> *Nor yet as **lording it over** those allotted to your charge but proving to be examples to the flock.* (1 Pet. 5:3)
>
> *Through love **serve** one another.* (Gal. 5:13)
>
> *The one who is the greatest among you must become like the youngest, and the leader like **the servant**.* (Lk. 22:26)

You may need to look at your relationships and determine how best to protect yourself from a destructive soul tie. You can go through the severing of soul ties but the soul tie will come back unless the relationship changes. It may be necessary to discuss with some people the need for boundaries for a healthy association. Your pastor/counselor will be able to help you when this is needed. There may be other relationships that are so unhealthy that you need to end them.

In a marriage, the soul tie could be passing both positive and negative energies. There may be love and concern, and yet there may be domination and control. So in this case you would only sever the ungodly aspect of the relationship, not the godly aspect. You are not severing the marriage contract. You are to be present to pray and minister God's grace into the relationship, if at all possible.

Caution: Ask your pastor/counselor for help if you are in an abusive (physically or mentally) relationship. You must do what is necessary to protect your life and the life of your children. Some churches are legalistic and tell you that you must stay in such a relationship. I do not necessarily believe this is God's will.

ASSIGNMENT—MAKE A LIST OF UNGODLY SOUL TIES

Ask God to remind you of people with whom you have ungodly soul ties. Tune to flow. Jot down all names and faces which flash across your mind. You may awaken during the night or in the morning with additional names which have come to mind. You may end up with 20 or 30 names; that is fine. On this list you will include everyone you have had a contractual relationship with, a sexual or fantasy relation with, or an ungodly soul tie, where you passed back and forth negativity rather than Kingdom realities.

You will be praying the prayer below **for each one** on your list, so it may take up your morning devotional time for several days.

PRAYER TO SEVER UNGODLY SOUL TIES—PRAY THIS FOR EACH PERSON ON YOUR LIST

1. **I confess** and repent of my sin of an ungodly soul tie with (person's name), and of any anger and resentment against You, God, for allowing this to happen in my life.
2. **I forgive** (person's name) for their involvement in this sin. I ask You, God, to forgive me, and I receive Your forgiveness. I forgive myself for participating in this sin.
3. **Action:** Lord, I take the sword of the Spirit and cut the ungodly soul tie between me and _____. I cut it. I cut it. I cut it. (See a sword in your hand and swing it several times at the cord connecting you to this person until you see the cord, chain or cable snap, and the negative energy fall to the ground). **Comment for counselor:** I do not always have the

person cut the ungodly soul ties; sometimes I ask the Lord to cut the soul tie for them. Do this as the Lord leads.

4. **Action:** (Lay your hand on your heart)—Lord, remove anything evil that was deposited in me through this ungodly relationship and restore anything precious that has been stolen from me. (Feel and see Him doing this). **Get even more specific: The client prays,** "Lord, show me if there was any label put on my spirit as a result of this soul tie." Listen for one or two flowing words from the Spirit. Prayer: "Lord, cleanse my spirit from this label." Labels are ungodly structures.

House cleaning: You will need to destroy pornographic material and any mementoes or keepsakes of ungodly relationships. Net Nanny is a good protective program which can shield you from pornographic websites. The Bible says, "Do not go near the door of a harlot" (Prov. 5:1-8; 7:7-27). Well, now her door is one click away on your computer. Let Net Nanny close that door.[1]

BREAKING CHAINS WHICH BIND

A soul tie, as we have said, is like a wire, cable or chain which connects two individuals. After a relationship between me and a church was severed in a very unhealthy way, the Lord asked me to do a symbolic act of breaking the ungodly soul tie between me and this church. He had me buy a chain that was light enough for me to break with my hands. He told me to go to the office door during off hours and break the chain in front of the door, symbolizing and crystalizing my freedom from the ungodly forces which were coming at me from this unChristlike separation. I did, and I felt a release within me. I had noted that others who were forced out in a similar unhealthy way had severe calamity and death occur in their lives in the months which followed. No such thing happened to me. I believe by completing this prophetic action in faith, I was released from all such negative forces.

THE POWER OF PROPHETIC ACTIONS

Normally when severing ungodly soul ties, I see a sword in my hand and I swing it, cutting the soul tie. I do this in faith that God is moving and cutting this tie. Faith in this prophetic action releases divine power.

Elisha prophesied to King Joash that he was to do a prophetic action to destroy the enemy. Elisha said, "Strike the ground," and he struck it three times and stopped. So the man of God was angry with him and said, "You should have struck five or six times, then you would have struck Aram until you would have destroyed it" (2 Kings 13:18-19).

Therefore when I am cutting an ungodly soul tie, I see a sword in my hand and I swing it at the soul tie five or six times to make it fully effective.

KEYING IN ON MY CLOSEST RELATIONSHIPS (PARENTS, SPOUSE, CHILDREN)

Let's delve deeper into strengthening our most important relationships; that is, those with our parents, our spouse and our children.

No parent, spouse or child is perfect and we can focus on the imperfections, judge them and dishonor them, or we can ask God to show us the gifts each of these are in our lives, and how we are to be a gift back to them. Mercy can triumph over judgment (Jas. 2:13), honor over dishonor (1 Pet. 2:17) and friendships over resentment (Lk. 6:37). Parents sometimes provoke their children to wrath (Eph. 6:4). Children sometimes fail to honor their parents (Lk. 18:20).

Improper training can easily damage our relationships. Men are taught to cut off their emotions, which results in those close to them not feeling loved. Women often feel emotions strongly, but are rarely taught how to guide them by carefully selecting only pictures which come from God. So their emotions can be all over the place. (Of course, men can be overemotional and women can cut off their emotions, but that is culturally less common.) Can God's grace cover such issues? Yes, it can.

Listen to God's voice by using the four keys discussed in Chapter 1 (stillness, vision, spontaneity, journaling), and see how the Wonderful Counselor tells you to strengthen your key relationships. Let His light pour in, dispelling all darkness.

TWO-WAY JOURNALING EXERCISES

Play the instrumental visionary meditation "A Stroll Along the Sea of Galilee." The biblical imagery with soft soaking music will assist you in using the four keys.[2]

1. The quickest way to build healthy, godly relationships is to let the Wonderful Counselor speak to us about them. Go through each of your closest relationships one at a time, and ask the Lord:

- What is the gift I receive through this relationship?
- What is the gift You want me to be in this relationship?
- Are there areas where I have walked in judgment, and I need to forgive and show mercy toward my key family relationships and toward myself?
- Journal out what He says to you. Receive it with faith and gratitude.

RESTORING HEALTHY SOUL TIES—MY STORY OF LOVING MY FATHER

Godly soul ties release blessings into one's life. Just as an ungodly soul tie releases death, godly soul ties release life. Below is a story of how God re-established a strong godly soul tie between me and my father and the blessing that flowed into my life as a result.

Many years ago, after I had just become charismatic, I got into discussions with my father who was not a charismatic. I was trying to convince him to embrace the charismatic movement and he was resisting. This meant our relationship became tense.

I remember saying to myself, "I'm glad we live 1500 miles apart. I am leaving him to the pastor of his church to minister to him, because I sure can't." You know, it's hard to bring up your parents in the nurture and admonition of the Lord! I was careful not to have anger toward him, as I knew that would be wrong.

However, while worshiping one evening in a small home group meeting, I felt the Lord say to me, "Mark, you don't love your father." My immediate response was, "I don't hate him." The Lord spoke back, "That is not what I said. I said you don't love your father. You are neutral. Love is not neutral. Love is passionate."

So I repented on the spot and confessed my sin to the home group after the worship was over and we were sharing what the Lord had spoken to us.

Two days later I received a letter in the mail from my dad. The letter dealt with a loan my parents had given me several years earlier to help purchase the home we were living in. He was charging interest on the loan, which was fine with me. However, the Lord convicted him that this was not right and he wrote to let me know that he was forgiving all future interest, and applying all past interest paid toward the principal. This amounted to a huge gift to me of many thousands of dollars.

So was this a coincidence or did I just observe spiritual forces which were set in motion through repentance and compassionate love? You decide. I know what I believe.

ENDNOTES

1. NetNanny.com
2. Freely downloadable from cwgministries.org/galilee

Chapter Five

RENOUNCING UNBIBLICAL BELIEFS AND INNER VOWS

I suspect we all hold some unbiblical beliefs along with our biblical beliefs. I sure have in the past and likely still do, as growth is an ongoing process. I've actually written a book about 49 of the lies I repented of. It has 100 pages of two-way journaling where God spoke to me and transformed my thinking. As we pay attention to what God is saying, the light gets brighter and brighter until the dawning of the full day of Christ in our hearts (2 Pet. 1:19). I **love** this process!

What we believe in our hearts expresses itself in our words and actions. Sometimes consciously but more often unconsciously, we make decisions about how we will respond to life based on the beliefs we hold. For example, I may believe that things never work out and all I ever get is disasters. So I respond with a decision to not stretch myself or attempt great things in the future.

In reality, the Bible is clear that God is working all things out for good, and I am to continue pressing forward until I am fully experiencing the Promised Land He has for me. If I truly am experiencing disasters, it would be prudent to ask the Lord if I am doing something wrong which is causing them, and then act on whatever He tells me. If the pressure of these adversities has driven me to my knees seeking God's revelation, then this is indeed working out for good, as I am growing and learning the ways of God, being conformed more closely into His image (Rom. 8:28-30).

So in this example, I have an unbiblical belief (things never work out well) and an inner vow (I will not stretch and attempt things), which was replaced by a biblical belief (God is working this out for good) and godly purpose (I will press forward in faith and enter my Promised Land). Let's explore these steps in greater detail.

LET'S DEFINE OUR WORDS

An **ungodly** or **unbiblical** **belief**, also called a **negative expectation**, is any belief which I hold which is contrary to God's truth as revealed in the Bible or by His spoken word to me. Two of the great Bible teachers in my life have provided this counsel.

- "Never hold any thought about yourself that God doesn't hold about you."
- "Never say anything about yourself that God has not said about you."

Well, that sure cleans up my mouth and my thought processes! These unbiblical beliefs can be against yourself, others, authorities, institutions, or God. Most of these are established on the unconscious level, so we are generally not even aware that we are holding them. Yet all must be repented of.

Negative expectations can also come from someone preaching unscriptural opinions which you accept as true and seek to live out. Negative expectations may come from your heart digesting a negative experience and then creating a negative belief from the experience. For example, if you share your ideas and are ridiculed for it, you could begin to believe the lie that, "If I ever open my mouth, I will be put down."

The list of negative beliefs is endless. For example: "I will probably fail. I will probably end up in divorce. Nobody likes me. All politicians are evil. The government is out to get me. A godly man can't succeed in business. Women don't like making love. All men want is sex."

An **inner vow** is a promise I make to myself of the action I will take in light of the ungodly beliefs I hold. Inner vows are decisions I make to protect myself from the things I fear (the unbiblical/negative beliefs). Therefore they are ungodly thought structures which are separated from the wisdom, grace and empowerment of the Holy Spirit. These beliefs and vows may be against myself, others, authorities, institutions, or God. Generally these are on an **unconscious level**, so I am not even aware that I am holding them. We must bring them to the conscious level so we can repent of them and replace them with godly beliefs and godly purposes in the Spirit.

One of the easiest ways to discover the inner vows you have made on an unconscious level is to ask yourself, "What **action** do I take? What am I **doing** that is contrary to God's desires for me?" Discerning your current actions allows you to then ask, "What vow would I have had to take to end up with this action?"

EXAMPLES OF UNGODLY BELIEFS/WORD CURSES AND THEIR POSSIBLE CORRESPONDING VOWS

	LORD, WHAT NEGATIVE EXPECTATIONS ARE CONTRIBUTING TO (NAME OF HEART WOUND)? **I expect/believe that ...**	LORD, WHAT INNER VOWS ARE CONTRIBUTING TO (NAME OF HEART WOUND)? **Therefore I vow to do this (an action) ...**
1.	I'll probably fail	give up and die
2.	I will not have financial freedom—never enough	equate poverty with godliness
3.	my sin is unforgivable	hide from God
4.	I don't deserve God's blessing	make it on my own
5.	my children will rebel	seek to control them
6.	life is unfair & God doesn't intervene	distrust and withdraw
7.	people won't accept me	put up a protective wall
8.	I must be perfect.	try hard
9.	men don't cry	stuff my feelings
10.	I'm no good	act out my evil impulses
11.	I'm not very gifted so I can't succeed	not try to accomplish great things
12.	the forces around me are too powerful	stay invisible so I am not squashed
	I repent for the ungodly belief that ...	**I repent for the inner vow that I will ...**

Once you list your negative beliefs and inner vows, you then work down through each list and repent individually for each item on your lists. You ask God's forgiveness for believing these lies and for vowing to act in a corresponding ungodly manner.

A BIBLICAL EXAMPLE OF AN UNGODLY BELIEF AND INNER VOW THAT WREAKED HAVOC IN PEOPLE'S LIVES

The Israelites had been delivered from Egyptian slavery through the miracle-working hand of God, including ten plagues sent upon Egypt. Now, as God leads them through the wilderness to their destination, which He called their "Promised Land," this story unfolds.

God made this promise to the leaders: "Go and gather the elders of Israel together and say to them, 'The LORD, the God of your fathers, the God of Abraham, Isaac and Jacob, has appeared to me, saying ... I will bring you ... to a land flowing with milk and honey.'" (Ex. 3:16, 17).

God made the same promise to the Israelites: "It shall be when the LORD brings you to ... a land flowing with milk and honey..." (Ex. 13:5).

So God's promise to them was clear: He was going to get them through the wilderness and into a land flowing with milk and honey. They had a spoken word from God concerning their amazing future. All they had to do was come into agreement with it, and say "Yes, Lord." God showed His love to them by providing manna, a cloud by day and a pillar of fire by night. They were being supernaturally sustained in the wilderness.

The godly belief for them would have been, "God is taking us to a land flowing with milk and honey. I trust in God." This should have been their confession. This should have been what they pictured in their hearts. Had it been, they would have received what God stated was theirs. However, rather than come into agreement with what God had spoken to them, they agreed with the enemy of their souls, the accuser, and the results were disastrous.

THE STORY CONTINUES—GOD TESTS TO SEE IF THERE IS BELIEF IN OUR HEARTS

*"You shall remember all the way which the LORD your God has led you in the wilderness these forty years, that He might humble you, **testing you, to know what was in your heart**, whether you would keep His commandments or not. He humbled you and let you be hungry, and fed you with manna which you did not know, nor did your fathers know, that He might make you understand that man does not live by bread alone, but man lives by everything that proceeds out of the mouth of the LORD."* (Deut. 8:2, 3, 16)

Ok, so they are going to encounter some God-ordained tests to see if their hearts believe the words spoken to them by God.

*When they came to Marah, they could not drink the waters of Marah, for they were bitter; therefore it was named Marah. So the **people grumbled** at Moses, saying, **"What shall we drink?"** Then he cried out to the LORD, and the LORD showed him a tree; and he threw it into the waters, and the waters became sweet. There He made for them a statute and regulation, and **there He tested them**. And He said, "**If you will give earnest heed to the voice of the LORD your God**, and do what is right in His sight, and give ear to His commandments, and keep all His statutes, I will put* *none of the diseases on you which I have put on the Egyptians; for I, the LORD, am your healer."* (Ex. 15:22-26)

Now, they could have believed, "God will make a way," but instead they chose to grumble. **They failed this test.**

GOD REMINDS THE ISRAELITES OF HIS FAITHFULNESS TO THEM

God reminds them of His past goodness to them and that they need to heed both His voice and His commandments. His commandments are recorded for us in the Bible and His voice we hear daily in our hearts ("My sheep hear My voice"—Jn.10:27).

"Your clothing did not wear out on you, nor did your foot swell these forty years. Thus you are to know in your heart that the LORD your God was disciplining you just as a man disciplines his son. Therefore, you shall keep the commandments of the LORD your God, to walk in His ways and to fear Him." (Deut. 8:4-6)

We too need to recall God's faithfulness to us over the years so we do not become accusative and grumble against God and against spiritual leaders when the pressure is on. We need to know that God disciplines us to increase our faith. Remember, "discipline" means "activity, exercise, or a regimen that develops or improves a skill; training." To see how well we have learned, He tests us to see if we have **believing hearts** and we will obey Him.

GOD REITERATES HIS PROMISE AND PLAN FOR THEIR LIVES

> *"For the LORD your God is **bringing you into a good land**, a land of brooks of water, of fountains and springs, flowing forth in valleys and hills; a land of wheat and barley, of vines and fig trees and pomegranates, a land of olive oil and honey; a land where you will eat food without scarcity, in which you will not lack anything; a land whose stones are iron, and out of whose hills you can dig copper. When you have eaten and are satisfied, you shall bless the LORD your God for the good land which He has given you."* (Deut. 8:7-10)

Once again, it is imperative that we continually go back to God's promises to us and repeat them to ourselves so that our hearts and minds speak only the promises of God and not the lies of the enemy.

WE MUST NEVER FORGET THAT IT IS THE HAND OF GOD THAT CONTINUALLY SUSTAINS US

> *"Beware that you **do not forget** the LORD your God by not keeping His commandments and His ordinances and His statutes which I am commanding you today; otherwise, when you have eaten and are satisfied, and have built good houses and lived in them, and when your herds and your flocks multiply, and your silver and gold multiply, and all that you have multiplies, **then your heart will become proud** and you will forget the LORD your God who brought you out from the land of Egypt, out of the house of slavery. He led you through the great and terrible wilderness, with its fiery serpents and scorpions and thirsty*

> ground where there was no water; He brought water for you out of the rock of flint. In the wilderness He fed you manna which your fathers did not know, that He might humble you and that He might test you, to do good for you in the end." (Deut. 8:11-16)

IF I FORGET THAT IT IS GOD'S HAND THAT SUSTAINS ME, I WILL HAVE THIS ADDITIONAL UNGODLY BELIEF

> "Otherwise, you may say in your heart, **'My power and the strength of my hand made me this wealth.'** But you shall remember the LORD your God, for **it is He who is giving you power to make wealth, that He may confirm His covenant** which He swore to your fathers, as it is this day."
>
> (Deut. 8:17-18)

God's blessing makes me prosper. I can *never* think it is my greatness that makes me prosper.

I WILL PERISH IF I DON'T LISTEN TO THE VOICE OF GOD BUT BELIEVE THE LIES OF SATAN

> "It shall come about **if you ever forget the LORD your God** and go after other gods and serve them and worship them, I testify against you today that you will surely perish. Like the nations that the LORD makes to perish before you, so **you shall perish; because you would not listen to the voice of the LORD** your God."
>
> (Deut. 8:19-20)

THE ISRAELITES APPROACH THEIR FINISH LINE

They are ready to cross into their promised land. First they send ten spies to check out the land. They return saying:

"'We went in to the land where you sent us; and ***it certainly does flow with milk and honey***, and this is its fruit. Nevertheless, the people who live in the land are strong, and the cities are fortified and very large... We are not able to go up against the people, for ***they are too strong for us.*'** So they gave out to the sons of Israel a bad report of the land which they had spied out, saying, 'The land through which we have gone, in spying it out, is a land that devours its inhabitants; and all the people whom we saw in it are men of great size... and **we became like grasshoppers in our own sight...**'" (Num. 13:27-33).

MY PROMISED LAND IS AWESOME BUT I HAVE A "GRASSHOPPER COMPLEX"

Well, we have settled the fact that God did indeed lead us to our promised land. However, there are challenges to take it. Evil forces to be dealt with. Battles I need to fight and win. Gee, I thought this was going to be handed to me on a platter. Fight? Yuck.

Evil forces are big. I am small. I am a grasshopper. I cannot win. Well, right there is an ungodly belief and an inner vow. I don't have enough power to succeed. I am a grasshopper, therefore my vow/action is to not even enter the fight or engage the enemy. I will just sit down and grumble about how poorly God has provided for me.

BUT WAIT—HAVE FAITH—WE CAN WIN BY DRAWING UPON THE STRENGTH OF THE LORD!

*Then Caleb quieted the people before Moses and said, "We should by all means go up and take possession of it, for we will surely overcome it. The land which we passed through to spy out is an exceedingly good land... If the LORD is pleased with us, then He will bring us into this land and give it to us—a land which flows with milk and honey... Only **do not rebel against the LORD**; and do not fear the people of the land, for they will be our prey. Their protection has been removed from them, and **the LORD is with us; do not fear them.**"* (Num. 13:30; 14:8, 9)

THE ISRAELITES CLING TO THEIR UNGODLY BELIEF AND INNER VOW

*All the sons of Israel grumbled against Moses and Aaron; and the whole congregation said to them, "**Would that we had died** in the land of Egypt! Or would that we had died in this wilderness! Why is the LORD bringing us into this land, to fall by the sword? Our wives and our little ones will become plunder; would it not be better for us to return to Egypt?"* (Num. 14:2, 3)

Their **ungodly belief was** that God was not going to fight and win for them, and their **inner vow was**, "I vow it would be better for us if we return to Egypt." Their **resulting action** was, "**We will not fight.**"

Wow! How's that for lack of faith? So much for their wilderness training experience. It doesn't appear that they learned at all that they can trust God in the midst of adversity.

GOD DECLARES THAT THEIR DESTINY IS NOW CHANGED

> "Surely all the men who have **seen My glory and My signs** which I performed in Egypt and in the wilderness, yet have **put Me to the test these ten times and have not listened to My voice**, shall by no means see the land which I swore to their fathers, nor shall any of those who spurned Me see it. But My servant Caleb, because he has had **a different spirit** and has followed Me fully, I will bring into the land which he entered, and his descendants shall take possession of it. How long shall I bear with **this evil congregation who are grumbling** against Me? I have heard the complaints of the sons of Israel, which they are making against Me. Say to them, 'As I live,' says the LORD, '**just as you have spoken in My hearing, so I will surely do to you**; your corpses will fall in this wilderness, even all your numbered men, according to your complete number from twenty years old and upward, who have grumbled against Me. Surely **you shall not come into the land** in which I swore to settle you, except Caleb the son of Jephunneh and Joshua the son of Nun.'"
>
> (From Num. 14:22-38—please read the entire passage.)

Wow! Talk about the beliefs in one's heart, the words of their mouth, and the actions they take ripping away their God-ordained destiny! Their action brings a resulting action from God. Now God declares they **will receive exactly what they are believing for and confessing and acting on**. They are going to die in the wilderness rather than enjoy the land of blessing He had prepared for them.

The beliefs in their hearts, the confession of their mouths, and the resulting actions determined their destiny. The same is true for us!

THIS HAPPENED FOR OUR INSTRUCTION—SO WE DON'T MAKE THE SAME MISTAKES

> Nevertheless, with most of them God was not well-pleased; for **they were laid low in the wilderness**. Now **these things happened as examples for us**, so that we would not crave evil things as they also craved. Do not be idolaters, as some of them were; as it is written, "THE PEOPLE SAT DOWN TO EAT AND DRINK, AND STOOD UP TO PLAY." Nor let us act immorally, as some of them did, and twenty-three thousand fell in one day. Nor let us try the Lord, as some of them did, and were destroyed by the serpents. Nor grumble, as some of them did, and were destroyed by the destroyer. Now **these things happened to them as an example, and they were written for our instruction**, upon whom the ends of the ages have come... (1 Cor. 10:5-22)

Well, this is clear: I need to make sure I learn from the mistakes of the Israelites in the wilderness. I need to not hold ungodly beliefs or inner vows and lousy actions. I need to not see myself as a grasshopper, for now that I am filled with the Spirit there are nine supernatural manifestation of His Spirit always available to me (1 Cor. 12:7-11). By the power of the Spirit, I have the victory in each path that God leads me into. My victory is not because of my greatness. It is because the anointing of the Spirit flows through me, gifting me with what I need to be successful. "In all these things we overwhelmingly conquer through Him who loved us" (Rom. 8:27)!

WHY EVEN "GOOD" INNER VOWS ARE SO DESTRUCTIVE

Inner vows are decisions we make to protect ourselves from the things we fear—the unbiblical/negative beliefs—and therefore they are ungodly structures. They are always harmful even when they seem to be good. For example, take the inner vow that "I will never become an alcoholic." This is harmful because it is very likely based on bitterness and judgment, and therefore it defiles us (Heb. 12:15). In addition, such vows are most often relying on the strivings of our flesh to accomplish them, and Jesus is clear, "The flesh profits nothing" (Jn. 6:63). We are to be constantly trusting in the empowering of the Spirit to accomplish rather than the strength of our flesh. "The words that I have spoken to you are spirit and are life" (Jn. 5:30, 6:63). That means I am acknowledging Christ present with me always, and am asking for and tuned to His flowing thoughts, pictures and power.

NEGATIVE EXPECTATIONS, INNER VOWS AND SIX POWERFUL LAWS

Law One—Negative expectations activate the Law of Faith (also called the Law of Belief)

Often these expectations are self-reinforcing, for whatever you expect and believe will happen, most likely will happen. The Bible is clear to say that whatever one believes for he will receive.

According to your faith be it unto you. (Matthew 9:29)

All things are possible to him that believes. (Mark 9:23)

One's faith makes even what appears impossible, possible. So even if it were unlikely that I would fail in life, if I believe I will, I will. Because I have embraced a belief system in my spirit that I am going to fail, the Law of Faith is activated in my life.

Law Two—Negative expectations activate the Law of Judgment

The Law of Judgment says, *"Do not judge so that you will not be judged. For in the way you judge, you will be judged; and by your standard of measure, it will be measured to you"* (Matthew 7:1-2).

Therefore, there is now an opposite force that is activated in the universe that comes back against me and performs the judgment on me which I have made about others.

If you judge (or expect) people to be unfriendly, they will be unfriendly toward you. If you judge (or expect) them to be friendly, they will be friendly toward you. Obviously, it may take some extremely unfriendly people a while to warm up to your friendliness. This is where the Law of Sowing and Reaping comes in. You sow into a person's life for a while and eventually you reap a harvest.

Law Three—Negative expectations activate the Law of Sowing and Reaping

According to the Law of Sowing and Reaping, I will reap a harvest in light of what I have sown.

Do not be deceived, God is not mocked; for whatever a man sows, this he will also reap. (Gal. 6:7)

RENOUNCING UNBIBLICAL BELIEFS AND INNER VOWS

Sow with a view to righteousness, reap in accordance with kindness. (Hosea 10:12)

Those who sow trouble harvest it. (Job 4:8)

This means that I should expect judgments to come back to me in the same areas I have made them. For example, if I have made a judgment against people who are overweight, then I may find that I have put spiritual laws in motion which end up in me becoming overweight. Or I might find that I draw an overweight spouse to myself. Even if she is slender when we marry, my gale-wind judgment being constantly sent forth from my spirit that I don't like people who are overweight, and that I won't approve of her if she becomes heavy, will cause a constant belittling of her self-worth as I criticize any and every activity that I see her doing that could cause her to gain weight. Eventually she succumbs to the constant criticism and the negative expectation that she will become heavy and, sure enough, I have received back exactly what I have judged. I now have an overweight spouse.

Law Four—Negative expectations activate the Law of Multiplication

They sow the wind and they reap the whirlwind. (Hosea 8:7)

When sowing a negative expectation, I have sown to the wind and now I must reap the whirlwind. You may only sow a small seed of anger, but you will reap an entire crop of wrath, because one little seed sown produces multiplied fruit in return.

Law Five—The Law of Delay—don't be deceived, give the Law of the Harvest time to work
It may take a while for the harvest to grow, so your initial sins may not bring you back a negative recompense immediately. This deceives some people into believing that "God doesn't care that I am sinning; nothing bad is happening to me." But the Bible says, "Do not be deceived, God is not mocked; for whatever a man sows, this he will also reap" (Gal. 6:7). Don't let the fact that there is a delay between the sowing and reaping processes make you think things are not happening in the spiritual world. They are—either good things or bad things, depending on what seeds you have sown.

Law Six—The Law of Honoring, Loving, Fearing
Rather than a negative judging of others, the Bible tells us what our attitude is to be:

> "Honor all men. Love the brotherhood. Fear God. Honor the king." (1 Peter 2:17)

Remember, we will receive back the judgment we send out. Wouldn't it be nice to receive back honor and love from others and blessing from God, because we reverence and obey Him?

When we disdain others, we cut ourselves off from any gifts or blessings God may have planned for that person to give us. Honor obviously begins with our parents, as that is one of the Ten Commandments. God even has a promise for keeping this particular commandment: "Honor your father and mother…that it may be well with you and that you may have a long life on the earth" (Eph. 6:2, 3).

RENOUNCING UNBIBLICAL BELIEFS AND INNER VOWS

In any area we judge our parents, our lives will not go well. To generalize this principle, in any area we judge anyone, our lives will not go well for us.

Summary: The seed of judgment or negative expectation sown in my spirit obediently sends out a message to all within its reach. My spirit might say, "I am programmed to fail; please respond to me in that light." In this case, everyone else's spirits hear and receive that message and respond in kind. Their spirits say, "Let's do everything we can to ensure that this directive is fulfilled." And so I continue to attract events, people, and situations to my life which ensure my failure over and over again. I draw to myself that which I believe to be true. I create my own lifestyle based on the beliefs I hold within.

Clearly, the fruit I am harvesting in my life can become an important clue to guide me as I search for possible expectations I hold, whether good or bad. I can discover unconscious negative expectations **by observing the fruit my life is producing**, and then tracing back to possible roots which might be causing this fruit.

I will want to examine the conscious and unconscious beliefs and judgments I hold and ensure that they all line up with the Bible. Those that don't will need to be repented of and renounced and replaced with a more biblical belief system.

APPLICATION EXERCISE—PICTURE JESUS NEXT TO YOU IN A COMFORTABLE SETTING AND TUNE TO FLOW

The exercise below gets you started discerning unbiblical beliefs and inner vows and praying properly to remove them. If you prefer not writing in this book, then put your answers in your journal or use our freely downloadable "Replacing Ungodly Beliefs" prayer worksheets.[1]

	LORD, WHAT NEGATIVE EXPECTATIONS ARE CONTRIBUTING TO _____? I expect/believe that ...	LORD, WHAT INNER VOWS ARE CONTRIBUTING TO _____? Therefore I vow to do this (an action) ...
1.		
2.		
3.		
4.		
5.		
6.		
7.		
8.		
9.		
10.		
11.		
12.		
	I repent for the ungodly belief that ...	I repent for the inner vow that I will ...

PRAYER OF REPENTANCE

Starting with row number 1, speak the following in prayer: *"I repent for the ungodly belief that.... I repent for the inner vow that..."* Do this for each of the items you list above. Pray from your heart (i.e. tuned to flow, pictures and emotion). If you need more space than 15 lines, get out a sheet of paper and extend this exercise so you are completely freed from the energy of negative beliefs.

TWO-WAY JOURNALING EXERCISE

Use the four keys to hearing God's voice, taught in Chapter 1: stillness, vision, spontaneity and journaling. Play the instrumental visionary meditation, "A Stroll Along the Sea of Galilee." The biblical imagery with soft soaking music will assist you in using the four keys.

- Journal God's answer to this question: "Lord, what would You like to say to me concerning the truths in this chapter?"

Coming up next: The Law of Belief works just as well, if not better, in the positive. If you expect God's promises of blessing and provision and His watchful care over you, you will receive them. According to your faith be it unto you, and what you say, you get. In the next chapter we will explore the Law of Belief as it works in the positive in your life.

ENDNOTES

1. Worksheets available at the close of this article: cwgministries.org/Prayer_Worksheets

Chapter Six

REPLACING UNGODLY BELIEFS WITH GODLY BELIEFS

RECALLING THE MESS OF THE LAST CHAPTER
The Israelites had confessed over and over that they were going to die in the wilderness. They expected to die. They said they would die, and sure enough, God said, "I am going to give you exactly what you have been believing for and confessing. You will die in the wilderness." This actually countered God's plan for their lives, for God had intended to give them the Promised Land. But their negative expectations and inner vows and unbelieving confession brought them destruction rather than God's plan of Promised Land blessings. What a sobering truth for our own lives. We can miss God's choice blessings for our lives by believing for and confessing demonic lies.

WHAT I BELIEVE DETERMINES MY SUCCESS OR FAILURE, AND THROUGH THAT, MY IDENTITY

My corresponding inner vow ensures that all the spiritual energies being developed in my heart by my expectation have a focused avenue of release into the outer world. The message is sent out loud and clear from my spirit: "Do this to me, for I am expecting with all my heart and all my energies for this to happen, so please come alongside me and help me accomplish this goal."

Whatever I have believed for, I will receive. It is that simple. I receive exactly what I believe for and exactly what I have promised myself. This fruit of life then speaks back to me, causing me to crystalize my identity.

REPLACING UNGODLY IDENTITIES WITH GODLY IDENTITIES

If my ungodly belief is "I'll probably fail," then it is reasonable to ask, "What does this reveal that I believe about myself?" The underlying identity may be "I am a failure," or "There's something wrong with me." Then we ask the Lord to speak the truth to that ungodly lie and true identity to replace the false identity built upon lies.

God's truth is, "I can do all things through Christ Who strengthens me" (Phil. 4:13). The **new identity** that this truth produces in me is, "I am a victor. I always triumph in Christ Jesus" (2 Cor. 2:14).

Wow, my entire identity is built upon what I believe! Astounding. I can have a godly identity built on what God says about me or I can have a faulty identity built upon lies. It is absolutely crucial I replace all lies and all false identities with God's truth and the true identity I have in Him! I am able to move from failure to success simply by letting God **replace** the false beliefs and false identities within me. So let's get at it. How do I get this job done?

HOW DO I KEEP UNGODLY BELIEFS (LIES) FROM RETURNING TO MY MIND?

Have you ever tried to push darkness out of a room? Of course not. To even picture such an attempt is absurd. To remove darkness you must turn on the light. This is true in the natural as well as in the spiritual. The darkness of sin in my life is only removed as the light is turned on. Jesus is the Light of the world, so we invite *Him* into these darkened ungodly beliefs. Jesus speaks and I say "Yes, Lord," and His light floods this darkened area. Many years ago I gave up attacking sin in my life. Instead I focus on abiding in Christ, for if I am abiding in Christ, sin is automatically removed.

The only way to remove an ungodly belief is to **replace it** with a godly belief. There are no vacuums in the spirit world. What the Holy Spirit doesn't fill with His light and truth is quickly filled with the darkness of an evil spirit. For example, I could battle against lustful pictures in my mind, and be unsuccessful. However if instead of battling lust, I fix my eyes on Jesus (Heb. 12:1, 2; Acts 2:25; Ps. 16:8), lust is **automatically removed as a**

byproduct of living in the light! Therefore I am not going to attack any ungodly beliefs and try to beat them out of my life. I am simply going to ask God what His godly belief is that replaces it, then write down what is coming to me by way of flowing thoughts and flowing pictures. I will start with a brief statement from Jesus which directly confronts the ungodly belief with God's divine truth. This hits the nail squarely on the head.

Then I will often come back to that statement and have an extended time of two-way journaling so I fully see and integrate God's revelation to me in this area, while removing any blocks which would hinder me from completely embracing His truth.

Jesus said, "The words (*rhemas*) that I **speak** unto you, they are **spirit**, and they are **life**" (Jn. 6:63).

His *rhema* words to us break the yoke of satan's lies. Jesus' *rhema* words turn on the light within us.

I do not overcome my grasshopper complex of weakness by saying, "I am no longer a grasshopper; I am no longer weak and insecure and inferior," for in so doing I would be focusing on what I am not. The problem with this approach is that we are drawn into whatever we focus on. The Lord said to me in my journaling, *"Whatever you focus on grows within you, and whatever grows within you, you become."* So I am not going to confess that I am not a grasshopper in the face of my strong enemies. I am going to tune to flow and get something like this.

Simple statement: "I rule and reign with Christ!"

Extended journaling: "Mark, I have anointed you with strength and power. You are seated with Me in heavenly places to rule and reign with Me over the forces of the enemy. Hear what I am saying about the circumstances, see what I am doing, and speak that truth into the situation. I have come to destroy the works of satan. Now you are My hands and feet, also destroying the works of the enemy. Their power is completely under My control, and now also under your control. So speak that they are cast down. Their power is stripped from them through the victory of the cross. You have authority to speak into the situation and to transform it. So speak now as I tell you to speak...." (The dialogue with Jesus continued on.)

Since it is clear that **a picture is worth a thousand words** and it produces heart faith (Gen. 15:1-5), I will ask for a picture from God of His victory through me in this particular conflict. I will gaze upon that picture and I will speak aloud the revelation of God over the situation as I pray and intercede for God's divine will to be released and His kingdom to come to earth as it is in heaven.

RATHER THAN FOLLOWING UP A GODLY BELIEF WITH A GODLY VOW TO REPLACE THE UNGODLY VOW...

I am *not* going to make a new vow as to how I am going to live in light of my newly-held belief. Jesus said, "I say to you, **make no oath** at all" (Matt. 5:34). So rather than vowing to do something, I say, *"I purpose by the power of the Holy Spirit to..."* This is as close as I would ever come to making a vow.

So exactly what is the difference between "a vow" and "a purpose by the power of the Holy Spirit"? When I make a vow, I have my eyes fixed on me and my power to accomplish this feat. This will result in failure, as I don't have enough power to overcome the works of the enemy. I end up striving and grunting, using my own strength. The Bible is clear to cease my labors and enter into His rest (Heb. 4:10, 11).

So when I purpose by the power of the Holy Spirit to accomplish, I am not looking to self at all. I am acknowledging that is it God who accomplishes, not me. It is the power of His indwelling Spirit which empowers me and grants me wisdom and everything I need for life, godliness and success (2 Pet. 1:3).

It is no longer a striving of my flesh. I no longer have this ungodly picture that "I" am in the center of any process. I am now holding a godly picture that Jesus is at my right hand (Acts 2:25), giving me direction, wise counsel and comfort, and His Spirit **flows within me**, anointing me with the power to overcome. This change in focus is the difference between a dead work, something "I" come up with and I try to do (Heb. 6:1, 2), and a live work, a work commissioned, empowered and culminated by the Holy Spirit. It is the difference between religion and Christianity.

EXAMPLES OF GODLY BELIEFS AND GODLY PURPOSES

Below are twelve godly beliefs and godly purposes which can replace the twelve ungodly beliefs and ungodly vows of the last chapter. Take the time to compare the twelve from the last chapter to the twelve listed here. Get a feel for how this process works, because next it will be your turn to do the same.

	However, God says ...	So I purpose by the power of the Spirit to...
1.	"I make your way prosperous"	step out in faith
2.	"I give you the power to make wealth"	believe God for financial prosperity
3.	"I have offered you a land of milk and honey"	possess my promised land
4.	"My blood washes away all your sin"	repent and be cleansed
5.	"...will not depart from the way he should go"	train my children, not provoke them
6.	"I work all things out for good"	trust that God rules over all
7.	"Give My love away to others"	stay open and loving
8.	"I am the perfect One"	trust in God's perfection, not my own
9.	"Jesus wept"	be responsive to my heart's emotions
10.	"You are righteous through Christ"	put on Christ's righteousness
11.	"You can do all things through Christ"	see Christ within empowering me
12.	"You are seated with Christ in heavenly places"	rule with Christ over the forces of evil
	I accept what God has spoken that ...	**I purpose by the power of the Holy Spirit to ...**

PICTURE JESUS NEXT TO YOU IN A COMFORTABLE SETTING AND TUNE TO FLOW

The exercise below helps you replace unbiblical beliefs and vows with godly beliefs and purposes. If you prefer not writing in this book, then put your answers in your journal or use the freely downloadable prayer worksheets.[1]

Review your ungodly belief and inner vow number 1 from the previous chapter. Then ask the Lord what He wants to say that counters these. Tune to flow and write down what comes to you in line one on the chart below. Repeat this process for each of the fifteen ungodly beliefs you have previously recorded.

REPLACING UNGODLY BELIEFS WITH GODLY BELIEFS

	However, God says ...	So I purpose by the power of the Spirit to...
1.		
2.		
3.		
4.		
5.		
6.		
7.		
8.		
9.		
10.		
11.		
12.		
13.		
14		
15.		
	I accept what God has spoken that ...	**I purpose by the power of the Holy Spirit to ...**

DO THIS APPLICATION NOW—PRAYER TO EMBRACE WHAT GOD HAS SPOKEN

Starting with row number 1, speak the following in prayer: *"I accept what God has spoken that... (insert godly belief) and I purpose by the power of the Holy Spirit to... (insert godly purpose)."* Do this for each on the list above. Pray from your heart (i.e. tuned to flow, pictures and emotions).

It would be helpful to renew this prayer in your morning devotions for a few days until your heart says, "I've got it." Also expanding each godly belief into a two-way journaling exercise is a wonderful way to deepen it.

GOD HAS ANOINTED YOU WITH THE SPIRIT TO SUCCEED IN EVERY SITUATION: HOME, MARKETPLACE AND CHURCH!

I want to hone in on removing satan's two biggest lies which are found in the first words out of his mouth in the Garden of Eden: "You will be like God, knowing good from evil" (Gen. 3:5).

"**YOU**" became the belief that everything centers around me. I am a self-contained unit. I should look to my strengths and my abilities to succeed. This is contrary to God's view, which is that I am a vessel, empty on the inside, needing to be filled by His Spirit which flows mightily within me.

"**Know**" became the belief that I am supposed to reason everything out rather than listen to and follow the voice and leading of God, relying on my own reasoning rather than anointed reason. Anointed reason is when I reason together with God (Isa. 1:18). Rationalism (relying on reason) became my god, rather than honoring the voice of God leading me from my heart (Jn. 7:37-39).

THESE LIES SET ME UP TO FALL INTO THE UNGODLY BELIEF THAT GOD SPOKE ABOUT

> '*My power and the strength of my hand made me this wealth.*'
> "But you shall remember the LORD your God, for **it is He who is giving you power to make wealth, that He may confirm His covenant** which He swore to your fathers, as it is this day.
> (Deut. 8:17-18)

It is God's blessing that makes me prosper. It is never my greatness that made me prosper.

I WILL PERISH IF I DON'T LISTEN TO THE VOICE OF GOD BUT BELIEVE THE LIES OF SATAN

> *"It shall come about if you ever forget the LORD your God and go after other gods and serve them* (e.g., rationalism & humanism) *and worship them, I testify against you today that you will surely perish. Like the nations that the LORD makes to perish before you, so **you shall perish; because you would not listen to the voice of the LORD** your God."* (Deut. 8:19-20)

I NEED TO KNOW THAT THE LOVES AND PASSIONS AND GIFTINGS I HAVE ARE ANOINTINGS FROM GOD

Did you know that there is *no* sacred/secular split in God's eyes? The earth is the Lord's and all it contains (Ps. 24:1), so nothing on this earth is secular. Nothing is satan's. It is *all* God's. So any job I do is my ministry unto the Lord and His service through me to all of humanity (Col. 3:23,24). This includes everything from construction to sewing, as well as teaching others how to do the same. When you read the covenant blessings of Deuteronomy 28:1-14, they take your breath away. They touch every area of your life. I encourage you to read them now.

CRAFTSMEN ARE ANOINTED WITH GOD'S WISDOM AND KNOWLEDGE

> *Now the LORD spoke to Moses, saying, "See, I have called by name Bezalel... **I have filled him with the Spirit of God in wisdom, in understanding, in knowledge,** and in **all kinds of***

craftsmanship, to make artistic designs for work in gold, in silver, and in bronze, and in the cutting of stones for settings, and in the carving of wood, that he may work in all kinds of craftsmanship...in the hearts of all who are skillful I have put skill, that they may make all that I have commanded you" (Exodus 31:1-6).

"You are to instruct all the skilled craftsmen, whom I have filled with a spirit of wisdom, to make garments for Aaron's consecration, so that he may serve Me as priest" (Exodus 28:3).

*Then Moses said to the Israelites, "See, the LORD has called by name Bezalel son of Uri, the son of Hur, of the tribe of Judah. And He has **filled him with the Spirit of God, with skill, ability, and knowledge in all kinds of craftsmanship**, to design artistic works in gold, silver, and bronze, to cut gemstones for settings, and to carve wood, so that he may be a master of every artistic craft.*

*And the LORD has given both him and Oholiab son of Ahisamach, of the tribe of Dan, **the ability to teach others**. He has filled them with skill to do all kinds of work as engravers, designers, **embroiderers in blue, purple, and scarlet yarn and fine linen, and as weavers**—as artistic designers of every kind of craft"*
(Ex. 35:30-35 Berean Study Bible).

I am struck by the fact that even sewing, weaving and embroidering were done under the anointing—so it's not just "men's work." Also, the ability to teach others these crafts is a gift and calling from God. Success is not about me. It is about the anointings placed within me by Almighty God, and me listening to His voice and following His lead. **Remember:** His voice is experienced as flowing, spontaneous thoughts while my eyes are fixed on Him. A pretty simple way to live. Very childlike, and totally countercultural. However this is the way we are designed to live. This is where success rules and reigns. This is where the passion of my heart meets the gifts and anointings in my life and I serve society well, being amply rewarded for my gift to them. This is success!

JOURNALING APPLICATION

Use the four keys to hearing God's voice, taught in Chapter 1: stillness, vision, spontaneity and journaling. Play the instrumental visionary meditation, "A Stroll Along the Sea of Galilee." The biblical imagery with soft soaking music will assist you in using the four keys.

1. Lord, what are the skills You have placed within me?
2. Lord, what love and passion have You put in my heart?
3. Lord, how do You want to combine this love, passion and skill to fulfill the **specific destiny** You have for my life, that destiny which allows me to serve humanity well through all You have placed within me?
4. Show me a vision of what my life looks like as I fulfill the destiny You have for me.
5. Lord, what do You want to show me from the lives of the heroes of faith (Heb. 11), and how that relates to where I am in my life now?
6. What is the next step You want me to take?

The vision of the destiny God has for your life, built upon the gifts and anointings He has graced you with, should be something you gaze upon steadily, for from it flow strength and power and the direction to keep you on course. You may want to write it out in detail and post it in a visible spot, or even create a picture of it which you can post and gaze upon. Clean godly pictures displace satan's pictures.

RESOURCES

1. **Business Prayers**—cwgministries.org/ways-to-pray-lord-how-do-i-pray-today#Business
2. **Biblical Gift Mix Profile**—cwgministries.org/giftmix
3. **How to Build a Winning Team**—cwgministries.org/iwork4him

I can do all things through Christ who strengthens me!

(Phil. 4:13)

ENDNOTES

1. Worksheets available at the close of this article: cwgministries.org/Prayer_Worksheets

Chapter Seven

REPLACING WORD CURSES WITH BLESSINGS

Blessings and curses can come from words spoken about you by yourself or others. A parent or teacher may label you as stupid, or you may call yourself stupid. Both these word curses will likely produce a negative expectation that you should act as if you are stupid.

I used to speak a word curse over myself as a result of my experience throughout my school years. In both high school and college, I was a straight "B" student. So I would speak that word curse over myself, declaring that I have a "B-level" brain. One day when I was journaling the Lord said to me, "Don't ever again say 'I have a B-level brain,' for now that you have the Holy Spirit, you have an AAA brain. You have the mind of Christ. You have words of wisdom and knowledge. You have My wisdom flowing within you as you ask, turn to Me and receive My flowing thoughts and ideas."

I repented immediately and now confess that I have a AAA brain. I am brilliant! And now that I believe I am brilliant with God's wisdom, I am willing to expect to do great things for God, far beyond the limitations of my flesh. Yay God! And of course, **we all** have this same Holy Spirit!

I had unending digestive issues, and the Lord brought to my attention that one of the phrases I have used throughout my life is, "That makes me sick to my stomach." How's that for a word curse!

Or have you ever said about someone, "He is such a pain in the neck"? What do you think that says to your body?

I doubt many of us consider the seriousness of the words we speak. Whether these words are about ourselves or others, they carry great weight and have the power to influence destinies.

> *The tongue is a fire, the very world of iniquity; the tongue is set among our members as that which defiles the entire body, and **sets on fire the course of our life**, and is set on fire by hell.* (Jas. 3:6)

Can there be any stronger statement concerning the power of our speech? It is a fire, set on fire by hell, can defile my entire body, and set the course of my life on fire. So what I say is what I get! I got it!

"DEATH AND LIFE ARE IN THE POWER OF THE TONGUE" (PROV. 18:21).

> *"There is one who speaks **rashly** like the thrusts of a sword, But the tongue of the wise brings healing."* (Prov. 12:18)

> "A soothing tongue is a tree of life, But **perversion** in it crushes the spirit." (Prov. 15:4)

Word curses—Rash, perverse words spoken over me by myself or others which produce death.

Word blessings—Words of potential, fulfillment and destiny spoken over me by myself or others which produce life.

EXAMPLES OF WORD CURSES

You dummy. You are such a loser. You'll never make it as a _____. You're so fat. You are just lazy. You'll never amount to anything. This is the computer nerd, or any other negative nicknames.

I just can't excel. I can't catch a break. I'm a failure. I can't succeed. I can't fulfill the needs of my spouse. My marriage is headed for the rocks. I will probably get sick. My immune system is weak. I have (name any disease). And the list goes on and on.

EXAMPLES OF WORD BLESSINGS

Jesus spoke words of blessing and spiritual power was released: "Arise, take up your bed and walk." "You are healed…." "Your sins are forgiven. Go and sin no more." "Your name is Peter, and upon this rock I will build My church."

I can speak words of life and blessing about myself: I have triumphed in Christ Jesus. I have overcome by the word of my testimony. I can do all things through Christ who strengthens me. I am an overcomer. I will continue to press in until I succeed. I only do what I hear my Father speaking. I am anointed to release healing to the broken, to heal the blind, to set the captive free. I have been blessed with every spiritual blessing in Christ Jesus.

I am seated with Christ in heavenly places and I rule and reign with Him. God has given me the power to create wealth.

SPIRITUAL FORCES WHICH CREATE OR DESTROY LIFE ARE RELEASED BY THE WORDS WE SPEAK

God spoke the worlds into being. Breath and spirit are the same word in both the Greek and the Hebrew languages. So when I speak, the breath which is coming out with my words is spirit and contains the energy of the spirit which birthed the words.

If they are accusative words, they have been birthed by the accuser and I am releasing the energy of satan and his evil spirits (demons). If they are comforting words, they have been birthed by the Comforter, and I am releasing the energy of Jesus and the Holy Spirit. So the power of evil spirits and the power of the Holy Spirit are released through the words I speak.

Remember Ananias and Sapphira? Satan put it in their hearts to speak lies, and the result was their death (Acts 5:1-10).

WHICH OF MY THOUGHTS COME FROM THE ENEMY AND WHICH FROM THE HOLY SPIRIT?

The tenor of thoughts reveals who birthed them. We are in spiritual warfare and are to **take every thought captive** (2 Cor. 10:4, 5), because some thoughts are coming from the enemy. If I speak the thoughts which have flowed into my mind from the enemy, I am speaking death over the situation. That is why the Bible says that life and death are in the power of the tongue.

The thoughts and words which line up with the names of satan we will assume came as spontaneous flowing thoughts from his evil spirits, and those which line up with Jesus are coming from the Holy Spirit. In the Bible, one's name reveals one's character. Ask if a thought you have lines up with the left column which details the nature of satan, or the right column which details the nature of Jesus. Reject any thought which lines up with the nature of satan. Do not let it dwell in your heart or mind or come out of your mouth to curse you or those around you.

SATAN DESTROYING	HOLY SPIRIT BUILDING UP
The Accuser (Rev. 12:10)	The Comforter (Jn. 14:16)
The Father of Lies (Jn. 8:44)	The Spirit of Truth (Jn. 16:13)
The Adversary (Matt. 13:39)	The Edifier (1 Cor. 14:3)
The Condemner (Rom. 8:1)	The Exhorter/Teacher (1 Cor. 14:3; Jn. 4:26)
Thief—Steals, Kills, Destroys (Jn. 10:10)	Giver of Abundant Life (Jn. 10:10)

ALL MY CELLS LISTEN AND RESPOND TO WHAT IS SPOKEN

The trillions of cells within me also hear and respond to what I say, so I am speaking life or death to them. If I say, "I am sick," they say, "OK, we are sick." If I say, "By His stripes I am healed," they respond, "OK, Jesus has healed me." They react in accord with what I speak. Truly life and death are in the power of the tongue.

SEE GOD'S PASSION THAT WE SPEAK ONLY WORDS OF LIFE SO WE RELEASE ONLY THE HOLY SPIRIT

- *Let no unwholesome word proceed from your mouth, but **only such a word as is good for edification** according to the need of the moment, so that it will give grace to those who hear.* (Eph. 4:29)
- *In everything by prayer and supplication with **thanksgiving*** (Phil 4:6)

- ***In*** *everything give thanks* (1 Thess. 5:18)
- *Always giving thanks **for** all things* (Eph. 5:20)
- *Continually offer up a sacrifice of **praise** to God* (Heb. 13:15)
- *Overflowing with **gratitude*** (Col. 2:7)
- *You will also **decree** a thing, and it will be established for you* (Job 22:28)
- Seek to speak in tongues and prophesy (1 Cor. 14:1-5)
- *Honor all people, love the brotherhood, fear God, honor the king* (1 Pet. 2:17)

If we are honoring and loving, we will not be judging and speaking negatives. We will be praying for people with a heart of compassion, just as Jesus did. If we sow words of life, we receive life back. If we send out death with our mouths, death comes back to us. Whatever we sow, we reap.

WORDS UNLEASH THE LAW OF SOWING AND REAPING

Do not judge, so that you will not be judged. (Matt. 7:1)

Do not be deceived, God is not mocked; for whatever a person sows, this he will also reap. (Gal. 6:7)

They have sown the wind, and they shall reap the whirlwind. (Hos. 8:7)

The principle of sowing and reaping flows throughout life. We see it in crops in the field, and it is also evident in words we say. If I speak works of judgement, I will receive judgment back. If I speak words of anger, I receive anger back. If I speak words of peace,

I receive peace back. And the harvest is greater than the seed sown. I can sow out just a few seeds and reap much fruit in return.

I know what I want in life; I want peace, joy, happiness, blessing, prosperity, mercy. Therefore I need to sow these things with my lips.

THE HEBREW MINDSET COMBINES WORDS WITH PICTURES—I NEED TO DO THE SAME

It is not just what I am **saying** that blesses or curses me; it is also the pictures attached to my words which exert tremendous influence over me. It is true that a picture is worth a thousand words. Consider Jesus, who always used parables or picture stories in His teaching (Matt. 13:34). Consider the fact that the Bible is written most largely as a book of stories of people's lives, which evoke pictures within us as we read them. Consider that when the Bible commands us to reason, even our reasoning is to be centered in pictures.

> *"Come now, and let us reason together," says the LORD, "Though your sins are as scarlet, they will be as white as snow; though they are red like crimson, they will be like wool.* (Isa. 1:18)

As a westerner, I see reasoning as a logical procedure. However, Isaiah 1:18 is the only verse in the Bible telling me to "reason," and the instructions for reasoning are: 1) make sure God is guiding you, and 2) make sure pictures are central to the process.

I make sure God is guiding the process by seeing Jesus at my right hand. I relax by putting a smile on my face, asking Him for His thoughts and pictures concerning the situation. I tune to flowing thoughts and pictures, which I write down, believing they are God's voice and God's vision to me. Finally, I honor them by acting on them. If I have any doubt, I submit them to my three spiritual advisors.

WHY WORDS *WITHOUT* PICTURES DID NOT WORK FOR ME

God led me to a Word of Faith church so I could grow strong in faith. They taught me to confess truth, such as, "I am the righteousness of God in Christ Jesus" (1 Cor. 1:30). Unfortunately, I said the words hundreds of times, while at the same time picturing myself as a lowdown sinner. I found my confession was short-circuited by the ungodly picture I was gazing upon. My inner being was **not congruent**. It was in discord and thus shorting out the power of God within me. I was picturing one thing and speaking another.

When I added the godly picture that I am clothed with Christ's righteousness, then my confession released life because my picture of myself adorned in a robe of white was **in agreement** with the words of my mouth (Gal. 3:27).

The Bible is clear that transformation occurs **"while we look"** (2 Cor. 3:18). Jesus spoke to me and said, "Whatever you fix your eyes on grows within you and whatever grows within you, you become."

So each of us must make sure we have complete congruency within ourselves. This congruency requires the alignment of biblical **thoughts**, biblical **pictures** and biblical **confessions**. When these three align, we then can release the life of the Holy Spirit, and this amazing life transforms us and all whom we touch.

BAD SPEECH IS REALLY A HEART PROBLEM

If my mouth speaks negatives which line up with the names of satan, rather than positives which line up with the names of Jesus, then I need to fix this problem. But trying to control what I say is not enough. It is more than a mouth problem. The mouth speaks out of that which fills the heart, so this is really a **heart** problem.

> *The mouth speaks out of that which fills the heart. The good man brings out of his good treasure what is good; and the evil man brings out of his evil treasure what is evil. But I tell you that every careless word that people speak, they shall give an accounting for it in the day of judgment. For **by your words you will be justified**, and **by your words you will be condemned**."* (Matt. 12:34-37)
>
> *The things that proceed out of the mouth **come from the heart**, and those **defile** the man.* (Matt. 15:18)

Negative words are proof that I believe the lies of satan more than I believe the truths of God's word. What a terrible situation to be in. What a slap in God's face. What a way to cut off God's blessings in my life.

So how do I get a deeper revelation of God's will concerning a situation? I do this by using the seven-step Bible meditation which we will explore in Chapter Ten.

A FATHER'S BLESSING IS AN EXAMPLE OF SPEAKING WORDS OF LIFE

A father's blessing is a wonderful way of conferring destiny, anointing and power from one to another. This blessing can come from your heavenly Father, your earthly father, or a spiritual advisor.

Abram received a Father's blessing from his heavenly Father:

Now the LORD said to Abram, "Go forth from your country, And from your relatives And from your father's house, To the land which I will show you; And I will make you a great nation, And I will bless you, And make your name great; And so you shall be a blessing; And I will bless those who bless you, And the one who curses you I will curse. And in you all the families of the earth will be blessed." (Gen. 12:1-3)

Isaac gave a father's blessing:

Now may God give you of the dew of heaven, And of the fatness of the earth, and an abundance of grain and new wine; May peoples serve you, And nations bow down to you; Be master of your brothers, And may your mother's sons bow down to you. Cursed be those who curse you, and blessed be those who bless you." (Gen 27:28-29)

I received this blessing from the Lord through journaling:

Mark, we are going to saturate the world with the message of communion with God. I want you to be like Abraham. He was a man of great faith, a financial leader, and a political leader.

My spiritual advisor, Roger Miller, provided me this life-transforming counsel at a point in my life when I was very negative. It was like a father's blessing to me, directing the steps of my present and future:

Leadership is automatically passed to those who remain optimistic.

PRAYER EXERCISE

This exercise helps you begin discerning word curses and God's countering truth, and praying properly to remove them. If you prefer not writing in this book, then put your answers in your journal or use the downloadable prayer worksheets.

"Lord, what word curses have I or others spoken over me?" (Picture Jesus with you and tune to flow…)

	WORD CURSE	GOD'S COUNTERING TRUTH IS …
1.		
2.		
3.		
4.		
5.		
6.		
7.		
8.		
9.		
10.		

PRAYER TO BREAK WORD CURSES

	STEPS	SPECIFIC ACTIONS
1.	I forgive, release and bless the person (you or another)	Picture them and speak directly to them
2.	I repent for accepting this ungodly belief	And I believe instead what God has said which is …
3.	I break off all spiritual forces in Jesus' name	I embrace God's blessing which is …

JOURNALING ASSIGNMENT—BLESSING SELF AND OTHERS

Use the four keys to hearing God's voice, taught in Chapter 1: stillness, vision, spontaneity and journaling. Play the instrumental visionary meditation, "A Stroll Along the Sea of Galilee" to assist you.

The opposite of word curses are word blessings. Continuing and expanding the journaling from the last chapter, ask the Lord for His spoken word of blessing over you concerning your gifts, purpose and destiny. Write out what you receive. This could easily take an entire page or two, and becomes something you can post on a mirror to re-read from time to time to stay encouraged and focused. Then ask God what blessings He wants you to speak over your family members and others close to you. Write these down and share them as appropriate.

CAREFULLY CLEANSE YOUR HOME OF OBJECTS CARRYING CURSES

- **Cursed objects:** *"The carved images of their gods you are to **burn with fire**; you shall not covet the silver or the gold that is on them, nor take it for yourselves, or you will be trapped by it; for it is an abomination to the Lord your God. And you shall not bring an abomination into your house and become designated for destruction, like it; you are to utterly detest it, and you are to utterly loathe it, for it is something **designated for destruction**."* (Deut. 7:25-26)

Application: Ask the Lord to bring to your attention any objects in your home with potential curses on them so you can remove and destroy them immediately (Acts 19:19). Tune to flow and record what you receive.

Repentance: Lord, I come to You concerning cursed objects and any demon infestation in my possessions and home. I understand that this is idolatry and I ask Your forgiveness for having any such items.

Action: Remove and destroy them. (Do not give them away or sell them!)

BEGIN TO BLESS OBJECTS WITH THE POWER OF THE HOLY SPIRIT

- **Blessed objects:** *"God worked special miracles by the hands of Paul: So that from his body were brought unto the sick **handkerchiefs or aprons**, and the diseases departed from them, and the evil spirits went out of them"* (Acts 19:11-12).

CONSOLIDATION—IF YOU HAVE NOT ALREADY DONE SO...

Download these free prayer worksheets from this website: cwgministries.org/Prayer_Worksheets

- Replacing Ungodly Beliefs—**Completed Sample**
- Replacing Ungodly Beliefs—**Worksheet** (make copies so you have plenty of space)
- Replacing Ungodly Beliefs—**Edit Enabled**
- Contributing Strands Worksheet—**PDF**
- Contributing Strands Worksheet—**Edit Enabled**
- Seven Prayers Overview Sheet (to print on standard 8.5x11 letter size paper and fold in half)

The worksheets above allow you to list:

- All ungodly beliefs and inner vows **and** countering godly beliefs and inner purposes.
- You can **also list** all word curses and accompanying actions, followed by God's truths and your new purposes in the Holy Spirit.

All the personal applications from Chapters 5-7 are combined on this one chart. You may copy the applications you have completed from these last three chapters into this **one place**. However, stay open to flow as God may have you **clarify and perfect** some of the answers you previously gave, adding detail and precision to maximize the healing process.

Once everything is listed, complete the prayers which are given at the bottom of the four columns. Stay tuned to flow and vision and emotion so this is a deep spiritual encounter. If you have already prayed them, **do so again** since repeating a prayer a second and third time deepens the impact and release of power.

Chapter Eight

TRAUMATIC PICTURES HEALED THROUGH INNER HEALING

Inner Healing may be defined as: *"allowing God to replace the pictures in the art gallery of your mind, removing pictures that do not have Jesus in them and replacing them with those that do have Jesus in them."* I gleaned this definition for inner healing from Rita Bennett's book *Emotionally Free*. For over 30 years, I have used this approach continuously in my own prayer times and with those I counsel. It allows the Wonderful Counselor direct access to the wounds in our hearts, inviting Him to show us what He was doing and what He was saying in the trauma we experienced. These new pictures and ideas replace the corrupt pictures and lies within and heal us by bringing light into these darkened areas. I love the power, effectiveness and simplicity of inner healing.

Inner healing is a very simple three-step process. You go back to the painful scene, invite Jesus into it and allow Him to move freely. You tune to flowing thoughts and flowing pictures, and record what He is speaking and showing you. The chart below lists these three steps along with a biblical example.

THE INNER HEALING PROCESS

	THE STEP TAKEN	A BIBLICAL EXAMPLE PETER (LK. 22:54-62 & JN. 18:18; 21:2-17)
1.	Using vision, go back and re-enter the hurt.	Charcoal fire Dawn Three-fold confession
2.	Using vision, bring Jesus into the scene.	"Jesus stood on the beach…"
3.	Using vision, let Jesus move freely, healing the hurt with His loving presence.	Jesus' statements of affirming love: "Tend My lambs; Shepherd My sheep; Tend My sheep"

JESUS HEALED PETER'S WOUND USING THIS INNER HEALING PROCESS

In Luke 22:54-62 and John 18:15-18, we have the story of Peter's greatest heart wound. (I encourage you to go back and read it now.) After promising Jesus that he would never desert Him, he denied Him three times. It happened near a charcoal fire in early morning, just before a rooster crowed. This hurt him so deeply that he went out and wept bitterly.

The next time Jesus sees Peter is in John 21:2-17. (Please read it now.) Instead of simply telling Peter, "You are forgiven," He takes the time to completely recreate the painful scene. It is again early morning, beside a charcoal fire and it involves a threefold confession: "Do you love Me?" In this new, revised scene, rather than Peter seeing and believing that he is now forever rejected and can never be used in the ministry again, Peter sees and hears

Jesus' words of love, compassion and re-commissioning. These are coming directly from the mouth of Jesus. So from the midst of the painful scene being replayed in Peter's mind, Jesus has appeared and ministered grace, love and acceptance. This is inner healing. This is healing of the heart. This is Jesus replacing the pictures in the art gallery of our minds, removing pictures that do not have Jesus in them and replacing them with pictures that do.

Had Peter's heart not been filled with guilt and his eyes filled with tears when he denied Jesus, Peter could have probably seen His love, compassion and forgiveness even then (Lk. 22:61). However, in the midst of our hurt, we often are not looking to see Jesus. All we can see is the painful situation and perhaps feel guilty about our imperfect response to it.

REPLACING PICTURES OF LIES WITH PICTURES OF TRUTH

In inner healing, you are moving from a picture that **contains a lie** ("Jesus isn't present, watching over and protecting His children") to a picture that portrays the truth ("Jesus is always there, watching over and loving His children"). *Any picture in my mind must have Jesus in it to be legitimate and true!*

WE SAY A PICTURE IS WORTH HOW MUCH?

We say a picture is worth a thousand words. I believe the Bible concurs. A picture has 1000 times the power to impact and change us. Pictures are the **language of the heart**. To heal the heart, we must use the language of the heart.

The Bible says we are "transformed **while** we look" (2 Cor. 3:17, 18). So whatever we are gazing upon transforms us for good or for evil, depending if it is a picture of kingdom reality or an evil picture of lust, fear or separation from God.

Right pictures produce **faith**. Abraham saw a vision of thousands of stars and his faith was inflamed. That affirms my belief in the power of a picture.

> "**Look** now toward heaven, and count the stars if you are able to number them." And He said to him, "So shall your descendants be." And **he believed** in the LORD, and He accounted it to him for righteousness. (Gen. 15:5, 6)

Obviously his faith in God's promise was deepened by this image of numberless stars.

Wrong pictures move us **backward**.

> "But they hearkened not, nor inclined their ear, but walked in the counsels and in the **imagination** of their evil heart, and **went backward**, and not forward." (Jer. 7:24)

Wow! How's that for the power of pictures? Holding fast to a godly picture makes me the Father of Faith, while holding a wrong picture moves me backward.

According to Hebrews 12:1, 2, our eyes are always to be fixed on Jesus Who is at our side (Acts 2:25; Ps. 16:8). Jesus continually looked to see what His Father was doing.

> "Truly, truly, I say to you, the Son can do nothing of Himself, unless it is something He **sees** the Father doing; for whatever the Father does, these things the Son also does in like manner. For the Father loves the Son, and **shows Him all things** that He Himself is doing." (Jn. 5:19-20)

THE CONNECTION BETWEEN EMOTIONS AND PICTURES

My emotions are **guided** by the pictures being held in my mind. If my spouse is late coming home and in my mind's eye I see an accident, a crushed car and an ambulance, then the emotions of fear and dread will fill me. If instead I ask the Lord for His picture, and the flowing picture that lights upon my mind is an angel seated on the hood of her car, having a good time while she is stuck in traffic, that picture too produces an emotional response—faith, peace and joy that all is well.

Elisha's servant saw enemy chariots surrounding his city and he was filled with fear (2 Kings 6:15, 16). However when his eyes were opened, and he saw heavenly chariots between him and the enemy chariots, his fear was gone (2 Kings 6:17-19).

APPLICATION: STEP 1—IDENTIFY PAINFUL SCENES WHICH NEED GOD'S HEALING PRESENCE

Ask, "Lord, what negative pictures of people or experiences am I holding which are contributing to the heart wound we are dealing with today?" Tune to flow and summarize the scene in the left column below. Do not look at the scene any longer than 1-2 seconds, because you do not want to become re-traumatized. *Only* use *three* words to describe the scene (approximate age, place and person), for example, "7, kitchen, mom." Going into a long, detailed description of a painful memory is counterproductive. Gazing at it longer than one second is also counterproductive. The healing comes in the next step, Step 2 below, where we invite Jesus into the scene.

	PAINFUL SCENES IN 3 WORDS	INNER HEALING—RECORD WHAT JESUS SAYS AND DOES IN THE SITUATION
1.		
2.		
3.		
4.		
5.		
6.		
7.		

APPLICATION: STEP 2—ASK JESUS TO APPEAR IN THE SCENE

Process each of the painful scenes above, one at a time, beginning with the **least intense**. For a rape situation, go back to **after** it was over, **not** to the middle of it. Also, see Part Two of this book under "Inner Healing for Hellish Situations."

Begin each scene by affirming what you know to be true, "Lord, I know **You were there** in that troubling scene. Jesus, please show me where You were and what You were doing." Watch and see what Jesus does and says as He appears in the scene. Stay tuned to the Holy Spirit's flow and vision as you write. Do not manipulate the scene yourself. Follow Jesus' lead. Forgive, release, honor and bless as the Lord instructs. Those that wounded you were themselves wounded. We pray for those who mistreat us (Lk. 6:27, 29).

You may use additional paper to expand what Jesus is saying and doing. You may want to re-read Jesus' comments over the next couple of days. Submit any questionable scenes you receive to the Bible and to your spiritual counselors to ensure they are from God.

HOW A COUNSELOR TAKES A CLIENT THROUGH THE INNER HEALING PROCESS

I find inner healing to be the simplest, most effective counseling method I know. Here are the steps I take.

1. Have the client ask the Lord what scenes need His healing presence. I tell them, "Tune to flow and tell me what picture pops into your mind. Don't go digging; allow the Lord to bring to your mind the one He knows needs healing today."
2. I say, "Now, in three words, tell me the scene (age, location, person present). You will only look at this for 1-2 seconds, then..."
3. I lend my faith to the client by praying, "Lord Jesus, we know You **were** present in that scene. You are Immanuel. You **are always** with us. Allow us to see You in that situation."
4. I instruct the client to be relaxed, and look around for Jesus in the scene, and to let me know when they can see Him.
5. I am silent for 15-20 seconds as the client looks. Then client says, "I can see Him."
6. I respond, "Good, now tune to flowing thoughts and flowing pictures and see what He does. Describe it to me as you see it happening." Again I wait silently for 15-20 seconds, until the client speaks.
7. As the client begins describing what Jesus is saying and doing, I write quickly, capturing all the key elements of what Jesus is doing.
8. As I write, I encourage the client, *"That is good; now keep your eyes fixed on Jesus and tune to flowing thoughts and flowing pictures and tell me what Jesus does next."* This sentence should be memorized as it contains **key coaching**.

a. "That is good"—builds their faith that what they are seeing is a valid vision.
   b. "Keep your eyes fixed on Jesus"—if they aren't reminded, they will look other places.
   c. "Tune to flowing thoughts and flowing pictures"—if they aren't reminded, they will tune back to reason, logic, doubt, fear and judgment.
   d. So every element in this coaching sentence is crucial, important, and must be said.
9. We repeat the above steps for scene after scene until healing is complete.
10. I encourage the client to continue this process at home with the Lord, as He brings up additional scenes.
11. I send the completed notes home with the client for them to review.
12. Finally, I instruct them that from now on, they **only look at the new scenes**, those with Jesus present, **never** the old lying scenes. This is essential! If they go back to gaze on the old pictures, the wound re-emerges, and the emotions of pain come back.

PRAYER EXERCISE—INNER HEALING FOR AN ORGAN WHICH HAS BEEN TRAUMATIZED

If you have had open heart surgery or any other organ damage, or a broken bone or injured joint, the following prayer will be of great value. See Part Two of this book for an extended teaching on "Inner Healing for an Organ."

1. Lay hands on the organ.

2. Ask—"Jesus, come in and minister grace, peace, healing and Your calming touch."
3. "Jesus, cleanse the cellular memory of trauma from this organ."
4. See Him sweep out the trauma and fill the organ with peace and light.

PRAYER EXERCISE—RESTORING CELLULAR DNA

Each cell has an individual life with a brain, memory, emotions and relationship. Each cell functions according to its identity. As we ask Jesus to restore each cell to its original purpose and DNA, He will.

Prayer:

- Holy Spirit, would You please cleanse each cell in my body and would You please give it the identity of Jesus Christ?
- If you know certain cells have been specifically damaged, then pray this prayer specifically for those cells.

DISCOVER THE GIFT GOD HAS BROUGHT TO YOU THROUGH EACH PAINFUL EXPERIENCE

"A hurt is healed when you can see the gift God has produced in your life through the experience."

When I pray for inner healing of a painful memory and Jesus walks in and speaks and acts, and I forgive, then what? Isn't it enough to just say I have forgiven a person for this travesty they have committed against me? No, because forgiveness only brings me from the darkness of anger, bitterness and hatred to a **neutral** position. Neutral isn't really where I want to end up because everything God doesn't fill with His divine light is quickly filled with satan's darkness.

So let's turn on the light. We do this by journaling and letting God speak to us concerning the following question: "Lord, what is the gift you have produced in my life through this experience?" You tune to flow and write, and He shows you the gift. Now you can get excited and **thankful** for this wonderful gift. Now you are no longer neutral, but full of excitement, joy and life because you see God has turned this situation around for good. The Bible says God works all things out for good (Rom. 8:28).

Notice carefully: I am not saying you are thankful for the traumatic experience (although He may bring you to that place of grace). I am not saying we rejoice when others sin against us. However, we have a God Who redeems! What the enemy means for evil in your life, our God will use for your good (Gen. 50:20). No matter what has happened to you, God wants to redeem it to His glory. If you allow Him to, He will use your trials to conform you to the image of His Son and even bring honor and esteem and glory to you as well (Rom. 8:28-30). Nothing that happens to you can prevent His purposes and destiny for you from being fulfilled, as long as you continue to obey and submit to Him in every circumstance.

Let me share a personal example of this. One of the most traumatic experiences of my life was when I was abruptly fired from my position as one of the 12 pastors at a very large church. I loved working there and planned on spending the rest of my life on staff at that church as a teacher in their church-centered Bible school.

TRAUMATIC PICTURES HEALED THROUGH INNER HEALING

They called me up one evening and asked if a couple of the senior level staff could have breakfast with me. I said sure, assuming it was because they had discussed a new project I had presented to them, and that they had approved it. I had suggested they set up a Christian incubator for businessmen in the church, as that would cause their businesses to prosper, bless a greater number of customers in the area, and increase the tithe to the church. Win, win, win.

In the morning at the restaurant, three men from the board sat around a table with me. They informed me that they had terminated my position at the church and I was to clean out my office and leave today.

I was dumbstruck. I could not believe what I was hearing. I had worked there five years and blessed the church by building for them a print shop which had brought a quarter million dollars income to the church in the preceding twelve months. I had taught in their Bible school and people's lives were changed. I had counseled many people and seen healing and growth in their lives and marriages.

I cleaned out my office, boxed up my books, and went home. I was so angry that even though I am a theologian, I didn't unbox my books for six months. However, after six months of anger, I had arthritis in my fingers and knees, and I was only in my 30s! I knew it was caused by my anger and hatred of them, so I prayed and forgave them about 50 times, but I still hated them. Obviously this prayer wasn't working.

So I did inner healing prayer one morning in my journaling/devotional time. I asked Jesus to show up at the restaurant table in the scene in my mind. Pictures flowed in, along with flowing words. I saw Jesus standing off the end of the table laughing hilariously and slapping His knees. I asked, "What is so funny? I am bleeding to death over here!"

I WAS TUNED TO FLOW AND I JOURNALED OUT THE FOLLOWING

Jesus responded, "Don't you know I set this whole thing up?"

I said, "Don't tell me that or I will be mad at You, too."

Jesus said, "I have told you for two years to get on the road and teach communion with God around the world, and you wouldn't go. So now I have thrown you out of the nest."

I said, "I was going to go. I just wanted to first pay off the bills I have and get some money in the bank." (At the time, I was $15,000 in debt on top of my house mortgage.)

Jesus said, "It would have taken you years to do that, so I have thrust you out of the nest."

I explained to Jesus that my family and I were now going to starve to death.

Jesus said, "Not if you trust Me."

So after a bit of a battle I told Him I would trust Him, but if we starved to death, it was His fault.

The next day in my journaling/devotional time the Lord explained to me, "Mark, you can see these men as evil or as instruments in My hand which have thrust you into the fulfillment of your destiny. If you see them as evil men, your spirit, soul, body and ministry will shrivel up. If you see them as instruments in My hand, you will feel honor and respect, and your health and ministry will expand. The choice is yours."

I chose to see them as instruments in God's hands, thrusting me into the fulfillment of my destiny.

So now "I see the gift in this trauma." God wanted me on the road teaching the Church how to hear His voice. I was afraid I could not survive without a salary so I was unwilling to go. He forced me out so I could fulfill my destiny, which I am now doing.

A hurt is healed when you can see the gift God has produced in your life through the experience. Now I see the gift. I am fulfilling my destiny. Now I can be thankful to the men who fired me. Within 24 hours, half the arthritis pain was gone and within a week it was all gone. It is now 32 years later, and there is still no arthritis pain or any kind of pain in my body. Praise the Lord!

I have asked that senior pastor to be on my board of advisors. He has hosted me back at his church teaching the seminar on How to Hear God's Voice. I have traveled the world for 32 years teaching this message. Currently my online video events are viewed by thousands every month in over 100 nations. I have done seminars on hearing God's voice every other weekend for three decades. I can thank God for the gifts He has produced in my life through this painful experience. There is no other way I would have ever left the "security" of a regular weekly paycheck and gone on the road to live off freewill offerings. God knew that, so He threw me out of the nest and showed me that I could fly.

JOURNALING ASSIGNMENT

"Lord, what is the gift You have produced in my life through the various traumas I have listed earlier in this chapter?" Let Him show you and then be *thankful*. Never be neutral. Be filled with light!

Chapter Nine

DELIVERED FROM DEMONS

Let's begin by reviewing what we have accomplished so far. We have been dismantling all the negative energy streams which have been contributing to your heart wound.

OVERVIEW OF SEVEN POSSIBLE ROOTS OF SIN ENERGIES OR DEMONIC ENERGIES WHICH CONTRIBUTE TO HEART WOUNDS

1. **Generational sins and curses**—negative energy coming down through the family line
2. **Ungodly soul ties**—negative energy coming from close, bonded relationships
3. **Negative expectations**—negative energy coming from unbiblical beliefs
4. **Inner vows**—negative energy coming from the strivings of my flesh

5. **Traumatic pictures**—negative energy coming from unbiblical pictures
6. **Word curses**—negative energy coming from unbiblical spoken words
7. **Demonic oppression**—negative energy coming from evil spirits

A HOUSE FIT FOR A DEMON

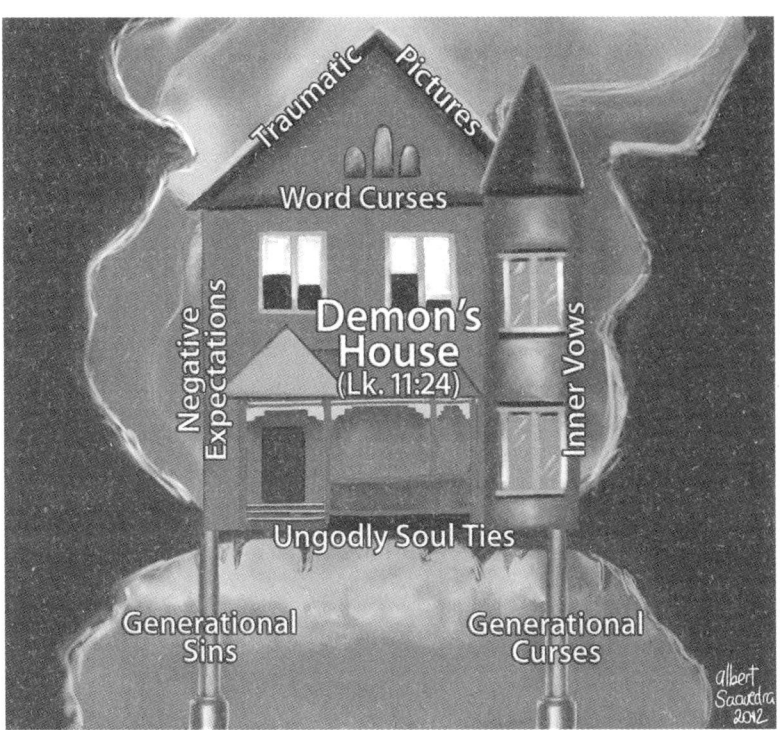

REMOVING THE DARKNESS OF DEMONS WHICH ATTACH TO HEART WOUNDS

Now that we have torn down the house, it is quite easy to remove the demon since it was anchored to us by our unbiblical beliefs, traumatic pictures, word curses, etc.

I picked up a demon of fear of stroke through a traumatic experience in my childhood. My favorite grandfather died of what I believed to be a stroke. This was not completely true, but in my childhood brain, that is what I believed. At this traumatic point in my life, a demon of "fear of stroke" attached itself to me, and I woke up for the next 15 years most mornings with the sensation that my arms and face were paralyzed. I would shake it off and then be fine for the rest of the day.

I finally asked my wife and the elders in our church to pray deliverance over me, and as they did, the demon manifested. A sensation of paralysis came over me; my tongue felt thick and sluggish. My wife said it looked like I was paralyzed. Tears flowed, and the demon of fear of stroke left. I was free of that terrible nightmare. I have never again had that sensation since that point in time. I was set free! Jesus came to set the captives free. Thank You, Lord!

SO MANY QUESTIONS—LET'S SEE IF WE CAN ANSWER THEM

What are demons? They are spirit entities which seek to enter people and manifest their evil personalities out through the human being.

Where do they come from? The Bible never addresses this question so we don't know, and there is no reason to guess.

CAN A DEMON POSSESS A CHRISTIAN?

Demons **don't possess** Christians. The word translated "demon-possessed" in the King James Version of the Bible is *daimonizomai* in the Greek. The literal definition of *daimonizomai* is *"under the* *influence of*" or *"vexed with."* This is a very different picture than that of possession. Yes, a demon can influence a Christian, as you can see from my story earlier in this chapter. The demon was able to manifest itself in one particular way in my life, although I surely was not possessed (totally controlled) by a demon.

Using the correct definition of *daimonizomai*, being—under the influence of—really clears up the **unbiblical picture** in our minds of a person being "possessed by" (totally controlled by) a demon. So let's drop the unfortunate translation of this word, and remove "possessed by" from our vocabulary, along with the unbiblical picture. Let's adopt a new phrase, "under the influence of," and a new biblical picture of "an area of my life is under the influence of a demon."

The word *daimonizomai* is used 25 times in the Greek New Testament. The King James Version only translates it "possessed" 11 of the 25 times. It is translated as simply "devil(s)" 13 times and "vexed" once. Well, having a devil or being vexed by a devil is a whole lot different in my mind than being "possessed" by a devil. So more than 50% of the time it is **not translated "possessed."** *Young's Literal Translation* (which I love for its precision) ***never once*** translates *daimonizomai* as "possessed."

THE GADARENE DEMONIAC

The story of the Gadarene demoniac is probably the most extreme case of demonization we see in the New Testament, and the narratives given by Luke and Mark are the most detailed accounts of deliverance in the Gospels. It is instructive to look closely at the precise words used to describe the man's condition. Because of its accuracy, I am going to use the *Young's Literal Translation*.

We are introduced to the suffering man in Mark 5:2 as "a man with an unclean spirit." Luke uses a similar expression in Luke 8:27, "a certain man...who had demons for a long time." Notice that it is the man who has demons, not demons that possess a man.

In describing how he was tormented, Luke continues, "many times it had caught him," with the result that he broke the chains and shackles with which he had been bound. The implication is that there were times when he was not under its power or influence.

Finally, Jesus cast the demons out, they entered the swine which rushed into the lake and were drowned. When the news of the swine's demise spread, many people came out to see what had happened. There they saw "the demoniac, sitting, and clothed, and right-minded" (Mk. 5:15, Lk. 8:35). Here, at last, we see the word which is often translated as "demon-possessed." Young uses the word "demoniac."

Again, there is a big difference between the images evoked by the expressions "having demons" and "being demon-possessed." Yet both expressions are used to describe this individual. In fact, Mark and Luke each use the more mild terms of "with demons" or "having demons" to describe the man when he was at his worst.

Unfortunately, even when the text clearly states someone *had* an unclean spirit or demon, Bible translations are not always accurate. For example, in the Greek, Luke 4:33 clearly says, "In the synagogue was a man, having a spirit of an unclean demon...." Yet the New American Standard (which is my preferred translation because it is usually so accurate) and several other versions say, "In the synagogue there was a man possessed by the spirit of an unclean demon...." It is no wonder that there is so much misunderstanding in the Church about demonization.

Christians' spirits are joined to the Holy Spirit. It is God who possesses the Christian's spirit. The demonization is not a possession; it is an infiltration of the enemy armies into one's castle. They might capture control of a "room" or two where they can express themselves, but they don't take over the castle. These enemy spirits must be thrown out again so that the Lordship of Christ can reign supreme throughout easch and every area of one's being, body and soul and spirit. That is what the deliverance ministry is all about—casting out the invaders.

IS THERE ANY BIBLICAL EXAMPLE OF A CHILD OF FAITH HAVING A DEMON?

Yes. Here is the story.

> *And there was a woman who for eighteen years had had a **sickness caused by a spirit**; and she was bent over double, and could not straighten up at all. When Jesus saw her, He called her over and said to her, "Woman, you are freed from your sickness." And He laid His hands on her; and immediately she stood up straight again, and began glorifying God.* (Lk. 13:11-13)

When the Pharisees challenged Jesus for doing this miracle on the Sabbath, Jesus responded...

> *And this woman, a **daughter of Abraham** as she is, whom **satan has bound** for eighteen long years, should she not have been released from this restraint on the Sabbath day?"* (Lk. 13:16)

Here is a woman who is a woman of faith since she is a daughter of Abraham, the Father of Faith, and satan has bound her, causing an infirmity for 18 years. Jesus loosed her and she was healed.

DO SICKNESS AND EVIL SPIRITS GO TOGETHER VERY OFTEN?

They sure do. Here are several biblical examples showing that Jesus and the apostles cast out demons as an integral part of their healing ministry.

> *Jesus rebuked the unclean spirit, saying to it, **"You deaf and mute spirit**, I command you, **come out** of him and do not enter him again." After crying out and throwing him into terrible convulsions, it came out; and the boy became so much like a corpse that most of them said, "He is dead!" But Jesus took him by the hand and raised him; and he got up.* (Mk. 9:25-27)

> *Then one was brought to Him who was **demon-possessed, blind and mute**; and He **healed** him, so that the blind and mute man both spoke and saw.* (Matt. 12:22)

> *There met Him out of the tombs a man with an unclean spirit, who had his dwelling among the tombs; and no one could bind him, not even with chains, neither could anyone tame him. And always, he was **cutting himself** with stones. Jesus said to him, **"Come out of the man, unclean spirit!"*** (Mk. 5:2-8)

> *"Lord, have mercy on my son, for he is a **lunatic** and is very ill... and Jesus rebuked him, and the **demon came out of him**, and the boy was **cured** at once.* (Matt. 17:15-18)

> *They brought to him all having ailments, pressed with manifold sicknesses and pains, and **demoniacs**, and lunatics, and paralytics, and he **healed** them.* (Matt. 4:24)

*They brought to him many **demoniacs**, and he did **cast out the spirits** with a word, and did **heal** all who were ill.* (Matt. 8:16)

At the hands of the apostles *many signs and wonders were taking place among the people...people who were sick or afflicted with unclean spirits... were all **being healed**.* (Acts 5:12,16)

If I follow my Master's example, I will cast out demons as I minister healing. Can I really improve on the way Jesus did things?

IN SUMMARY—DEMONS CAUSE MENTAL, PHYSICAL AND EMOTIONAL ISSUES

- Deafness (Mk. 9:25); blindness, muteness (Matt. 12:22); infirmity (Lk. 13:11, 12); madness, anti-social behavior (Mk. 5:1-20); and epilepsy (Matt. 17:14-18).
- "And there was a woman who had a **sickness caused by a spirit** ... You are freed from your sickness. And He laid His hands on her; and immediately she was made erect again and began glorifying God" (Lk. 13:11).

WHAT ARE THE FOOTHOLDS WHICH ALLOW DEMONS TO ENTER?

Continuous sin; addictions; traumas; faulty belief systems; involvement in false religions; fears/phobias; immorality; pornography; occult involvement; self-pronounced curses; unforgiveness; ungodly soul ties (Jn. 14:30; 2 Cor. 2:10,11; Eph. 4:25-27).

ARE DEMONS THE ROOT OF A PROBLEM?

Demons compound a problem. They are allowed entrance when darkness is present in one's heart. To rid yourself of the pain of a heart wound, you remove the darkness. You remove negative energies from a combination of all of the following: 1) generational curses, 2) soul ties, 3) negative expectations, 4) inner vows, 5) traumatizing pictures of "reality," 6) word curses and 7) demons.

Fighting these seven issues by setting your will to overcome will not accomplish the task. You must **set your will to come to Christ and the power of the Holy Spirit**, releasing Him through the seven biblical prayers we have discussed in this book.

HOW PREVALENT SHOULD DELIVERANCE PRAYER BE?

I really don't want to overlook the role of demons, nor do I want to focus my life on them. So let's go back to our Lord and Savior, Jesus. How many of His prayers included deliverance? Between one-quarter and one-third of Jesus' prayers for healing were deliverance prayers. (See Part Two of this book, "How Often Did Jesus Minister Deliverance?") ***Let's maintain the balance of Jesus*** as we pray for people's needs. If we don't use His balance, whose will we use? I'm sure not going to let my culture or my brain dictate how much emphasis should be placed on deliverance. Jesus is my guide.

Deliverance is not just for Jesus to do. The commission for Christians to cast out demons is given in Matthew 10:8; Mark 3:15; 6:7, 13; 16:17, 18; and Luke 9:1, 2.

HOW DO I DISCOVER THE NAMES OF DEMONS PRESENT?

Knowing the names of demons being cast out helps in several ways. First, they come out easier when named, and second, you know what you now need to build a strong defense against them so you don't invite them back.

Demons are named by the infirmity, weakness or sin-pattern that they cause. The three or four words you used to describe your heart wound would be the demons' names. I consider them to be the ruling demons, which then have a host of supporting demons contributing to the heart wound.

To find additional demons' names I ask, "What demons would be behind the ungodly beliefs listed earlier?" For example, if an ungodly belief is "I will fail," then put down demon names of "failure" and "fear of failure" on the list to cast out. If the ungodly belief is "I will be rejected," then put down demons' names of "rejection" and "fear of rejection."

List demons' names in the space below or on a separate sheet.

Since you can easily cast out two or three closely-related demons as a group, you can arrange them in clusters of two or three and cast them out in these mini-groups. Make the group that causes the biggest problem for you number 1. Number 2 group is the next biggest problem, etc. During deliverance, you begin with the group with the highest number and work your way down to group number 1, which is most likely the strongest demon group. These demons are left for last because by then they will be greatly weakened, having lost the support of all their underlings.

When a counselor is working with a client, have a sheet printed out in front of you and scan down over it, asking the Holy Spirit to highlight on the page those demons which need to be dealt with. The link below provides an extensive list of demon groups to prayerfully consider: cwgministries.org/demon-groupings

I have created a shorter list of potential demon groupings which can be found in Part Two of this book under "**Common Demon Groupings.**"

HERE IS AN EASY, SIMPLE DELIVERANCE PROCESS

It is best if one or two prayer counselors are praying deliverance for the client. It is really nice when one counselor is gifted in discernment and seeing, and the other counselor is more administrative. Their gifts flowing together promote huge, quick victory.

1. Pray for a protective covering of Christ's blood over all (self, family, property, others present).
2. **Place wedges between the client and the demons.** Since the demons are only allowed entrance if the client has agreed with them and their darkness, we **break that agreement** with the following three wedges.
   a. **Wedge 1:** Have the counselee repent of the sin the demon is contributing to, and state their intention to live in holiness in the area. For example, "I repent of my sin of being judgmental, and from now on I choose to express mercy toward all I meet."
   b. **Wedge 2:** Counselee tells the demon, "I will no longer give you a place. I command you to leave me in Jesus' name."

c. **Wedge 3:** Counselee sets their heart against the demon(s), but no longer speaks. The reason the counselee stops speaking is because frequently the demons leave through the breath (remember spirit and breath are the same word in the Greek). So we don't want the counselee's talking to hinder the release of the demon. I encourage them that if they feel something rising within them, don't hold back. Let it come out. And if it comes out with a sigh or a burp or whatever, that is fine.

   The counselor calls the demons by name and commands them to leave in the Name of the Lord Jesus Christ. The counselor commands the demons to shrink in size, detach themselves from each other and from all other spiritual forces and from the counselee and to come out in Jesus' name.

4. After commanding several times, ask the client what they are sensing within. If there is partial movement of the demon but it has not come out, repeat the three wedges above.
5. If the demon still resists coming out, ask, "Holy Spirit, what is this demon attached to?" Counselee and counselor tune to flow and receive the answer from the Holy Spirit. Then using the appropriate prayer approach, remove this demon's anchor so he will readily be cast out.
6. Once the demon has left, ask the Holy Spirit to come and fill this vacated area.
7. Counselee and counselor tune to flow and vision throughout the entire process, sharing what they are seeing and experiencing. I tell the counselee before we begin the deliverance that they should keep me informed of all

flowing thoughts, flowing pictures and flowing emotions that are coming to them. This will include things like, "I saw it leave," "I felt it leave," "a picture came to me of a time my father made me angry." (In this case, they will need to forgive their father and state that they choose to honor him, as their unforgiveness is an anchor that is still present which the demon is using as its legal right to remain.)

8. I tell the client, "You don't need to raise your hand and ask to speak. Just interrupt me with what is going on inside you so I can track with it." So in the above case, the client may simply interrupt and say, "I choose to forgive my father and love, honor and bless him." This can keep the deliverance session moving along quickly, smoothly and easily.

9. Since demons cause physical infirmity, you may be aware of the need to command the demon of infirmity, or arthritis, or pain, etc. to leave in Jesus name. You can expect to see amazing transformation as these leave.

The above process is used for each of the several clusters of demons. (Remember, you can easily cast out a group of 2-3 closely related demons simultaneously.) Normally the client will feel a freedom as the demons leave. However, if the client has cut off all feeling for many years then it is possible they will feel nothing. In this case, you will need to continue moving forward in faith, casting out each cluster of demons and trusting that the job is done, and then filling each area with the Holy Spirit. If you have a prophetic counselor teamed up with you in the counseling process, they can most likely see the demon leave, and let you know the demon is gone.

Once these steps are completed, we are then ready to move on to building a wall of defense so the demons cannot come back. Some new patterns of living need to be established which we discuss in the next chapter. However, let me say this for now.

House cleaning: You will need to destroy occult books and objects, pornographic material, New Age books and objects, objects associated with eastern religions, Freemasonry objects, objects associated with idolatry, and anything else connected to the demons. It is suggested that you have your pastor/counselor assist you with this task. THIS IS NOT OPTIONAL—IT IS A REQUIREMENT.

PRAYER APPLICATION

If you are doing this study in a group, take time to pray for each other for deliverance with two prayer counselors working with a client. Some of these prayer sessions may be scheduled over the next week or two as convenient. You may be able to have several mature prayer teams ministering deliverance so things move more quickly. Clients should have the freedom to select who they would like to minister deliverance to them. When I do seminars in churches, we normally have half a dozen prayer teams located in prayer stations all around the church sanctuary, and people are welcome to go to whomever they desire. Soft worship music plays in the background. While they wait to be prayed for, they review their first six prayers, deepening them so they are fully ready to be easily released from any and all demons.

WHERE CAN I FIND DELIVERANCE PRAYER MINISTERS?

Check with your church and other churches in your community by asking, "Does your church offer inner healing and deliverance prayer ministry?" When you reach a church receptionist who answers "yes," follow up with the question, "How may I make an appointment to receive this ministry?"

TWO-WAY JOURNALING EXERCISE

Lord, what would You like to say to me concerning the truths in this chapter?

RESOURCES

See Part Two of this book, "What If I Get Stuck?" and "Available Training for *Prayers That Heal the Heart*."

Chapter Ten

MAINTAINING THE VICTORY BY STAYING FILLED WITH THE HOLY SPIRIT

One gentleman I prayed for described the aftermath of his deliverance this way: Before his deliverance from a demon of lust, there was a compulsion to lust continuously, regardless of the amount of rebuking, fasting, Bible memorization or prayer that he did. Once delivered, he found that lust became like any other temptation of the flesh. He could choose to resist it and it would go. The compulsion was now gone but the temptation of the flesh was still present. However, now he could easily win the battle with this sin.

YES, I WILL EXPERIENCE DEMONIC PRESSURE AGAIN, EVEN AFTER I HAVE BEEN DELIVERED!

I don't like this truth, but if I understand it, then I won't be caught off guard when I experience it.

> *"When an unclean spirit goes out of a man, he goes through dry places, seeking rest, and finds none.* ***Then he says, 'I will return to my house from which I came.'*** *And when he comes, he finds it empty, swept, and put in order. Then he goes and takes with him seven other spirits more wicked than himself, and they enter and dwell there; and the last state of that man is worse than the first. So shall it also be with this wicked generation."* (Matt. 12:43-45)

The guarantee by Jesus is that "You *will* be tested!" In the above verses, Jesus states that the demon says, "I *will* return to my house from which I came." He is talking about returning to you, and he will come knocking on your door and saying, "I'm back!" So you *will* feel the pressure of his ugly thoughts and emotions as he pushes to re-enter you. This is where you *must* make a key decision to rebuke him in Jesus' name.

Rather than again coming into agreement with the demon and crying, "Oh, no! It's back;" bind the demon in Jesus' name and declare, "Oh, no! You are **not** back and I command you to leave now in Jesus' name!" Stand firm in your victory and the enemy must obey. Maintain your freedom by not coming back into agreement with the lies of the enemy. When you submit yourself to God and resist the devil, he will flee from you. There is no way I can emphasize this enough. This sequence **will** happen, and when you feel the "squeeze" on, do not do what the Israelites did and grumble and forsake your faith in God. Instead, declare your faith in God and the fact that He has set you free and those whom the Son sets free **are free indeed!** Take your stand. Fight the battle. Rebuke the enemy in Jesus' name and uphold your freedom.

Daily, welcome and honor the Holy Spirit. Do nothing to quench the Holy Spirit (1 Thess. 5:19). Repent immediately of any sin. Make sure to avoid any of the entry points for demons explored in the first six of these Prayers That Heal the Heart.

SEAL THE VICTORY BY HEARING WHAT JESUS IS SAYING TO YOU ON A DAILY BASIS

> *"I am the vine, you are the branches; he who abides in Me and I in him, he bears much fruit, for apart from Me you can do nothing. If you abide in Me, and My **words** abide in you, ask whatever you wish, and it will be done for you.*
>
> (Jn. 15:5, 7—**Note:** "words" in this verse is the Greek word rhema which means spoken word)

Above is a truly mind-blowing verse. It redefines who and what we are. Satan says, "You can know; You can do; You can be" (Gen. 3:5), and my culture echoes his words. It's all about **me** and what **I think**.

God said in my journaling: *"No, it's not all about you. You are a vessel, a temple, a branch grafted into a vine. You are hollow and another fills you. It is to be My Holy Spirit, and you live out of what My Holy Spirit is ministering within you. So trust in Me and in My river, which flows from My throne and out through your heart. Apart from Me you can do nothing. Anything you do which does not come from My river within is a dead work (Heb. 6:1, 2) and must be repented of, as it came from self and not from My Spirit.*

So I never assume I am going to battle and defeat demons with my strength. That would be a dead work. Instead, I simply turn to Jesus, see Him standing at my right hand (Acts 2:25) and I ask Him to rebuke the enemy together with me. I see Him doing that and I am at peace and set free, for I have not battled with the strength of my flesh to maintain freedom. Instead I have looked to Jesus, asked for Jesus' wisdom, power and strength, and watched what Jesus does. I do what I see Jesus doing. He is rebuking the enemy of my soul. This is so much easier than battling with my own strength.

MY HEART ESTABLISHES THE BOUNDARIES OF MY LIFE

Keep thy heart, For out of it are the outgoings of life
(Prov. 4:23 YLT).

Living from my heart involves the following: 1) it begins with being tuned to the voice of the Holy Spirit. What He speaks we embrace by 2) affirming it as our 3) personal and 4) present tense reality. In addition, the heart's language is 5) visual, 6) emotional, 7) and utilizes biblical meditation to frame in our spirits the things God desires to birth in our lives.

You can read through the Psalms to see how often David prays using *affirmative* statements which are *personal* and *present tense*. A few examples from Psalms chapter 3 will get you started: You, O LORD, **are** a shield about me (Ps. 3:3). The LORD **sustains** me (Ps. 3:5) You **have** smitten all my enemies (Ps. 3:7). David is not asking for this to happen. He is stating it is his present tense reality.

SEVEN STEPS IN WRITING GOD'S WORDS ON OUR HEARTS

1. **Everything begins with revelation from the Spirit:** The Holy Spirit, Who resides in our innermost being (Jn. 7:37-39), communicates to our hearts through flowing thoughts, flowing pictures and flowing energy. The spoken word of God within our hearts (*rhema*—Rom. 4:17) provides revelation and power (1 Cor. 12:7-11). So I live tuned to flow.
2. **I personally apply what God is speaking:** Jesus told the lame man to get up. The lame man got up, thus making God's power personal and real to him (Matt. 9:6, 7). Truth that is not personally acted upon is dead (Jas. 2:17). Meditation on the word of God must result in us **applying it** in order for it to benefit our lives (Josh. 1:8). Christ's death on the cross will not benefit anyone who does not personally apply His blood to wash away their sins.
3. **I live in the present moment:** We know the spirit world is present tense only, in that in the spirit world there is no past or future. God, Who is Spirit (Jn. 4:24), says; "I Am Who I Am" (Ex. 3:14). He is not an "I was" or an "I will be". He is always present tense. Time is part of our world, but not part of eternity. When we are meditating and lost in spirit, time disappears from our awareness. There is only "now."
4. **I make positive affirmations:** When we thank God that the promised miracle is already provided, we open the door for it to be realized. Mark 11:22-24 instructs us to pray, asking, believing, and **speaking that it is done.** Negativity

is prohibited. Those who are not thankful lose everything (Deut. 28:47, 48). Instead, an attitude of gratitude and thankfulness is commanded (Col. 3:15, 16; Col. 2:7; Heb. 12:28). **In** everything we give thanks (1 Thess. 5:18) and **for** everything we give thanks (Eph. 5:20; Phil. 4:6; 2 Cor. 2:14) because we know that God is big enough to work everything out for good (Rom. 8:28).

- The statement, "I am sick" is affirmative, but it is affirming the kingdom of darkness' "facts" rather than the Kingdom of God's Truth (Isa. 53:5).
- The statement, "I am not sick" is a Kingdom truth but it is not stated in the affirmative.
- The statement, "I will be healed" is positive, but not stated in the present tense now.
- "I am healed and walking in health" is a positive, present tense, affirmative Kingdom truth.

5. **I see the promise already fulfilled:** Pictures are the language of the heart (1 Chron. 29:18). *I pray that the **eyes of your heart** would be enlightened* (Eph. 1:18). Pictures move the heart and ideas move the mind. Since Jesus spoke to people's hearts, He constantly taught using parables, which are picture stories (Matt. 13:34). Also, note that the Bible is essentially a picture book, telling the stories of people's lives. Holding a picture of the promise fulfilled (Gen. 15:5) promotes faith for transformation of one's life and the release of a miracle (Gen. 15:6).

6. **My emotions agree the victory is won:** We have emotions in our hearts. God was *grieved* in his *heart* (Gen. 6:6). One amazing discovery the Lord showed to me was that *"emotions*

*are very often **by-products of pictures***" and here is one place where this principle is asserted: *"The steadfast of **mind** You will keep in **perfect peace**"* (Isa. 26:3). Peace is an emotion, and is a result of what? "Mind" in this verse is *yetser* in the original Hebrew. According to *Brown-Driver-Briggs Dictionary, yetser* means **imagination** and **frame up**. *Yetser* shows up nine times in the Bible. **Only** in Isaiah 26:3 is it translated mind. It should more correctly be translated "**imagination which frames up**" realities for us. In the King James Version *yetser* is translated "imagination" five times (Gen. 6:5; Deut. 31:21 twice; 1 Chron. 28:9 and 29:18) and "frame" twice (Ps. 103:14; Isa. 29:16). So Isaiah 26:3 correctly understood is... **A steadfast imagination** frames up and creates my reality, allowing me to live in an emotional state of perfect peace.

If we choose to imagine God's pictures, we are framing up pictures which produce peace and faith for a miracle (Gen. 15:5, 6). If we choose to imagine satan's pictures, we are framing up pictures which produce fear and bring destruction (Ex. 14:11, 12, 35). *We choose the picture we gaze upon, and accompanying emotions follow. When we select God's pictures, we experience Kingdom emotions and frame up Kingdom realities.*

Thoughts of our minds are *powerless* against the pictures we hold in our hearts. I can say 1000 times that I am the righteousness of God in Christ, but if I am picturing myself as a miserable sinner, the picture wins over the 1000-fold confession. I can say I have forgiven a person 1000 times, but until **I hold a picture** with the eyes of my heart of Jesus alive in the scene, anger remains (Eph. 1:17, 18).

7. **Bible meditation frames God's pictures in my spirit:** Meditation is something we do in our hearts (Ps. 19:14; 49:3; Josh. 1:8). "Imagine" is part of the definition of the Hebrew word "meditate" (*Strong's Exhaustive Concordance* #H1897). Meditation involves prayerfully reflecting and allowing the Holy Spirit to illumine the eyes of our hearts (Eph. 1:18) so we see from God's perspective. Our hearts burn with revelation as Jesus opens Scriptures to us (Lk. 24:32).

Meditation frames God's pictures in our spirit, so they can be birthed through our spirit into our world. Biblical meditation promotes miracles.[1] Rather than vacillating between meditating on God's promised provision part of the day and satan's fear of failure the rest of the time, we choose to be steadfast and single-minded, meditating only on God's promise, visually seen as being fulfilled. No double-mindedness, as that means I get nothing (Jas. 1:6-8).

To successfully write a message on our hearts, we must use the language of our hearts, which means it is 1) birthed by the Spirit, 2) personal, 3) present tense, 4) positive (affirmative), 5) visual, 6) emotion-packed and 7) something we meditate on continuously. Do this and you will walk free.

THE FATHER OF FAITH WRITES GOD'S MESSAGE ON HIS HEART AND BIRTHS A MIRACLE

An example of a message of faith being written on one's heart is that of Abram, the Father of Faith. At age 99, God spoke and changed Abram's name to Abraham, which means father of many nations (Gen. 17:5). This was at a time when Abraham had no children with his wife.

From that moment, when Abraham thinks of or speaks his name, saying, "I am Abraham," he is writing God's promise on his heart by making God's spoken word to him 1) personal, 2) affirmative, 3) present tense, 4) visual (it was based on a picture of millions of stars) which evoked 5) a deep emotional response within Abraham. 6) Abraham pondered God's promise (Rom. 4:17-22). He didn't spend his days, thinking, "This will never happen."

Notice Abraham is not saying, "I have a **goal** of being the father of..." nor is he saying, "I **ought** to be..." nor is he saying, "I am becoming...." Each of these statements *pushes the transformed reality off to some future date*, and effectually is saying, "I am not this now."

Instead Abraham is saying, "I *am* the father of a multitude of nations." He has entered the state of **heart faith**. He has heard a promise from God saying this is his destiny (Gen. 12:1-3), and seen a vision from God as the promise fulfilled (Gen. 15:5, 6). He has chosen to ponder it, speak it and act in faith. Now in the fullness of time, God can bring it forth. Isaac was born to his wife one year later, and the earth was blessed through his seed about 1500 years later, when Jesus was resurrected from His death on Calvary.

BUILD A WALL OF DEFENSE AGAINST DEMONS BY MEDITATING ON THE BIBLE

> *This Book of the Law shall not depart from your mouth, but **you shall meditate in it day and night**, that you may observe to do according to all that is written in it. For then you will make your way prosperous, and then you will have good success.* (Josh. 1:8)

Meditation: It is a much deeper process than Western study. For an examination of the six Hebrew or Greek words in the Bible which are translated meditate or meditation and the 68 verses containing these words, check out this article: cwgministries.org/Meditate_Hebrew_Greek

We can build up a strong wall of defense against demons by doing a Bible meditation on topics which are *opposite* to what we have been delivered of. For example, if delivered of...

- Fear, doubt and unbelief; do a meditation on verses which build faith, belief and courage.
- Anger, hatred and rage; do a meditation on forgiveness, mercy and love.
- Failure, fear of failure and rejection; do a meditation on success, victory and acceptance.

In doing this, we are infusing our hearts with light so the darkness cannot return.

A 7-STEP BIBLE MEDITATION PROCESS EXPLAINED

Bible meditation defined: *"God's Spirit utilizing every faculty of my heart and mind, resulting in revelation which ushers in transformation."*

1. **Write:** I copy the verse by hand onto a piece of paper or 3X5 card (Deut. 17:18) and keep it with me to meditate on, memorize and mutter throughout the day(s). I also record this verse in my meditation journal (which can be written, typed or verbally recorded).

2. **Quiet Down:** I become still in God's presence, loving Him through soft soaking music (2 Kings 3:15, 16) and/or praying in tongues (1 Cor. 14:14), or putting a smile on my face and picturing Jesus with me (Acts 2:25). I tune to His *flowing* thoughts, pictures and emotions (Jn. 7:37-39).
3. **Reason Together With God:** Come let us reason together (Isa. 1:18), meaning the Spirit guides my reasoning process. I ask, "Lord, what do You want to show me from this verse?" I tune to flow and revelation from the Holy Spirit bubbles up within me.
4. **Speak & Imagine:** I ponder the Scripture, personalizing and speaking it to myself softly over and over again until I can say it with my eyes closed. As I repeat the Scripture, I allow myself to see it with the eyes of my heart. I note what the picture is in my mind's eye as I repeat the Scripture.
5. **Feel God's Heart:** While seeing the above picture, I ask, "Lord, what does this Scripture reveal about Your heart toward me?" I feel His heart and journal it out.
6. **Hear God's *Rhema*:** I put myself in the picture of this Scripture in my mind. I ask, "Lord, what are You speaking to me through this Scripture?" I tune to flowing thoughts and flowing pictures (God's voice and vision) and I record this dialogue in my two-way journaling.
7. **Act:** I accept this revelation, repenting of any sin that is opposite of it and roaring at any obstacle that stands in the way of implementing it. I then speak it forth and act on it.

Our hearts burn within as He walks with us, opening Scriptures to us. (Lk. 24:32)

THE HOLY SPIRIT GUIDES THE ABOVE PROCESS

The Holy Spirit may lead to more or less emphasis on any of the various steps, according to God's wishes for the present moment and the personal needs one has. So we remain dependent upon Him throughout. For example, I may need more or less time to quiet myself in His presence, or more or less time in Spirit-led "reasoning," or more or less time in speaking it, or feeling God's heart in it, or doing two-way journaling about it, or roaring at the enemy to get his lies out of my head and his hands off my being. So I allow the flow of the Holy Spirit to guide me through the steps of this meditation process.

TOPICAL BIBLE MEDITATIONS PRODUCE DEEPENED REVELATION

Below is my approach to a topical meditation. Two sample Bible meditations I did after my deliverance can be found in Part Two of this book, "Bible Meditation on Judging" and "Bible Meditation on Sex."

Throughout my life, when I have encountered any kind of blockage that prevented me from moving forward in the Lord, I have immersed myself in meditating on everything I could find in the Bible on the topic. As a teacher I am eager to pass these revelations on to you, believing that if you follow in my footsteps you can learn much more quickly than I did. As a result, many of my books are simply topical Bible meditations, and you can use them to give you a head start on your own meditations.

1. **Be led by God to the topic:** God will show you the topic He wants you to explore by bringing it to your consciousness through thoughts, the comment of a friend or a book, or a presenting need in your life which demands the revelation and power of God to overcome (Jn. 16:13). Some examples of topics one might meditate on include a deepened revelation: that God works all things out for my good; that by His stripes I am healed; that I can do all things through Christ Who strengthens me (faith); the power of compassion; overcoming judementalism; the beauty and value and gift of being part of my new family, the body of Christ; how do I live by the Spirit?... the list is endless.
2. **Be cleansed by His blood:** Approach your meditation time by drawing near to the Lord, repenting of all sins, and asking for and receiving the cleansing of His blood (Heb. 10:22).
3. **Be humble and teachable:** Ask for the Holy Spirit to reveal truth to you (Eph. 1:17, 18). Be willing to discover and embrace His truth, no matter what it costs (reputation, pride, ego, job, financial security, etc.).
4. **Be fearless:** Some churches will excommunicate, terminate employment or shun a person who disagrees with the church's belief. Thus fear hinders many from pursuing truth. Put your whole trust in God to sustain you, even if you are shunned or rejected by organized religion. As I was turning charismatic, I was told by the denominational pastor I was working under that I would be thrown out of the church and lose the security of a denomination supporting me. I felt fear,

but I also felt faith that God could and would provide for me. Now, 48 years later, I can affirm to you that God has kept me.

5. **Be wholehearted in your search:** Seek the Lord with your whole heart (i.e. presenting all your faculties to the Lord to fill and to use) and you will find Him (Jer. 29:13). Ask the Holy Spirit to guide and fill your heart and then tune to flowing thoughts, flowing pictures, flowing emotions.

6. **Let the Holy Spirit guide you in the use of the following Bible tools:**
   - A good concordance such as *Strong's Exhaustive Concordance* and the *King James Concordance* (gives you every verse where a specific Hebrew or Greek word is used).
   - Some good Bible dictionaries such as *Strong's Hebrew and Greek Dictionaries, Brown-Driver-Briggs Dictionary, Vine's Complete Bible Dictionary of New Testament Words, Vine's Complete Dictionary of Old Testament Words.*
   - Miscellaneous analytical tools such as *Nave's Topical Bible,* and *Manners and Customs of the Bible,* etc.
   - Interpretive tools such as exegetical commentaries, expository commentaries and devotional commentaries.
   - These tools plus many more are available electronically in the free software e-Sword (E-sword.net). I use this software all the time. Our online e-learning module "The Art of Biblical Meditation" provides training on how to research a topic using these tools (cluschooolofthespirit.com/meditation).

7. **Receive counsel:** Wisdom and safety come from receiving counsel, input and confirmation from the fivefold team God has given to you (Prov. 11:14; Eph. 4:11; 2 Cor. 13:1).

PERSONAL APPLICATION

1. Lord, what truth do You want to write on my heart? How do You want me to speak it, see it, feel it, ponder it and act upon it? Thank You, Lord.

2. Devotionals which guide you in imprinting messages on your heart can be freely downloaded from our website: cwgministries.org/SpiritualTransformations. The various meditations available are:
   - New Creation Celebration—Replacing Emotions (40 minutes)
   - New Creation Celebration—Replacing Beliefs (22 minutes)
   - New Creation Celebration—Putting on Christ (13 minutes)
   - New Creation Celebration—Possessing Your Promised Land (9 minutes)

ENDNOTES

1. More on meditation can be found here: cwgministries.org/meditation.

Chapter Eleven

CLEARING CELLULAR MEMORIES

REMOVING EMOTIONAL ROOTS TO DISEASES
Have you ever said: "That person is a pain in the neck"? I have witnessed the pain of a stiff neck and shoulder immediately released when the person I was counseling forgave another who was "a pain in their neck." The book *Molecules of Emotion* by Dr. Candance Pert lays out scientific evidence that emotions are stored in our cells.

There is plenty of pain to be stored. In addition to the ongoing pains of experiencing rejection, losing a job, etc., research has shown that one in five Americans was sexually molested as a child; and one in three couples engages in physical violence. A quarter of us grew up with alcoholic relatives (Van der Kolk MD, Bessel. *The Body Keeps the Score: Brain, Mind, and Body in the Healing of Trauma*, p. 1).

You can easily turn your daily devotional times into amazing healing encounters with the Wonderful Counselor, allowing Him to pinpoint and remove emotional and physical trauma and restore health to your whole being. I regularly use this exciting process to help me abide in the true, Spirit-born Kingdom realities of peace and joy in the Holy Spirit (Rom. 14:17) displacing satan's fear, insecurity, anger, judgment and accusation.

CATCHING A MURDERER

Memories are stored in our cells: In one case study, a heart transplant recipient acquired the memories from the murdered donor, providing police with enough leads to arrest the killer.

It has also been noted that people receiving a heart transplant simultaneously take on the likes and dislikes of the donor. Clearly, our cells record much more than we ever imagined.

Emotional trauma leads to 90% of our health issues. Emotional trauma causes stress on our bodies. "The classic definition of stress is 'any real or imagined threat and your body's response to it.' Your body's natural stress response can have a significant impact on your immune function, brain chemistry, blood sugar levels, hormonal balance, and much more."[1]

The US National Library of Medicine hosts an article on stress which indicates up to 90% of illnesses are stress related. Quotes from the article include: "It is estimated that 80% to 90% of all industrial accidents are related to personal problems and employees' inability to handle stress (6)." "The European Agency for Safety and Health at work reported that about 50% of job absenteeism is caused by stress (7)...." "The Center for Disease Control and Prevention of the United States estimates that stress accounts for about 75% of all doctors' visits (7)..." "According to Occupational Health and Safety news and the National Council on compensation of insurance, up to 90% of all visits to primary care physicians are for stress-related complaints."

If stress wreaks that much havoc, imagine the overwhelming cumulative health effect of all our emotional issues! The prayer approach in this chapter is designed to help us receive Jesus' healing touch to release such memories.

How to discover a trapped memory: One great way to discover a root cause to an infirmity is to ask, *"Lord, what happened in my life just before this infirmity began?"* The thought which immediately lights upon your mind is a word of knowledge and will reveal a stored cellular trauma which needs to be processed in prayer. Another great way to recognize that you have a trapped memory is to notice when you have a negative reaction that is way out of proportion to the stimulus that triggered it. This indicates that you are reacting to the memory rather than the current issue.

I EXPERIENCED CLEARING OF CELLULAR MEMORIES

I was not as healed as I had hoped: My stimulus to explore this topic came from my decision to *fully* process the emotional traumas in my life which were stressing my adrenal gland (the fight/flight response). My naturopath had been telling me for years that my adrenal gland was stressed, and I adamantly told her "no," because I had learned to abide in Christ. Well, finally another naturopath told me a skin irritation which kept coming back was the result of a stressed out adrenal gland. So I decided it was time to get to the root of this and resolve it now, at the tender young age of 63, a good dozen years after first being informed of the problem. You don't need to be foolish and wait 12 years to process your issues. Be wise. Choose to get your release *now*.

My real stressors were stored cellular memories: I *finally* realized that the stress in my adrenals was not necessarily coming from my current life, as I had now learned to abide in Christ. It was more likely that this was stored stress in the memory of the cells of my adrenal gland from past issues in my life, and perhaps even stresses that had been passed down through my family line. This was a big "*Wow*" moment for me and gave me understanding of a whole new way to pray for healing! Do our genes 'remember' pain? Many scientists believe they do.

Your own healing encounters: Since this prayer approach can be freely done by yourself at home and I can guarantee that you will benefit from it emotionally, spiritually and physically, it is highly recommended that you complete this as part of a spiritual retreat or as daily devotions for a few weeks. Why live with stuff you don't need? You have come so far in healing your heart wounds; don't stop now! Don't let the enemy convince you to put off this healing process until a later date. There is so much of value in it. So satan, be gone!

EIGHT STEPS FOR CLEARING CELLULAR MEMORIES

1. **I enter His rest**—I put on some very soft soaking music to quiet my spirit before Him.
2. **I ask Jesus what needs healing**—"Lord, what needs healing in my life today? What stressed body organ or infirmity or abnormal emotional response needs to be dealt with?"

3. **I receive words of knowledge**—"Holy Spirit, please bring to my attention any event(s) which occurred at the inception of this physical, emotional or spiritual infirmity in my life or which added to it later on." I tune to flow and *make a list* of one line titles for each of the various events which light upon my mind. These are words of wisdom and words of knowledge revealing a root experience which will need to be resolved so the infirmity can be healed. A spouse or close friend can assist me in recalling traumatic events which need healing. *After* this list is created, we then apply steps 4-8 to each event on this list. Use the downloadable sheet mentioned in the next section to make this easy.

4. **I invite Jesus into the scene**—"Jesus, remind me of what I was feeling and where You are in this scene. What are You speaking, doing, and asking me to do?" I follow His instructions by repenting, forgiving, releasing, honoring and blessing the individuals (including myself and the event itself). John Arnott tells of asking a woman to forgive her horse for falling on her and crushing her hip. As soon as she forgave the horse, her hip pain vanished! Record what the Lord speaks and does, and what happens.

5. **Cellular emotional trauma is released by Jesus**—"Jesus, please remove the memory of this trauma which is stored in my (state specific body part)." Pause, watch, look, listen and feel as Jesus ministers healing grace. Conclude with a couple of deep breaths.

6. **Demonic entanglements are renounced in Jesus' name**—"I renounce and break off all demons, in the name of Jesus, which were attached to these events." I pause, watch,

look, listen and feel as Jesus ministers deliverance to me. Breathe out a couple of times forcefully and feel the release. Record what demons are rebuked and what you sense and see happening. The names of the demons will light upon your mind as spontaneous flowing thoughts, and generally correspond with what they are causing: anger, hatred, fear, inferiority, condemnation, shame, infirmity, arthritis, etc.

7. **Physical healing is received through Jesus**—"Lord Jesus, would You shine Your light upon (name body part)?" Watch Jesus touch, heal and restore the damaged body part. Then thank Him: "Thank You, Jesus, for Your healing, restorative touch. I receive it with gratefulness." Record what transpires.

8. **Divine gifts are revealed by Jesus**—"Lord, what is the gift You have produced in my life through this trauma/event?" Record what this gift is and see and speak only of this gift from now on!

APPLY STEPS FOUR THROUGH EIGHT TO EACH TRAUMA

Apply steps 4-8 to **each** event/item on the list you created in step three above.

- Now you process each of these events in a relaxed prayer time, performing all five steps for *each* trauma on your list. You can find a free "Clearing Cellular Memories Worksheet" to help you at: **cwgministries.org/Prayer_Worksheets**
- Reviewing your completed worksheet a second time allows God the opportunity to deepen and enlarge His healing presence in each one.

Seeing the gifts God has produced in your life through these traumas (Rom. 8:28) is the final step. Below are a couple of the gifts which God revealed to me from the traumas of my life.

- I am perfectly molded and positioned to fulfill God's destiny for my life.
- God used separation to bring me into my own, to function in the role He has called me to.

GO THE EXTRA MILE AND EXPERIENCE YOUR FULL HEALING

Receive *more* revelation: Apply the above healing process to the **various stages** of your life: In the womb, ages 1-5, elementary school, middle school, high school, college, marriage, after marriage. **Ask:** *"Holy Spirit, reveal traumas from my life during (state each specific period)."* Jot down one-line titles for each scene which lights upon your mind. For me, this resulted in a list of another 21 traumatic events.

No thinking allowed. You are to stay tuned to the flow of the Holy Spirit (Jn. 7:37-39), allowing *Him* to reveal what needs healing rather than digging around using self-effort (Jn. 6:63).

Process your list of events by applying the prayer worksheet which covers steps 4-8 to each event. I processed two scenes per day during my daily devotional time, covering all 21 traumas in 11 days.

How to deepen a revelation: Fully gain God's perspective by meditating on relevant Scriptures, asking God to explain them so your heart burns with revelation (Lk. 24:32). If you don't clearly see God's perspective, which results in **fully feeling** His emotions (since *emotions are by-products of pictures*), the hurt is not yet fully healed.

Emotion provides the stimulus for action. You need a significant emotional impetus to move you to the action of interrupting your current 65,000 thousand thoughts a day, of which 90% are automatic, and intersecting them with God's new thought processes which you hear, see, feel and speak. If this does not happen, you will not be healed!

Emotions can be created by pictures God gives you through journaling, Bible meditation or nighttime dreams. And if you hold a picture in your imagination of God's completed promise to you, as I'm sure the Father of Faith did (Gen. 15:5,6—thousands of stars representing thousands of descendants), that picture, too, can create the emotional stimulus to move you to action.

I received ongoing revelation: I would go to sleep asking God to reveal any additional situations which left trauma in my body. I would awaken each morning with one or two more, so the process continued until finally I awoke with no more scenes on my mind.

Healed!: This healing of my adrenal gland allowed me to begin sleeping eight hours every night, rather than six or seven, something I knew was healthy but had not been able to do for many years. And a skin irritation completely disappeared over the three weeks it took me to process these 35 traumas.

The rest of the story: During these three weeks I doubled my daily nutrition, and took Milk Thistle (to cleanse my liver), and added a few additional items my naturopath had recommended. I was truly ready to resolve this issue and do whatever was necessary.

FIVE TAKE-AWAYS

1. **I am committed to wholeness**—living in His presence which releases within me His love. I will take whatever time and effort is necessary to apply His healing presence to all emotional traumas, as these produce 90% of all sickness. I am emotionally healed when I manifest the fruit (singular) of the indwelling Spirit (Gal. 5:22-23). This fruit is a *real* emotion from God's heart which we receive whenever we are in His presence (i.e., "abiding in Christ"). It is compassionate love, which heals our entire beings. It has nine expressions:
   - **Love**
   - Joy is love rejoicing
   - Peace is love resting
   - Patience is love enduring
   - Kindness is love caring
   - Goodness is love motivating
   - Faithfulness (faith) is love trusting
   - Gentleness is love esteeming others (see Phil. 1:3)
   - Self-control is love restraining (power under control)
2. **I will use repetition to deepen the healing:** I will review my journaling, asking God to deepen and expand what He has shown me.
3. **I will gaze only upon pictures** of the *gifts* God has produced in my life through these traumas: Pictures are the language of the heart and the railroad tracks my life runs on.
4. **I will confess "I am healed":** I will speak life over myself. "My body is healed and functioning normally, in Jesus' name."

5. **I will restructure my thought processes:** I will pull down strongholds (2 Cor. 10:4,5—demonic, unbiblical thought processes) in my mind, and replace them with biblical thought processes which I arrive at by conducting Bible meditations on topics which are relevant to maintaining my new position of health. For example, to remove fear, I will look up verses on the opposite of fear, which is faith.

SATAN'S TOP LIES TO ENSURE YOU STAY SICK

	SATAN'S LIES	GOD'S TRUTHS
1.	This will take too much time.	This makes your devotional times revelation-based healing encounters with Almighty God, releasing spiritual transformation and complete healing into your life. Could anything be better?
2.	The prayer worksheet is too methodical for me. I'm free floating.	Farmers prepare for an outstanding crop by first completely tilling the soil, making sure they drag *every inch* and that *every weed* gets removed.
3.	I started with my biggest scene and it is too traumatic. I'm stuck.	Start with something smaller and work your way up.
4.	No one can be perfectly healthy.	Sure you can. Jesus *purchased* your health with His *broken body* on the cross (Isa. 53:5). Our goal is not just release of pain but vibrant health!

*Some find **an excuse** as to why they can't. Others find **a way** as to how they can!*

RESOURCES

- **Free downloadable "Clearing Cellular Memories Worksheet"**—cwgministries.org/Prayer_Worksheets
- **Clearing Cellular Memories MP3/Video Download Set**—This contains 23 minutes of Mark Virkler explaining

in detail the steps above, and how he has used them successfully to bring great healing to his life. cwgministries.org/cellmemories

---

ENDNOTES

1. Dr. Mercola, "Imaging Technology Finally Reveals How Emotions Manifest in Your Body"

Chapter Twelve

THE "TRAUMA PRAYER"

This chapter is written by a dear friend of ours, Jim Banks. His 23-minute "trauma prayer" which has been downloaded from his website over 3 million times, is written out verbatim in this chapter (jimandpatbanks.com/trauma-prayer). As you experience it, you will feel a release.

Everyone is familiar with the term trauma and yet only about 35% of trauma sufferers actually understand that they are experiencing some of the repercussions of it. How can that be? It is simply because to them this is just how their family functioned on a daily basis and they thought everyone else experienced exactly what they did. To them it was normal life. Dr. Jim Wilder has defined childhood trauma as falling into two general categories: Type A is what your parents do to you, and Type B trauma is what you don't get from your parents.

We are very familiar with stories of children who were abused by their parents, either continuously or episodically, and the resulting social and relational dysfunctionality that it produces. We are currently living in an age where the physical and emotional disconnection of parents has produced a generation of children who have little or no capacity to deal with the normal difficulties of life, much less the significant ones. A case in point is from the US Veterans Administration which cites that of those servicemen and women who served in a theater of combat in the last ten years, who have been clinically diagnosed with Post Traumatic Stress disorder, 60% of them never actually experienced actual combat. That means that these young adults do not have the capacity to function for any significant length of time under the stress of normal military life.

The 20-something daughter of a friend of ours recently took a job as a recruiter for a small mid-western college. The college's covid response had them all working from home for the first five months of her employment. When they returned to work in the office together she noted that those of her generation were not very good employees. On numerous occasions when told that they needed to follow established policies and protocols for admission, many of them stated, "That makes me very uncomfortable," as though everything should suit how they wanted to see how things were done. She was shocked to find that most of the co-workers of her generation were a bunch of emotional pansies!

It is my belief that the presence of an attentive father in the home, who daily interacts with his children, is attentive to them in that he responds to their needs for connection and conversation, who helps them navigate their problems and

THE "TRAUMA PRAYER"

difficulties (without doing it for them), is the primary means of establishing the identity of a child. When a child's identity is established, a confidence arises that allows them to weather storms pretty naturally. Tough times will come, but they will not be totally rocked in who they know themselves to be. It will take a traumatic disaster of significant import to accomplish that. I suspect that the profound lack of fathering that we find in our culture is the primary reason behind the VA's PTSD experience.

I have ministered to a number of combat veterans who were clinically diagnosed with PTSD whose combat responsibility was to take the lives of their enemies and who personally witnessed the death of fellow soldiers whom they knew and cared about. The common factor among these young men was that they had the God-given wiring of the Redemptive Gift of Mercy.[1] Individuals with this wiring tend to be more emotionally and spiritually sensitive than the general population, and are men and women who are driven (wired) to experience the depth of relationship with others. Consequently, such activities or experiences violate, run at direct cross-purposes to, their wiring and make a significant mark on their human spirits as well as their soul. Consequently, part of their trauma recovery process will require some healing prayer for their human spirits, as well as for their soul. Although the intricacies of this particular element of the recovery process are not covered here, it is worth mentioning because of the increasing population of veterans that we will each engage in general society.[2]

To give you a better picture of what Post Traumatic Stress is about and how it affects people, the following is a list of its specific symptoms. Understand that when a person has PTSD they may or may not exhibit all of these symptoms, and most often those who actually have PTSD don't think they do and consequently will not go for help to resolve it.

As noted in the opening paragraph, it is important for us to point out the symptoms to those who are struggling with PTSD because most of them are totally unaware of it. This is particularly true of hyper-vigilance and choosing to live in denial about their personal dysfunction. There is abundant help for recovery from it, but it can't be accessed if you believe you are not impacted by trauma.

DIAGNOSTIC STATISTICAL MANUAL IV, DEFINITION OF POST TRAUMATIC STRESS DISORDER BY THE AMERICAN PSYCHIATRIC ASSOCIATION

1. The person has been exposed to a traumatic event in which **both** of the following were present:
   a. the person experienced, witnessed, or was confronted with an event or events that involved actual or threatened death or serious injury, or a threat to the physical integrity of self or others.
   b. the person's response involved intense fear, helplessness, or horror. Note: In children, this may be expressed instead by disorganized or agitated behavior.
2. The traumatic event is persistently re-experienced in one (or more) of the following ways:
   a. recurrent and intrusive distressing recollections of the event, including images, thoughts, or perceptions.
   b. recurrent distressing dreams of the event.

THE "TRAUMA PRAYER"

    c. acting or feeling as if the traumatic event were recurring (includes a sense of reliving the experience, illusions, hallucinations, and dissociative flashback episodes, including those that occur on awakening or when intoxicated).

    d. intense psychological distress at exposure to internal or external cues that symbolize or resemble an aspect of the traumatic event (emotional triggers).

    e. physiological reactivity on exposure to internal or external cues that symbolize or resemble an aspect of the traumatic event.

3. Persistent avoidance of stimuli associated with the trauma and numbing of general responsiveness, as indicated by three (or more) of the following:

    a. efforts to avoid thoughts, feelings, or conversations associated with the trauma

    b. efforts to avoid activities, places, or people that arouse recollections of the trauma

    c. inability to recall an important aspect of the trauma

    d. markedly diminished interest or participation in significant activities

    e. feeling of detachment or estrangement from others

    f. restricted range of effect (e.g., unable to have loving feelings)

    g. sense of a foreshortened future (e.g., does not expect to have a career, marriage, children, or a normal life span).

4. Persistent symptoms of increased arousal as indicated by two (or more) of the following:

    a. difficulty falling or staying asleep

b. irritability or outbursts of anger
c. difficulty concentrating
d. hyper vigilance
e. exaggerated startle response.
5. Duration of the disturbance (symptoms in Criteria 2, 3, and 4) is more than 1 month.
6. The disturbance causes clinically significant distress or impairment in social, occupational, or other important areas of functioning.

Obviously, trauma presents some major difficulties for us to resolve, both functionally and relationally, whether you suffered from Type A trauma, a Type B, or you experienced it later in life as a single event or a series of them. What you need to understand is that trauma is a specific scheme of the enemy of your soul and spirit executed for several purposes:

1. for the purpose of future torment.
2. To divert you from entering into the fullness of your personal identity and therefore keeping you estranged from the God-ordained purpose of your life.
3. Causing you to become the collateral damage of the cosmic level war between God and satan such that His (God's) will is not fulfilled in the earth through you, thus further delaying satan's judgment.

Consequently, there are two components that must be resolved in the process of recovering from the traumas of life, the spiritual aspect(s) of trauma and the fleshly or soulish aspects of it, the former component being, breaking the demonic

THE "TRAUMA PRAYER"

attachments and access, the latter being the resolution of the lies and half-truths that the enemy of our soul was able to introduce at the time of the trauma, covered elsewhere in this book. Failure to deal with the spiritual aspects and implications of trauma will delay or even block a rapid recovery from the other aspects of trauma.

The Trauma Prayer Process was created in late 2008 and early 2009 when a dozen young ladies, all single and under 30 years of age, came to me for ministry separately, each complaining of tormenting dreams. All of their dreams were of a violent sexual nature filled with frightening demonic creatures. They were afraid to go to sleep knowing that the relentless terror-filled dreams would begin again. The effects of sleep deprivation were adding to the difficulties making it increasingly challenging to concentrate while at work and complete the basic tasks to keep body and soul together. At the time, I prayed everything I knew to pray, followed Holy Spirit as far as I could, dealt with every open door I could find, and all I could manage was to put a dent in the problem. Any freedom they experienced was short-lived.

So ... I spent time on my face before the Lord asking for His wisdom and understanding and how to deal with it. What occurred was an amalgamation of the two things I'd learned from others (Arthur Burk, Dr. Paul Cox and Dr. Tom Hawkins) and something I'd never seen before. When all were thrown into the mix, an amazing cake was formed.

In the last 11 or 12 years I've prayed that prayer over about 8 or 9,000 people on multiple continents and different cultures. The prayer not only immediately kills tormenting dreams for 95% of those I've prayed it over, but has also resulted in a physical healing for about 10% of those whose injuries occurred as a result of the trauma ... and has uniformly resulted in the best night's sleep any of them had experienced in years... among other things.

You can go to our website and listen to, or download a 23-minute prayer that was recorded at the conclusion of a training session in San Antonio, TX back in 2010, and/or you can view a video of a 40-minute version I did at a church in Tampa, FL in 2020.

There is also a book I wrote in 2009 and workbook entitled *The Effects of Trauma and How to Deal with It* available at Amazon.com that gives instruction on each of the items covered in the original 23-minute version of the prayer, as well as teaching which covers items I've since added to the prayer.

Because we tend to see in part and know in part, and because we tend to have a fairly narrow focus when we are trying to solve a specific problem—in this case it was simply to kill the tormenting dreams—the Lord delights in adding to our education as we continue to seek Him. The realization of the importance of the other things He's given me to aid sufferers' recovery from trauma came later because we always get more than we ask for when God delivers an answer. He knows all of what people need and is delighted to provide it, even when I was clueless that I needed it; such is the character of the awesome God we serve.

Below is a transcription of the 23-minute version of the Trauma Prayer. Prior to praying this over a group I always give them some instruction:

First of all, take care of yourself. When I reach the part where I will command your body to begin to release the memory of trauma stored in your body, you may experience a rise of emotion that is connected to it. If it feels to you that the emotion may become overwhelming, and that concerns you, you have our collective permission to get up and walk around, or leave the room if you feel you need to. There is no shame or condemnation in you taking care of yourself. You are the only one who knows where you are and what you need to do. Just take care of yourself.

Secondly, a number of you will start to cry as trauma is being accessed and released. Do not go to them in an attempt to comfort them. This prayer is for you personally, not to provide you an opportunity to show your concerned friendship. Let Holy Spirit do in them what He wishes.

Thirdly, anywhere from 5 to 10% of this group will fall asleep during this prayer. Some of you will begin to snore. Do not nudge them or attempt to wake them. Just try to ignore them as best you can. It's okay. That's what this prayer is all about, a means to cast all our cares on Him who cares for us. Let Him do His thing.

THE TRAUMA PRAYER TRANSCRIBED

(This is an accurate transcription of the 23-minute audio recording of the Trauma Prayer that currently appears on our websites: jimandpatbanks.com, traumaprayer.com, Vimeo and in multiple locations on YouTube.)

> "If you want to lay down on the floor, be my guest. Some of you are going to wind up there anyway. Pat and I may wander around and lay hands on you. If somebody touches you, don't freak out.
>
> [Starts prayer]

Father, we take authority over anything left over hanging around in this room that wants to insert itself, inject itself, or otherwise mess with what's going on. Father, we just kick to the curb anything that will not bow its knee to the Lord Jesus Christ. You have no place here, we give you none. Holy Spirit, we invite You. Come and minister to those that You love. We submit to You. We give You place. We thank You so much for what You have done for us. For what You've provided us. For what You've shown us.

Father, in Jesus' name, I take authority over this time, this space, this dimension, in the name of the Lord Jesus Christ. Father, I ask You to disconnect every one of them from every second heaven entity that's gained access to them for the purpose of inflicting torment and trauma. I specifically ask You to disconnect them from fear, chaos, death, destruction; anything that has bound or blocked development. Disconnect them right now, Father, in Jesus' name.

Father, I ask You to disconnect them from all of the schemes and contracts and agreements that (higher order) demonic entities have made with each other to torment and torture. Disconnect them, Father.

Father, I take authority over every (person's) body in this place, in Jesus' name, for a few minutes. I command their bodies to release all of the effects of trauma. Everything that it has held onto, down to the cellular level, from accidents, injuries, medical procedures, surgeries, invasive medical procedures, broken bones, cuts. I also command their bodies to release all of the effects of trauma with respect

THE "TRAUMA PRAYER"

to rejection, abandonment, death, divorce, loss of dreams, hopes, aspirations, every time they were robbed, stolen from. You'll come out without harm or injury. I just command you to release it all. Don't hang on to any of it. All of the pent-up stress and tension, anxiety, worry, results of fear.

I command your bodies to release all of the fear of the future. "How is this going to work out? What's going to happen?" All of the issues regarding health, business, children, spouses, I just command all of that out of your body, you can't hold on to it, in Jesus' name. Out of every bone, out of every piece of connective tissue, out of spines and muscle, hair, teeth, come out in Jesus' name.

I command your bodies to release all of the memories of aching loneliness; the feeling that you were all alone and helpless. Just be released right now, in Jesus' name. Let it go. Wherever you have hidden it, wherever you have allowed it to be stored up in your body, just let it go. Let it be released.

In this season of economic uncertainty, I just command your bodies to release all of the stress and tension of how it's going to work out. The plans that had been so diligently made, that seemed to have been undermined, just release, release, release. Just let it all go. All of the effects of unforgiveness, bitterness, of being cut off or abandoned. Just let it go. Just release all of the effects of shame, disappointment, and disillusionment. Everywhere that people have not lived up to their word, in fact, have done exactly the opposite. Every time you have been called a name, lied against, lied about, dishonored. Just let it all go. Release it. All of the physical effects, whether it was emotional, spiritual or physical, just release it all now in the name of Jesus. Every bit of it. Just let it go.

I command out of your nostrils and taste buds everything connected with defiling touch. Any place in your body that felt it or was impacted by it, I just command it to be released now in Jesus' name.

I take authority right now, in Jesus' name, over all witchcraft prayers that have been prayed against you, against the body of Christ, against your relationships, against your place in the body, even those who have been jealous of you for how you looked, how you acted, the favor you had, I just cut that all off right now, in Jesus' name. I release you from every bit of it. Father, we just call every one of those (words and prayers) null and void and we cast them to the ground. Have no effect. It's dust under their feet.

Father, we release them from all of the tension and anxiety and anything that it's imparted, too, and Father, we just break all of that off. Father, we even remove from them all of the heaviness of false responsibility. The stuff that others have told them that needs to be done, and they need to do it. I just release them from all of that, in Jesus' name. I release them from their expectations of what you ought to look like, how you ought to do it and how it ought to get done.

Father, if there's any portion of them that's been removed, stuck in prison, held captive, in any other time, space, place or dimension, as a result of the trauma that they've experienced, I ask You, Father, in Jesus' name that You would release them. Cause them to be recovered from wherever

THE "TRAUMA PRAYER"

that has been. I ask that You restore it to them. Cleanse it of any defilement of any place that it has been. Cancel the assignment of any familiar spirit that's been assigned to it to hold it there.

Father, if there's any portion of themselves that they have dismissed because they have believed it wasn't acceptable, was not worthy, caused them to be vulnerable, or felt like it allowed them to be taken advantage of, Father I, in Jesus' name, pronounce them forgiven for dismissing that part of them that they did not agree was good. I ask You, Father, to restore it. Reunify it so that it becomes part of them in this time, this space, this dimension.

Father, where there had been blockages to development in any area, particularly relationally, Father, I ask You to remove those dams. Allow them to grow. Father, I place my hand on every head and I pray for their brains. Father, any place that has become chemically imbalanced because of the trauma they suffered, I ask You, Father, to restore whatever connections are necessary, whatever enzymes are necessary, bring full functionality. Father, any pathways that need to be reestablished between hemispheres of the brain, or areas of the brain, so the fullness of who You created them to be can be directed towards the issues of life, Father, I ask You to restore it. If there's any deficiency in any gland in the brain, I ask You to restore it. Restore connectivity between areas of the brain. Father, specifically for those areas like the amygdala, Father, I ask You, in Jesus' name, that You would give them a new normal.

While we're at it, Lord, I ask You to move all of the memories of all of the traumatic and tormenting events to the back of the bus. Make them difficult to get to. Lord, all of those memories that speak to them of being loved, appreciated and understood, connected, belonging, Father, I ask You to move them so that they would be in the first place that they can get to.

Father, I ask You, in Jesus' name, that You would restore whatever memories are necessary for healing and the completion of what You said You started.

For those who have been horribly abused, I want to speak to your spirits and to your soul. I declare to you that those times are over. You do not have to remain on guard 24/7. The other shoe is not going to drop. You're safe now. You're no longer a little child. You can let down your guard. You can enter into the rest of the world. He has become your rear-guard. He is with you 24/7. I invite you to stand down. To enter into that place of rest that was designed for you.

Father, I ask You, in Jesus' name, to reestablish for each one of those here, the sleep patterns that You designed for them so that when they put their head on the pillow at night, they can do so with full confidence that they'll not be awakened with tormenting dreams. That the disconnection from the enemy will allow them to sleep peacefully, not reminded of where they've been rejected, abandoned, where they're helpless, hopeless. Father, that they know when they wake in the morning, their bodies will be rejuvenated, restored, and they'll have all of the energy that they need for the coming day.

THE "TRAUMA PRAYER"

Father, while You're at it, I ask You, in Jesus' name, that You would download into their spirits everything that they will need for the coming day because You know who they're going to run into, You know the circumstances they're going to be facing. Father, I ask You, in Jesus' name, that during that night season, that You will cause them to be prepared for everything that's coming.

[Pat speaking]

Now, Father, we ask that You will pour Your Spirit into every place where trauma has left. Spirit of life and light and truth will fill every cell, every bone, every tissue, every organ, every place where memories are stored, that You will fill it with Your truth. That You will restore broken places. That You will remove the bruises. Spirit of truth, Spirit of life, Spirit of God come and fill and renew the life that is within them. We invite You to come, Spirit, and to bring back to life the dead places. The places that have been given up on, set aside and ignored. The places where lies have been believed, Spirit come.

We call for a restoration and a redemptive work within each person, at a level they cannot cognitively get to. We thank You, Spirit, it's Your job. We thank You for filling. We thank You for renewing. We thank You for refreshing. We thank You for loving. We thank You for defeating the enemy on our behalf. We thank You for taking all of the effects of trauma on the cross. In the name of Jesus, we yield that to You right now. The effects of living in a fallen world, we yield that to You. The effects of stress of the busyness of life, we just release it to You. The burdens of ministering to broken people, we release it to You. The pressure, stress, or family members who are ill, and it leaves us brokenhearted, we release it to You.

Father, we release generational trauma. Trauma that has been passed down through the family line that caused the recurrence of trauma, we release it in Jesus' name, and we speak forgiveness over it. We stand as sons and daughters of the living God who declare dominion over the works of the enemy in ourselves first, in our family, in our body, in this town, in this nation and in this world, we declare he is defeated. You, Father God, are the victor.

Father, we bless each individual here. We bless their identity. We bless their future. We bless their destiny. We bless their dreams. We bless them. Their coming and their going. We bless them in the name of Jesus.

Amen.

As I wrote earlier, the authority of the believer praying this prayer will kill tormenting dreams in about 95% of the cases you are presented with. If it is not completely, or is only partially effective, it is usually due to cultic involvement on the part of the individual or a family member. Sorting out whether this was their desire, knowingly or unknowingly, or was forced upon them, or they were coerced into it ... or whether this came as a generational assignment or other outside force, is the responsibility of the minister to sort out. As our society becomes more and more godless, and the media bows to the introduction of witchcraft on TV and movies, we will collectively find more and more cases where you will have to become a sleuth to discern the entry point for the torment.

Fortunately, Holy Spirit is here to help us discover what we need to know to set the captive free of the effects of trauma.

While this prayer is generally very effective in dealing with the demonic—I have witnessed a number of spontaneous deliverances—I have also found that asking the Lord to disconnect the individual from any ties or strings that are attached to their personal identity is important to do. Oftentimes I run into people whose trauma occurred decades ago and they have come to incorporate its effects into who they are and they have absolutely no concept that how they currently see and interact with the world is completely dysfunctional. You could easily characterize this as the result of a victim spirit, perhaps an unloving spirit or the spirit of self-hate. No matter how you characterize it, there is a veil over their eyes that will not allow them to see the relational tragedy they've experienced for decades is actually their fault and compel them to do something about it.

SOME IMPORTANT CLUES

The final resolution of the effects of trauma requires the discovery of all the various lies and half-truths which were sown by the enemy during or immediately following the trauma. Anytime there is an emotionally charged event, the enemy is there to help people misinterpret it to their hurt. The lies generally come in one of three forms:

1. A lie about the individual suffering the trauma; I am not good enough, strong enough, smart enough, something enough.

2. A lie about God; He doesn't love me, care about me, won't protect me, isn't interested in me and won't talk to me.
3. A lie about those involved in the trauma; I can't trust men, I can't trust authorities, they don't love me nor do they have my best interests at heart, in direct opposition to what they said, etc.

There are numerous perturbations and varieties of these lies and some of them may have even been sown prior to the major trauma they experienced so as to cement a belief system and establish or fortify a stronghold of thought. Once the lie is implanted, the devil doesn't need to assign everyone a demon, not that he has that many anyway. (If you've forgotten, only one-third of the angels fell. That means there are twice as many good guys as there are bad ones. Are your angels bored?)

*Jesus therefore said to those Jews which had believed him, If ye abide in my word, then are ye truly my disciples; and ye shall **know the truth**, and **the truth** shall make you free.*

(John 8:31-32)

*Jesus saith unto him, **I am the way, and the truth**, and the life: no one cometh unto the Father, but by me.* (John 14:6)

In other words, the truth is able to refute the lie (about who you are, about God and the others surrounding your trauma) and firmly establish or re-establish your personal identity. And perhaps more importantly, the truth is also a Person. Whether it's in the person of Jesus or the Holy Spirit, implanted truth has the ability to restore order and bring freedom in a manner that is not only restorative, but also permanent. Whether you use

THE "TRAUMA PRAYER"

the tools of Sozo, the Immanuel Process, Theophostic or Heart-Sync, you will find that connecting a trauma sufferer with Jesus, the Father or Holy Spirit, is the most effective and rapid way of resolving all the residual issue of trauma that we have available to us thus far.

Since trauma is one of the main tools the enemy uses to damage, disrupt or cause us to alter our personal identity, our ministry is primarily directed toward removing all the things that hinder people from understanding and walking in who they were created to be. Among the tools we regularly use are understanding Redemptive Gifts, Ministry to the Human Spirit, a Mindfulness exercise keyed to design, breaking our performance and perfectionist mindsets, deliverance and disconnection from higher and lower order demonic schemes and strategies through the Trauma Prayer, and of course connecting the individual to a member of the Godhead for the purpose of healing wounds and implanting truth through the use of one of the tools noted in the previous paragraph.

This book not only covers the processes involved in ministry to trauma sufferers, but does a great job in pointing you to the ministries and the resources that will help train you to assist others in trauma resolution that sets the captive free.

If you would like to pray this prayer over individuals or groups, you can go to our website www.jimandpatbanks.com and download a free copy of the complete Notes for the long version of this prayer, that will give you specific items to remember and a short version of what to pray within each item covered.

My prayer for each of you is that you will embrace all of these tools and allow the Lord to teach you how to use them in a manner that is consistent with who He has made you to be, such that the fullness of who He is in you will operate authentically through you.

> *I thank my God upon all my remembrance of you, always in every supplication of mine on behalf of you all making my supplication with joy, for your fellowship in furtherance of the gospel from the first day until now;* **being confident of this very thing, that he which began a good work in you will perfect it** *until the day of Jesus Christ.* (Philippians 1:3-6)

The point of this is that you and I are part of the process, healing, and recovery for someone. I don't know how many steps there are in the process of helping to walk a trauma sufferer into wholeness. All I know is that I am responsible for taking them from wherever they are one or more steps down the line. If each of us does our little part in their process, hundreds of thousands will find the freedom that Christ set them free to live in. These are part of the "good works" that Ephesians 2 says we were created to accomplish before the Father created this globe we stand on and call home.

I hereby pronounce a blessing upon you to learn and grow into all that God has prepared for you to experience in this life, such that when you stand before Him on Judgment Day you will hear a resounding, *"Well done, good and faithful servant, enter into your reward!"*

ENDNOTES

1. See Arthur Burk's work at www.theslg.com, or Pat's teaching on Redemptive Gifts at www.jimandpatbanks.com.
2. See Pat Banks' video teaching on Ministry to the Human Spirit on our website.

Chapter Thirteen

THE KINGDOM LIFESTYLE

What a release we feel when the accumulated wounds to our heart have finally been healed! What a weight is lifted from our spirits! Wouldn't it be wonderful to be able to live in that feeling of lightness and peace and joy for the rest of your life? And then to use this new life you have been given to release miracles and healing to those around you who are hurting? That certainly would be the abundant life we were promised!

Is it even possible to maintain this freedom? We know that "in this world you will have tribulation." Life seems unfair. People, who are themselves wounded, wound others. People will say and do cruel things that cut our hearts again. We may face loss and trauma. So how can we live in this freedom we have found? Is there a way of living that can protect us, in the moment, from the arrows that would injure us?

I believe that God has provided a shield that we can employ that will minimize and even neutralize the painful effects of living in this fallen world. We don't have to let that poison go deep into our hearts, infecting our spirit, soul and body with its corruption. The Lord first showed me this revelation when I was trying to learn how to move more fully in His anointing, but as I walked in it, He demonstrated that it is also a secret to living in His peace and joy, as well as His power.

Throughout this book we have talked about the power of our thoughts and words to create our reality. Sadly, all too often that power has been used to trap us in ungodly lifestyles and prevent us from experiencing the abundant life Jesus promised.

We have emphasized the need to see and hear from God to move out of our brokenness and into His wholeness. If "it is no longer I who live but Christ in me," growing in Him means increasingly relying on His initiative in every situation. In this chapter we want to draw together these themes to demonstrate how the processes that have been working to keep you in pain and bondage can be used to elevate you to a life that is supernatural in every way.

THE REVELATION

While praying at the altar of my church, in a flash God showed me a revelation that clarified truths I had been learning from David Yonggi Cho and Kenneth Hagin. I have lived out of this revelation ever since.

In his book *The Fourth Dimension*, David Yonggi Cho teaches that there are the two things you need if you want to do great things for God: a rhema word and a vision from God. I fully embrace that, for it is my passion. On the other hand, Kenneth Hagin, "Father of the Faith Movement," said that if you want to release a miracle, you need to ponder God's promises, speak them and act on them. I agreed with this as well, and he had thousands of testimonies proving it worked.

God showed me that Cho and Hagin fit together perfectly like a hand and a glove. The keys Cho emphasized are where we begin, and the three keys Hagin highlighted nurture the *rhema* and vision until they bring forth fruit.

FILLING THE FIVE SENSES OF MY SPIRIT

We will look at how this process is used to release miracle-working power, then we will more closely examine how we can use it to release supernatural peace and joy.

Cho emphasizes the first two steps: 1) God **speaks to me** a *rhema* word that is His promise of how He is going to meet the need. 2) God then adds His **picture of the miracle already completed**. This plants God's purposes within my heart.

Hagin then adds the next three steps, which are the incubation process. Hagin advises me to: 3) **ponder** only God's *rhema* and vision, 4) **speak** only what God has spoken, and 5) **act** on what God has spoken. In the fullness of time God brings forth His miracle.

By following these five simple steps, God has birthed miracles as well as an international ministry out through my life, which is far beyond my wildest imagination. I know He will do the same for you as you let God fill all five senses of your spirit with Him.

How to have
Mountain-Moving Faith
by filling all five senses of your heart with God!

	SENSE	HOW USED	BIBLE EXAMPLE	STAGE
1.	Inner Ear (Jn. 5:30)	Receives God's Rhema	Gen. 12:1-3	Conception
2.	Inner Eye (Rev. 4:1)	Receives God's Vision	Gen. 15:5,6	Conception
3.	Inner Mind (Lk. 2:19)	Ponders God's Thoughts	Rom. 4:20,21	Incubation
4.	Inner Will (Acts 19:21)	Speaks on God's Rhema	Gen. 17:5	Incubation
5.	Inner Emotions (I Kings 21:5)	Acts on God's Rhema and Vision	Gen. 17:23	Incubation
End Result		Death of the Vision "I" am unable to bring it about	Gen. 16:2 / Gen. 17:18,19	Birth
End Result		Supernatural Resurrection of the Vision	Gen. 21:1,2	Birth
End Result		"In the fullness of time GOD brings it forth"	Gal. 4:4a	Birth

"Have God's faith [Greek literal translation].
Truly I say to you, whoever says to this mountain,
Be taken up and cast into the sea,
and does not doubt in his heart,
but believes that what he says is going to happen,
it will be granted him."
(Mk. 11:22,23)

ABRAHAM MODELS FAITH

Abraham is called the Father of Faith (Rom. 4:11-16). I believe that means he models all the key steps which we would need to take if we desire to follow his example and become children of faith. The Bible says we can cast mountains into the sea if we don't doubt in our **hearts** (Mk. 11:22-24). We really want to understand how to have **heart faith** so we can see miracles released out through our hands. We want to speak to mountains in our lives (i.e., sickness, poverty, demons, depression, fear, brokenness, etc.) and see them removed! So let's see what we can learn from the Father of Faith. How did Abraham grow so strong in faith?

Step 1—Faith Begins With a Spoken Word From the Lord

God spoke a promise into Abraham's heart.

> *Now the LORD **said** to Abram, "Go forth from your country, And from your relatives And from your father's house, To the land which I will show you; And I will make you a great nation, And I will bless you, And make your name great; And so you shall be a blessing; And I will bless those who bless you, And the one who curses you I will curse. And in you all the families of the earth will be blessed."* (Gen. 12:1-3)

When we need a miracle, we go to God in prayer and ask, "Lord, what do You want to say to me about this situation?" We listen for His voice, tuning to flowing thoughts, and we write down what He says back to us, as taught in Chapter 1.

Step 2—God Adds a Vision, a Picture of the Promise Fulfilled
God showed Abraham a vision (Gen. 15:1). And He took him outside and said,

> "**Now look** toward the heavens, and count the stars, if you are able to count them." And He said to him, "So shall your descendants be." **Then he believed** in the LORD; and He reckoned it to him as righteousness. (Gen. 15:5-6)

We say a picture is worth 1,000 words. According to the above verses, I would say the Bible agrees. You will note that as soon as God gave Abraham a picture of the promise fulfilled, the next verse tells us "**then he believed**." So I understand that in order to have miracle-working faith, I need two things from God: I need God to speak a *rhema* word to me, and I need God to show me a picture of this *rhema* word already fulfilled.

"So Lord, what does my healed body look like? What will I be able to do when You have restored me to full health? What does Your blessing of prosperity look like in my life? What does total freedom and release look like? Can You show me pictures of these things? Thank You, Lord!"

Once we have received a *rhema* word and a vision from the Lord concerning His promises and provision for any area of our lives, conception has taken place. We are now pregnant with the purposes of God for that area of our lives.

Step 3—We Ponder This Rhema and Vision From God—Nothing Else!

> *And not being weak in faith, he **did not consider his own body**, already dead (since he was about a hundred years old), and the*

*deadness of Sarah's womb. He **did not waver at the promise of God through unbelief**, but was strengthened in faith, giving glory to God, and being fully convinced that what He had promised He was also able to perform. And therefore "IT WAS ACCOUNTED TO HIM FOR RIGHTEOUSNESS."* (Rom. 4:19-22 NKJV)

Like Abraham, we must choose what we are going to look at and what we are going to believe. Abraham could have looked at the weakness of his aged body, and said, "Reality is, I can't reproduce anymore." But he chose not to *consider* (ponder and picture) his weakness, but instead to ponder and picture only the promise and vision of God.

Likewise, I choose carefully to daily, continuously ponder and see *only* God's promised blessing to me and not lack or need. As God spoke to me, "Whatever you fix your eyes upon, grows within you; whatever grows within you, you become." This changed my life. I no longer look at disease, self-effort, lack, weakness or law. Now I only fix my eyes on Jesus (Heb. 12:1, 2; Acts 2:25; Ps. 16:8), and His spoken promises and visions to me, and these grow within me and I step into these realities. I *am* healed! I *am* blessed! I *have* favor everywhere I go! I release effective ministry to those I touch! I have a blessed marriage and family! Thank You, Lord, for these amazing gifts!

What do you see in your mind's eye: lack or fullness, disease or health, division or unity, rejection or acceptance? We ponder and see something all the time. Make sure you are only seeing God's promises to you in each and every area of your life! We choose to meditate on God's promise and visions to us in both our morning and evening prayer meditations (1 Chron. 23:30) as well as throughout the day. I would recommend a meditation of thanksgiving morning and evening where you speak the promises God has made to you in the various areas of your life. Filling your heart and mind with His divine light causes darkness to flee.

Step 4—We Speak the Rhema and Vision God Has Given to Us.

When Abraham was 99 years old (Gen. 17:1) and still had no children by his wife, God asked him to speak a word of faith and call the promise into being:

> *No longer shall your name be called Abram, but your name shall be Abraham; for I have made you a father of many nations.*
> (Gen. 17:5 NKJV)

Now, every time Abraham speaks his name aloud, he is confessing the promise of God to him (the name Abraham means "father of a multitude"). Abraham was convinced that *"God... calls those things which do not exist as though they did"* (Rom. 4:17 NKJV), and *"by faith we understand that the **worlds were framed by the word of God**, so that the things which are seen were not made of things which are visible"* (Heb. 11:3 NKJV).

Our spoken words become the directives which **frame** the creative miracles we are going to see. *Breath* and *spirit* are the same words in the Greek and Hebrew languages. So when we speak what God speaks, the spiritual energy/realities which have been growing within us through our daily meditations on God's *rhema* and vision pour out with our spoken words and create that which we frame with the words of our mouths. Death and life truly are in the power of the tongue (Prov. 18:21).

God will tell us what words to say. We don't need to come up with them ourselves. We ask God what He wants us to speak over our situations, and He will tell us. God said to Abram, "Your name shall be Abraham," so God told Abram exactly what to say. Incidentally, God waited a period of time before telling Abram to confess this new name. We keep God in the center of the process at all times. We don't need to be doing things on our own initiative, when and how we think is best. Our only desire is to live like Jesus, out of divine initiative (Jn. 5:30).

> *So shall My word be that goes forth from **My mouth**; It shall not return to Me void, But it **shall accomplish** what I please, And it shall prosper in the thing for which I sent it.*   (Isa. 55:11)

Step 5—We Act on the Rhema and Vision God Has Given to Us

Faith without works is dead (Jas. 2:17). Take up your bed and walk (Lk. 5:24). We decide to get up and walk. We decide to walk on the water, to take risks, aware that God must and will come through. As long as our eyes stay on the Lord, our faith is intact and the miracle happens. Peter walked on the water as long as he looked only at the Lord Jesus Christ. When he looked at the wind and the waves, fear entered in, disrupting the flow of God's power, and down he went (Matt. 14:29-31).

Abraham grew *strong* in faith (Rom. 4:20). This brought him to the place of instant total obedience to God's ongoing directives to him. He **acted**, circumcising his family on the **very same day** God commanded him to do so (Gen. 17:23). His wife became pregnant immediately following, and within one year Isaac was born (Gen. 22:1, 2).

We, too, grow strong in faith through daily, prayerfully revolving in our hearts and minds the *rhemas* and visions of Almighty God, and in the fullness of time (Gal. 4:4) God brings forth a miracle.

Step 6—We Die to Self-Effort

The fullness of time... hmmm. It only took 24 years for Sarah to become pregnant! Personally, God, I don't want to wait 24 years for anything to happen. I prefer it to happen within 24 minutes or 24 seconds of the time God speaks it. His answer back to me was: "Who writes the rules of the universe, you or Me?"

So many times miracles require an incubation period before they are released from the invisible, spiritual world into the visible, physical world. I need to make sure that, while I wait, I stay tuned only to God's voice and vision, and don't come up with **my own ideas** of how to make things happen (Gen. 16:1, 2). If I do, I will birth an Ishmael, which will not be accepted by God (Gen. 17:18, 19). I must die to all self-initiated behavior (Jn. 14:10) and only do those things I hear and see the Father doing (Jn. 8:26, 38). Wow! This is a totally counter-cultural way of living, where I am taught to be all that I can be. In reality I want to become all that Christ is in and through me. Lord, teach me to live this way, I pray.

Step 7—In rhe Fullness of Time, God Brings Forth the Miracle

> *And the LORD visited Sarah as He had said, and the LORD did for Sarah as He had spoken. For Sarah conceived and bore Abraham a son in his old age, at the set time of which God had*

spoken to him.... Now Abraham was one hundred years old when his son Isaac was born to him. (Gen 21:1,2,5)

Wow! It only took 25 years for this miracle to get started, and the full manifestation of it (i.e., the earth being blessed through Abraham's seed) occurred 1500 years later when Jesus was resurrected from the dead! Yikes, now I really don't like the rules of the universe. However, I only have two choices: to say "Yes, Lord" or to become angry and bitter and fall away from the living Lord. Of course, whatever is not of faith is sin (Rom. 14:23).

OK, Lord, I believe, and I am willing to go to my grave believing in the *rhema* and vision You have given to me. I will be a worshipper until the day I die, and then I will continue worshipping You for all eternity.

A SUMMARY OF THE 7 STEP MIRACLE MODEL

1. Faith begins with a **spoken word** from the Lord.
2. God adds a **vision**, a picture of the promise fulfilled.
3. We **ponder** this rhema and vision from God—nothing else!
4. We **speak** the rhema and vision God has given to us, according to His directions.
5. We **act** on the rhema and vision God has given to us.
6. We **die to self-effort.**
7. In the **fullness of time, God brings forth** the miracle.

Heart faith is mountain-moving faith. It is conceived by a rhema and vision from God, which when incubated, through pondering, speaking and acting, births a miracle in God's fullness of time.

MY 25-YEAR MIRACLE

In 1979, the year I learned the four keys to hearing God's voice, the Lord spoke in my journaling, "Mark, we are going to saturate the nation with communion with God." A month or two later He said, "Mark, we are going to saturate the world with communion with God."

I asked, "Which one, Lord, the nation or the world?"

He said, "It is up to you. If you want to believe for the nation I will give you the nation. If you want to believe for the world, I will give you the world."

My response was, "I will believe for the world."

God gave me a vision of little lights in homes all across the world. These lights were people communing with God. The number of lights continued to grow. This was a vision of the promise fulfilled.

I have pondered this *rhema* and vision, spoken it and acted on it by teaching worldwide.

It is now 40 years later and we have "seeded" the world with communion with God. Our Christian Leadership University has students in 129 countries who have taken our college course "Communion With God." When we offer free monthly video events with online training about How to Hear God's Voice, people from over 100 nations watch them. Wow!

No, I wouldn't call the world saturated yet, but I believe it will be, if not in my lifetime, then after I die. The people lauded in Hebrews 11 died in faith believing the promise of God to them would come about even though they did not see it in their lifetime.

WE ARE ALL CONSTANTLY FILLING THESE FIVE SENSES WITH GOD OR SATAN

It is not a question of whether we will be imagining or pondering or speaking or acting. We are always using these senses. For example, everyone has an idea and picture of the quality of their marriage which they are pondering, speaking, acting and birthing. It could be "we have an exquisite marriage" or "we have a fair marriage" or "we have a terrible marriage." Which reality are you birthing in your marriage?

Everyone has an idea and picture of their finances which they are pondering, speaking, acting and releasing. It could be "God always provides more than enough" or "I generally have just enough" or "I never have enough." Which reality are you birthing in your life?

Everyone has an idea and a picture of their health which they are pondering, speaking, acting and birthing. As I go into my senior years, "God will renew my strength like an eagle," or "I expect to get sicker and weaker," or "I expect I will have a major health problem." Which reality am I releasing in my life?

Obviously only one outcome in each of the above examples is biblical and acceptable to be incubating and birthing. Only one is infused with the light, glory and power of Almighty God. We must deliberately offer these senses to the Lord if we want to walk in His light and life.

LIVING IN KINGDOM EMOTIONS

Back to our question at the beginning of the chapter, how can this process be used to help me maintain a healed heart? When I experience something painful or traumatic, how can I protect my heart from responding poorly, absorbing the negative energy and beginning to build a new house for demons?

First you must hear what God is saying about you and the situation. Your immediate reaction to a hurtful event should be, "Lord, where are You? Show me what You are doing and saying here. Let me see through Your eyes. Show me how You are responding, and give me the grace to let You express Yourself through me." As His words and visions fill your heart and mind, the spiritual world will become more real than the physical (2 Cor. 4:17, 18). In due course, you will be able to ask Him, "What do You want to accomplish in me through this? What gift do You want to give me? How do You want to redeem for good to me what others meant for evil?"

Write down what you hear and see, and embrace His view as reality. Allow His Truth to replace the temporal "facts" of the material world. Whenever your mind goes to the hurtful event, don't allow yourself to dwell in the negative but instead, immediately reflect on His *rhema*. Replace the movie that tries to dominate your mind with the vision God has shown you. Immerse yourself in the eternal truth that He has given you, leaving behind the lies that want to entrap you.

If you ever speak about the hurtful event, speak only what He tells you to say, when He tells you to say it. Refuse to be drawn into slander, gossip or negative speech of any kind. Speak only words that are edifying, giving grace to those who hear.

As you ponder and speak God's words of grace, you will find your actions also become filled with grace. You will not act out anger or hurt or vengeance, but will love, forgive and serve.

THE KINGDOM LIFESTYLE

You will become a walking miracle, demonstrating the supernatural power of being a new creation! You will not be "normal," responding as the world expects you to. You will be recognized as one who has been with Jesus and experienced His life-changing power.

But remember—don't try to accomplish any of this in your own strength, through your own self-will and self-control. To do so will just push the poisoned arrow deeper into your heart where it can do even more damage. You may look good on the outside but inside the infection will be growing until once again you are under the power of negative energies. Or, to say it another way, it will only produce an Ishmael—not the promise of God.

This is a supernatural work of the Spirit that begins, continues and ends only by His power. Hear His voice, see His vision, ponder His revelation, speak as He directs you and act as He leads you. Only then will you be filled with the *dunamis* that overcomes the world.

PERSONAL JOURNALING QUESTIONS

1. Lord, what are the dreams You have given me for my life, my marriage, my finances, my health and my ministry? You could discuss these separately for several days in your devotional time.
2. Have I given up on these dreams?
3. Am I pondering them in my heart?
4. Am I speaking them forth as You, Lord, are asking me to?
5. Am I listening and obedient to each word You, Lord, are speaking to me, thus freeing the way for its fulfillment?

6. Am I resting from my strivings and simply doing what You, Lord, are asking me to do?

GO DEEPER WITH THESE ADDITIONAL RESOURCES

For further teaching, order the inspirational sermon "Mountain Moving Faith". cwgministries.org/mountain_moving_faith

Be sure to download the free accompanying PowerPoint slides and PDF one-page handout. This allows you to teach this message easily in a home group or a Sunday service. The one-page diagram should be printed out and provided to all in the group who are receiving the teaching. They can take notes on it and take it home for review. I have had hundreds if not thousands of comments from listeners saying, "This really put it together for me. Thank you."

Help me spread this message and together get the Church moving constantly in mountain-moving faith.

Chapter Fourteen

PRAY FOR ONE ANOTHER

It is now time to begin praying with people in your group who need additional work with these seven prayers in order to achieve full freedom. In the weeks which follow, continue to meet with those who want private or corporate prayer ministry until all are prayed for and set free. The goal of your group that has come together to complete this *Prayers That Heal the Heart* training module is that each one understands and fully experiences these seven prayers. So, everyone should be offered the opportunity to continue meeting as a group, praying for those desiring it, or letting people meet with a couple of prayer counselors from the group to receive ongoing ministry as they press forward to experience full healing and deliverance. Let the Church be the Church!

I encourage you to listen to the 80-minute model prayer session in which I pray with a lady, using all seven prayers. This will give you a feel for the entire process from beginning to end. It is part of the audio and video series of *Prayers That Heal the Heart*.

KEY QUESTIONS I ASK WHICH PROMOTE QUICK HEALING

1. When did this physical or emotional problem begin?
2. What happened in your life at that time or just before that time? Tune to flow and the answer will pop into your mind. If it doesn't, then ask the question as you are drifting off to sleep, and within the first 30 minutes after awakening, the answer will be in your consciousness.

Very often there is a connection between the above two answers, and this provides the key as to what and how to pray. It could be a person or event which needs forgiveness, or a trauma which needs inner healing and cellular clearing. Listen to God and He will show you how to pray.

We have provided a *Contributing Strands Worksheet* which can be freely downloaded or purchased very inexpensively from Communion with God Ministries. I use this worksheet in a three-hour *Prayers That Heal the Heart* counseling session. We move through it quickly and I fill in each section as I lead the counselee through the prayers. It is then given to the counselee to take home and review and save as a memorial of the great work God has done in their life. Alternatively, and preferably, the counselee completes the *Contributing Strands Worksheet* prior to the counseling appointment. Then our time together can be focused on inner healing and deliverance.[1]

I use each of the above tools effectively as I pray these prayers for myself and with others in counseling sessions. It takes awhile to get healed, so you can use these yourself as necessary. It might be wise to do a spiritual check-up every January where you ask the Lord if there are heart wounds you have picked up over the last twelve months which need to be processed in prayer.

Some may need specialized prayer to break off Freemasonry curses or to heal deeply fractured parts within their heart. Jesus came to heal the brokenhearted, so seek out specialized prayer as necessary.[2]

YOUR LIFE IN CHRIST GIVES YOU AUTHORITY TO PRAY THESE PRAYERS OF RELEASE FOR YOURSELF AND OTHERS.

If the Son therefore shall make you free, ye shall be free indeed.
(John 8:36 KJV)

Jesus... spoke... saying, "All authority has been given to Me in heaven and on earth. Go therefore and make disciples of all the nations." *(Matthew 28:18-19)*

For in Him all the fullness of the Deity dwells in bodily form, and in Him you have been made complete, and He is the head over all rule and authority. *(Colossians 2:9-10)*

And raised us up with Him, and seated us with Him in the heavenly places, in Christ Jesus, in order that in the ages to come He might show the surpassing riches of His grace in kindness toward us in Christ Jesus. *(Ephesians 2:6-7)*

And as you go, preach, saying, "The Kingdom of heaven is at hand," heal the sick, raise the dead, cleanse the lepers, cast out demons, freely you have received, freely give. *(Matthew 10:7-8)*

> *I will give you the keys of the kingdom of heaven; and whatever you bind on earth shall have been bound in heaven, and whatever you loose on earth shall have been loosed in heaven.*
>
> (Matthew 16:19)

God has given you the spiritual authority you need to pray prayers of release from bondage. You may pray these prayers for yourself as well as for others. However, if you can find other people skilled in these types of prayers, it is often helpful to have a couple of others praying with you and for you. Their added prayers and insight from the Holy Spirit often speed the process and help you see things you may not otherwise.

TAKE THE TIME NECESSARY FOR YOUR HEALING TO BE COMPLETE

Do not rush through the prayer sections in this book. You may want to use your devotional times for the next few weeks or months to fully apply the healing prayers. If you hurry through it, you have missed the entire value of this book. So slow down and take your time.

THE IMPORTANCE OF USING THE RIGHT PRAYER

I was flabbergasted that I could have lived for forty years with workaholism in my system and not seen it as a problem. In addition, I had lived for a good many years with other problems like doubt and anger and fear. My deceptions went like this.

I assumed the doubt was just part of the process one goes through as he seeks knowledge, and that maturity was learning to live with doubt. Wrong! I needed a revised process for seeking knowledge, which I have now found. Then doubt stayed away permanently, as I learned to reason together with God (Isa. 1:18).

I assumed the workaholism was just part of my personality and part of my love for serving the Lord. Wrong! I needed to apply the prayers of "replacing negative expectations" and "repenting of inner vows." Then my workaholism (which was rooted in a very early working relationship) vanished.

I assumed the onslaughts of fear I experienced were just demonic attacks, so I would bind satan and command him to leave. However, fear never went very far away and would always return at the first sign of a threat of any kind. This was because the fear was being fed by a spirit of doubt, and the spirit of doubt was being fed by my faulty epistemology (system for knowing). I was wrongly interpreting the experiences of my life and thus not fully believing in God's protective hand over me, and therefore the spirits of doubt and fear were continuously fed in my life. I needed to change my interpretation of the experiences of life if I was going to permanently cut off the demons of doubt and fear.

I assumed the anger I felt was simply righteous indignation and it really wasn't a problem at all. However, I was noticing that I was angry more and more often, until eventually it was most of the time. Everything seemed to make me angry. I was angry at institutions such as Phariseeism, legalism, government, and stupidity wherever I found it. I was beginning to feel that anger was getting out of control.

When I was finally healed of the anger, I recognized a step in prayer which I had completely missed. I had not repented of my negative judgment (and thus anger) against institutions which I felt were in error. So I held a grudge against Phariseeism, for example. Every time I thought about Phariseeism, I became angry, for I had a negative judgment against it.

Therefore, my prayers for healing my negative expectations needed to include repenting of my negative judgments against institutions which I deemed were faulty. The institution could be alcoholism (i.e., the whole industry which creates and markets liquor), Phariseeism, government, legalism, Western education, the abortion industry, the justice system, the Church—you name it. I am not to live in a negative judgment concerning any institution. I am to give my judgments to God so that I can minister life to those individuals who are caught in these institutions. If I harbor a judgment against the institution, I will have a negative spirit when I communicate with people in that institution. This negative spirit will cut off my ability to minister effectively to them, and will leave me with floating hostility.

My earlier prayers (before Australia) would bring a temporary relief to my system, but I could feel that these things were not too far away and that just about anything could trigger them. So in reality they weren't gone, they were *just kept in abeyance*. That is one of the keys we can look for. Are our hearts really healed of the problem or is the problem just kept "under control"? Let's nail this down as one sure-fire way of determining the need for prayer ministry.

You will observe that the reason my prayers had not been working before I received ministry in Australia was because I was using the wrong prayer to try to solve the problem, or because I was leaving out key elements when I was using the right prayer (e.g. I didn't repent of my judgment against institutions I didn't respect.) The purpose of this chapter is twofold. The first is to get you using the right prayers to solve the problem. The second is to make sure you don't forget any parts of the prayer, so that the prayer can do its full and complete work in you.

I have prayed with people who have struggled with inappropriate sexual desire. Many assume that they will just have to learn to live with the situation. Their prayers to bind or rebuke their inappropriate sexuality do not work to release its controlling power, possibly because they are praying the wrong prayers. They should be breaking generational sins and curses, and praying to break ungodly soul ties from the earlier days of their lives, and then casting out demons. When they do finally pray the right prayers, a great release from inappropriate sexuality pressure generally sweeps over them.

However, never forget that we are by nature sexual beings, so do not assume that all sexual desires are going to disappear.

USE THE RIGHT HEALING PRAYER APPROACH, NOT THE WRONG ONE!

When in Australia, I came to the shocking realization that I had been using the wrong healing prayer approach with several issues I had been struggling with for years. Therefore, I was not healed. The problems remained, and I fought and fought against them. *You should not have to endlessly fight internal battles. If you are doing so, then you probably have not yet applied the right prayer approach.* Stop what you are doing, and pray and meditate in the Lord's presence, asking, "Holy Spirit, which prayer is the right approach for healing this problem I am struggling with?" As you feel His leading to use one or the other of the prayers, do so and see if indeed it has set you free. If not, repeat the process again and again until you are totally free.

If you cannot get your heart free by praying on your own, then go to a counseling team who is skilled in these kinds of prayers and receive prayer from them. Life is too short to live it in misery. Get yourself free so you can enjoy and celebrate life.

THE VARIOUS STRANDS OF FORGIVENESS—APPLY THEM ALL!

If we confess our sins, he is faithful and just to forgive us our sins, and to cleanse us from all unrighteousness. (1 John 1:9)

"Forgive, and ye shall be forgiven." (Luke 6:37 KJV)

God will forgive you as you forgive those who have hurt you. Thus, a key to your healing is to forgive deeply, thoroughly, and completely. This includes: confessing the sins of your ancestors (Lev. 26:40; Dan. 9:2-20); forgiving them for what they passed on to you, as well as forgiving others who have hurt you; forgiving yourself for living in the sin you find yourself in; and asking God to forgive you for any resentment you have toward Him for allowing this problem in your life in the first place. Without thorough, deep, and comprehensive forgiveness, your healing will be incomplete.

WHY FORGIVE A PERSON WHEN HE WAS CRUEL AND UNJUST?

One value of forgiveness is that it releases you from being a slave to the person you hate. If you don't forgive him, every time you think of him and what he did to you, you will be filled with anger and rage, and you will be whipped and beaten emotionally. This emotional slavery can go on for years and years, even until the end of your life, if you don't forgive him. He may be free and living a happy life, but you are a slave to him, as well as to anger, wrath and bitterness.

This anger, wrath and bitterness you feel will destroy your health. Not only will you be an emotional slave to him, but your physical health will be drained, also.

Forgiving a person frees you emotionally and physically from the control and domination of the one who has hurt you. Of course, forgiving others does much more than that. It opens up God's forgiveness, blessing, and anointing upon your life. It also keeps you from sending out the wrong message from your spirit to others, which would cause you to reap a harvest of unpleasant realities.

THINGS WHICH GO ALONG WITH THE CONFESSION OF SINS

Establishing fences: Ask, "Lord, what fences do You want me to construct around myself so that my susceptibility to ongoing temptation in this area is reduced?" List these fences and see that they are constructed. God may tell you to avoid certain situations which pose an extreme temptation to you. For example, the Bible does tell us to flee youthful lusts (2 Tim. 2:22). That would mean that one would put up a fence which instructed him to run away from situations which produced sensual lust. One might even list those particular situations that they are going to make it a point to avoid.

Hosea prayed for a hedge of thorns to be constructed around Gomer, his wayward wife, so that she could no longer find her way toward evil (Hos. 2:6-7).

Making recompense: The Lord may ask you to approach certain people and ask their forgiveness and make recompense to them. Do as He says.

> *Then he shall confess his sin which he has committed, and he shall make restitution in full for his wrong and add to it a fifth of it, and give it to him whom he has wronged.* (Numbers 5:7)

IF I KEEP FALLING BACK INTO THE SIN, THEN WHAT? PERHAPS...

1. I am in bondage to spiritual forces which I have not yet fully broken.
2. I don't really want to overcome the sin—I am enjoying it too much.
3. I need to confess the sin to a close spiritual friend and make myself accountable to them.

If there are spiritual forces operating within me, then diligently praying through the seven prayers taught in this manual will eventually release me from them. If I am enjoying the sin too much to really want to overcome it, then I need to discover how to add passion to my repentance.

IMPASSIONED REPENTANCE

Connect enough pain to an activity and it becomes repulsive. Connect enough pleasure to an activity and it becomes desirable.

Since pain and pleasure are both emotional responses, and emotions are the by-products of pictures, hold clear, detailed pictures of the effects of both sinfulness and righteousness in your mind as you walk through life.

Create a detailed picture of pain: To acquire a profound motivating revulsion against a specific sin in your life, see all the ways this sin damages, devastates and destroys your life, both now and in eternity. Try Deuteronomy 28:14-68 for a picture of pain. What effect does this sin have on my relationship with Jesus? On my marriage? My children? My health? My finances? My testimony? My character? My other relationships? **Principle:** The more detailed you make your picture, the more power it has to move you emotionally.

Create a detailed picture of blessing: To acquire a profound motivating passion toward righteousness in your life, see all the ways righteousness enriches, enhances and anoints your life, both now and in eternity. Try Deuteronomy 28:1-14 for a picture of blessing. **Principle:** The more detailed you make your picture, the more power it has to move you emotionally.

ASAPH'S LOSS OF PASSION TO LIVE RIGHTEOUSLY (PSALM 73)

Asaph lost his pure fervent heart and stumbled when he took his eyes off the Lord and gazed longingly upon evil (Psalm 73:1-2). He developed a detailed picture of the pleasures of sin. He became envious of the proud, saw their prosperity, their pain-free life, their well-fed bodies, their mockery of others including God, and he decided it was vain for him to maintain personal purity (verses 3-15).

Then he went into the presence of God, and through revelation, received a detailed picture of the devastation at the end of their lives. They were on slippery places, and would eventually fall and, in a moment, experience destruction and sudden terror and be utterly swept away (verses 16-20).

Asaph's first picture enticed him toward evil. His second picture enticed him toward righteous living. Watch over the pictures in your mind. Are they drawing you toward evil or toward righteousness?

THE ULTIMATE STEP—CONFESSING THE SIN TO A CLOSE SPIRITUAL FRIEND AND MAKING YOURSELF ACCOUNTABLE TO HIM

Confession of sin to a close spiritual friend, and personal accountability in a particular sin area, is a step reserved for stubborn sin areas in your life.

Repentance begins by praying through the seven prayers to break spiritual forces in your life. Then, if the sin problem is still persisting, you would impassion your repentance by creating a detailed picture of the devastation this sin will ultimately cause in your life if allowed to continue and grow, as well as a detailed picture of the blessings of righteousness.

If the sin problem still persists, then you need to add this final step of confessing the sin to a close spiritual friend and making yourself accountable to him.

> *Is anyone among you sick? Let him call for the elders of the church, and let them pray over him, anointing him with oil in the name of the Lord; and the prayer offered in faith will restore the one who is sick, and the Lord will raise him up, and if he has committed sins, they will be forgiven him. Therefore, confess your sins to one another, and pray for one another, so that you may be healed. The effective prayer of a righteous man can accomplish much.*
>
> (James 5:14-16)

Obviously, the above command to confess our sins to one another and to pray for one another is in the context of being healed of a physical sickness. One point to make here is that if a sin is allowed to continue and grow in our lives, it will eventually turn into a sickness. This is clearly exemplified in Job 33:13-22, where Elihu explains that God does tell us what is going on in our lives.

MY OBSERVATIONS CONCERNING THE CONFESSION OF SINS TO ANOTHER

1. All sins do not need to be confessed to my close spiritual friends, only those which are severe and persistent or have resulted in pain and sickness in my body. If we all confessed every sin we have to one another, we would spend most of our time groveling around in one another's sins, which would not be very uplifting.

   I might add this suggestion: Why would I want to wait and persist in my sin until my health breaks down? Why not deal with it while I still have my health? If I have a severe and persistent sin which I have not been able to overcome through praying the seven prayers of this book or impassioning my repentance with detailed pictures, then I should go to my close spiritual friend and confess my sin and be prayed for by him.

2. The values of confessing my sin before another are that: a) When I bring my darkness to the light, it weakens and removes the power of that darkness. Confessing my sin to my close spiritual friend brings an increased amount of light upon the sin and thus contributes to its dissipation; b) My friend will probably have counsel he can give me of effective ways to overcome the sin; c) Having two or three others standing with me in prayer multiplies the power available to overcome it. One can put a thousand to flight, and two, ten thousand. A cord of three is not easily broken (Eccl. 4:9-12).

3. Let God guide you in a careful choice of the close spiritual friend(s) to whom you confess your sins and become accountable. Make sure they are truly your friends and that they will join in supporting you in overcoming this sin, and that they will not publicize it to the church or the world, or come against you and attack you for it. If they are Pharisees or legalists, steer clear of them, for such people will berate you for your weakness, rather than coming alongside and strengthening you in your time of need (as God does).

   So ask God to show you a person to whom you can confess who will be a friend, a counselor, and a strengthener to you. God can show you who this person (or persons) is to be. Then approach that person, asking if he or she is willing to pray with you in the manner described in James 5:14-16. If so, then proceed. Note: The person or persons may or may not be part of the eldership team in your local assembly. Follow God's leading in this.

4. Accountability relationships: In addition to confessing your sin(s) to these close spiritual friends and receiving their prayers, you may want to ask if they would become partners who would hold you accountable. In other words, you are asking if they would ask you regularly how you are doing in this area. This will keep you on your toes, because you know that you will have to give an account to them whenever they ask. This added awareness will be one more impetus to assist you in putting off this sin.

   I stand convinced that these three steps in deepening repentance will work even against the most stubborn of sins.

1) Start by praying through the seven prayers. 2) Then, if necessary, impassion your repentance with detailed pictures of the consequences of both sin and righteousness. 3) Finally, if the sin is still persisting, confess it to your close spiritual friend(s) and establish an accountability relationship with that person or persons.

Do it. Don't let your sin continue, for if you do, it will lead you into pain and sickness and eventually death.

The soul who sins will die. (Ezekiel 18:4)

PERSONAL APPLICATION

1. Pray for one another using the seven prayers that heal the heart.
2. If you are facing a stubborn sin, work through the steps described in the "Impassioned Repentance Worksheet" which can be found in Part Two of this book, and may be downloaded from cwgministries.org/Prayer_Worksheets
3. If necessary, use the final step of confessing sins to a spiritual accountability partner.

ENDNOTES

1. See Part Two of this book, "Available Training on Prayers That Heal the Heart" for additional prayer worksheets and resources.
2. For a list of Spirit-anointed counseling ministries we recommend see: cwgministries.org/outstanding-links

Chapter Fifteen

TIPS FOR THE PRAYER MINISTER

> *The Spirit of the Lord GOD is upon me; because the LORD hath anointed me to preach good tidings unto the meek; He hath sent me to bind up the brokenhearted, to proclaim liberty to the captives, and the opening of the prison to them that are bound.*
>
> (Isaiah 61:1)

The prayer ministry counseling approach described in the previous chapters heals! It has healed my heart and the hearts of many for whom I have prayed. Christian counselors around the world have seen breakthroughs with their clients in a single three-hour prayer ministry counseling session (which, of course, must be followed up with the appropriate exercises given in the previous chapters).

I strongly encourage you to consider drawing together a small group to experience this training. DVDs or digital videos can be used, followed by appropriate prayer ministry at the end of each weekly session. Each participant should have a copy of this book as well as the *LEARN Prayers That Heal the Heart Workbook—Revised Edition.*

FOUR UNIQUE CHARACTERISTICS OF THE "PRAYER MINISTRY COUNSELING MODEL"

1. It is founded on and saturated with the voice and vision of God.
2. It integrates many healing prayer approaches.
3. All these healing prayer approaches are used together on a single heart issue in a single three-hour prayer ministry counseling session.
4. Most of the counseling session is devoted to prayer.

A TIME WHEN ONLY *ONE* PRAYER WAS NEEDED TO CAST OUT A DEMON

I was on the phone recently with a student enrolled in Christian Leadership University. She shared that she was having a great struggle with anger. I suggested it may be a demon and if she wanted I would pray and cast it out of her. She was a bit shocked, but she agreed to have me pray. So, with a simple prayer of deliverance and in less than two minutes, she was freed of a spirit of anger. She felt it trembling in her stomach as I commanded the demon to leave, and then felt it leave through her breath. She was astounded. I was thrilled.

A couple of weeks later I received a note which she has allowed me to share with you. In part it said:

I want to thank you for praying for me over the phone. I am so very thankful and so relieved to be free of that ugly spirit of anger. I have been carrying that with me for at least three years. At first I just thought it was mood swings... I felt so defeated as a Christian.... When I got hold of a teaching on "Forgiveness Therapy" and the book "Making Love Last a Lifetime," God began showing me how angry and bitter I had become. I did not like what I saw. I finally had come to the point of godly sorrow and repentance, but still couldn't disconnect the emotion of anger every time I had a memory of some of the things perpetrated against me. I walked around in pain every moment of every day. I cried a lot and was depressed to the point of wanting to die so all the pain would end. Then God led me to you with His perfect timing that I never take for granted. I see now how He was gently leading me to the point in time where you could be used by Him to do that which He has been wanting to do for me for such a long time.... Now I am interested in learning about deliverance, so I can be used by God in order that those I know and love who find themselves in need of deliverance, can be set free. The Scripture, "Those who the Son sets free are free indeed!" is so alive in me now!

Thank you for your sensitivity to my circumstances and for walking in obedience by faith. I can't thank you enough. I have that peace that passes all understanding, and joy has returned to my camp!

What a wonderful letter to receive! Can you see why only a simple deliverance prayer was necessary to set her free—why we didn't need to go through the other prayers to dismantle the demon's home? She had already taken the time to prepare her heart for deliverance. She hated the sin of anger. She had repented of it. She wanted it gone. She was standing against it. The stage was set. All we needed now was a simple deliverance prayer. So, yes, a person can be set free easily and quickly when they are in the right place. I am sure that is exactly what the situation was with the crowds which followed Jesus and sought His hand of deliverance. They had prepared themselves, and the deliverance came readily, especially when Jesus prefaced His healing and deliverance ministry with an anointed time of teaching.

GUIDELINES FOR PRAYER MINISTRY COUNSELING

1. **Rely upon the voice and vision of God** throughout the process. Tune to the Holy Spirit's flow and follow that flow of thoughts and pictures which alight upon you as you minister in the Holy Spirit. This flow will be instructing you how to proceed and will keep the prayers from becoming mechanical formulas. The Holy Spirit will guide you, giving you the names of all the demons in the cluster you are evicting. If you become stuck and nothing is happening, flowing thoughts and flowing pictures from the Holy Spirit will instruct you where the blockage is and where to retrace your steps in order to get things moving again. He may guide you to change the order of the prayers. The Holy Spirit will bring things to mind which have been forgotten or never known by the counselee. Honor "flow" in the counseling session!

> *"Jesus replied, 'I assure you, the Son can do nothing of Himself. He does only what he sees the Father doing... I do nothing without consulting the Father. I judge as I am told. And my judgment is absolutely just, because it is according to the will of God.'"* (John 5:19, 30, NLT)

- If Jesus did not feel He could speak or minister outside of direct guidance, then surely we can't.
- The Spirit-anointed counseling model is built upon the assumption that Jesus is alive today, speaking directly into the hearts of all believers, providing vision and healing if they will but receive and do what He says.

2. **For empowered and balanced ministry, use counseling teams of at least two**, including both a right-brain prophet and a left-brain teacher (Acts 13:1). Jesus insisted that the disciples minister in teams (Luke 10:1). The power of the agreement of two is that anything they ask will be done for them (Matt. 18:19). Make sure all counseling has the appearance of propriety (1 Thess. 5:22). Constantly guard your own heart in all counseling situations so that satan is not given a foothold (Prov. 4:23). If desired, a third person may be present to take notes, to be trained, and to pray quietly.

3. **Require a serious commitment by the counselee** toward healing and wholeness. This will weed out those who aren't ready yet to put forth the intensity of effort it takes to become and stay healed, and will keep the counselor from spending his valuable time on people who are not serious about being whole. Be aware of people just wanting sympathy and looking to rehearse their pain over and over.

The counselee must do the work, be able to hear God's voice and engage in two-way journaling. If they don't have that skill, they should learn it first, as God's voice is key to getting healed and staying healed. They have been listening to demons' voices. Now they must learn to listen only to God's voice. They must be willing to stay constantly filled with the Holy Spirit so they don't have an empty vessel which allows the demons back.

4. **Expecting and discovering demonic clusters:** Recognize that demons are in clusters. It may be helpful for you to be aware of likely clusters. On Page 266 of this book we have a list of typical clusters of demons. As you become more experienced and as you stay tuned to the flow of the Holy Spirit, words will just pop into your head of additional demons in a cluster which the counselee should rebuke and which you should cast out. If you have prayed for anger and seen partial release but not total freedom from anger, then ask the Lord, "What other demons are in this cluster with anger?" Tune to the Holy Spirit's flow and into your mind may come words like hatred, malice, resentment, or unforgiveness. These then are parts of the cluster which must also be removed.

5. **Tips on the deliverance prayer:** Address the demon several times, commanding it to leave. Generally, there will be evidence of its leaving in (a) heavy breathing or coughing by the counselee (so keep your eyes open and be observant) and/or (b) the counselee feeling a sense of release. You can ask the counselee if he senses it is gone. The word for "spirit" and "breath" is the same in the Greek, so often when spirits leave, they leave through the breath. I feel that if the prayers

have been effective then the counselee should, at a minimum, be feeling a sense of inner release.

Other demonic manifestations **during** the deliverance session may include trembling, shaking, lumps in the throat, pain in the stomach or chest or shoulders, bands around the head, etc.

If a demon is hanging on and not coming out, ask, "What is this demon anchored to?" Both the counselor and the counselee should then tune to flow and a response should be forthcoming. You can then pray through the issue indicated as the anchor. One deliverance was blocked by the fact that the counselee had, in his younger days, made a pact with the devil while listening to satanic music. This pact, of course, needed to be renounced in prayer and the effects of this vow in his life cut off in the name of the Lord Jesus Christ.

6. **Tips on receiving divine pictures:** If you have returned to the first traumatic scene that gave birth to the emotional problems the counselee is facing, and the counselee is so emotionally distressed that he cannot see Jesus in that scene, ask him to look for a later occasion in his life where he felt this similar emotion. Invite Christ into that scene. Once healing of this less traumatic incident is complete, repeat the process with another future event. Then you should be able to return to the initial scene and bring Christ into it after some of the intense emotion has been dealt with.

If the counselee has disconnected or dissociated himself from his childhood and is therefore unable to go back and picture it (probably because it was so painful), ask Jesus to meet him as an adult, take his hand, lead him back to a childhood scene, and show him the scenes necessary to heal the particular heart emotion being dealt with. We have seen that the Lord does honor that prayer and the counselee sees a vision of himself either as an adult together with Jesus watching a movie of a scene in which Jesus is ministering to the child in a troubling situation, or he may go back and actually be in the scene. We have seen both happen with good results. Often scenes appear which the counselee has forgotten or pushed from his mind.

7. **Working backwards from a sickness:** Often sicknesses and infirmities have contributing strands coming from our souls and spirits. 3 John 2 offers a prayer that we would prosper and be in good health just as our souls prosper, indicating a link between our souls' health and our bodies' health. Jesus healed "all who were oppressed by the devil," indicating that many sicknesses have a spiritual and/or demonic root (Acts 10:38). James 5:14-16 says we should confess our sins so we can be healed, also indicating that outer infirmity is a result of inner infirmity.

Therefore we need to learn to look at a sickness or infirmity as an outgrowth of a disturbance in our souls and our spirits. To heal the infirmity, we would heal the underlying disturbance on the level of the soul/spirit.

Or, we could say it another way. Problems in our spiritual or soul area cause reactions which must be stored some place in the body. Various parts of the body store various spiritually-caused illnesses.

It is like a family of maggots. Will they live in a new, clean area or do they thrive in places of filth and impurity?

The same principles apply in the spiritual realm. If our bodies are whole and clean, we will not only prevent germs from entering and taking root in us, but by cleaning the soul and the spirit, demons or other uncleanness no longer find it a nice habitation and are much more willing to flee the area.

You may therefore start with a sickness and work backwards, asking the heart, "What is causing this sickness?" The heart knows, and, if you tune to flow, your heart and the Holy Spirit within your heart will light a thought spontaneously upon your mind. Then you can process the issue revealed, using the seven prayers.

HOW MUCH TIME SHOULD BE GIVEN TO LETTING THE COUNSELEE TELL HIS STORY? (ANSWER FROM KAY COX)

In regard to the counseling sessions, Mark, I tend to take things as they fall. Yes, in my normal counseling sessions (which last for two hours), I would listen to the counselee telling his/her story with as little interruption as possible. I would work through the prayers regarding generational sins and breaking soul ties. Then I would isolate a particular issue, discuss this and then pray into that area, forgiveness and repentance being the major focus. I would concentrate on inner healing prayers after that, then go on to the next issue, discuss, forgive, etc., with prayers for that, and so on.

If I only had two-and-a-half hours with someone, and that was all I was likely to get, I would approach it as I did with you: listen, discuss, break soul ties, repent, forgive, pray, as we went along. A sort of short version, so to speak.

Many a time, when we are in the middle of a dinner party with our friends, someone will say something, recognize there was an issue in what he had said, repent, forgive and ask for prayer right at the table. It all depends where I am, who I am with, what the time limit is, how eager the person is, what is happening, what degree of confidence they need. At church, people approach me and want prayer right at the front step. When a soul is hurting and wants to repent of some particular sin, I just do what is necessary at the time. The inner healing first usually allows the demonic to come away very gently without much fuss and bother. Most of the deliverance sessions are very quiet.

DOES PRAYER MINISTRY WORK WITH DRUGGED CLIENTS?

The following answer was provided by Mike Chaille from Ellel in Canada.

I don't know if you are familiar with the ministry of Jackie Pullinger in Hong Kong with drug addicts, but she has people praying in tongues for the addicts in their presence around the clock for one week. She has remarkable success because the prayer in the Spirit is going up to God, but also into their human spirits and building their spirits up to stand against the addiction.

One thing we are always careful about is to make sure we don't pray for anyone who doesn't understand what we are praying for. We never pray for anyone against their will. I guess my question would be, "Is the client aware of what you are praying and does she choose to be free?" The addicts in Hong Kong have chosen to leave their addictions and Jackie is praying for them to build up their spirits so they will have the strength to fight in their spirits against the desire of their soul to remain addicted. It is the battle of Romans 7 in which the spirit is strengthened to rule over the desires of the flesh.

We deal all the time with persons on anti-depressants. The anti-depressants affect body and soul, not spirits. We always pray the Lord causes the drugs to work to His advantage and they serve the proper purpose. We deal with any spirits of addiction attached to the drugs as well.

The main thing in all cases of depression is to get to the roots. It is usually rejection, self-rejection, or fear of rejection. Also, they usually have damaged or sick spirits from deep rejection or abuse. That is why we pray into their spirits a lot of Holy Spirit life. It would be helpful for you to read the book, Healing the Human Spirit by Ruth Hawkey.

SOZO HEALING PRAYER MODEL

Patti and I had the joy of spending a mealtime together with Dawna De Silva, who heads up the Sozo prayer healing model used at Bethel Church in Redding, CA. The conversation was so invigorating I want to share with you a few of my key take-away points from it. My essential conclusion was that for a person trained in the seven prayers that heal the heart, and needing to minister these prayers in a 90–120 minute period, the SOZO approach is a way to accomplish this.

Several aspects of Sozo which caught my attention during our discussion together:
1. The ministry time is completely Spirit-led and focused 100% on leading the counselee into a divine encounter where Jesus is speaking directly to the client.
2. The counselee is continually instructed as to exactly what to be asking Jesus.
3. The counselee is continuously led in the wording of the proper prayer to pray next.
4. Jesus reveals the root event of the problem, the lie that was embraced, and the truth which will now replace that lie.
5. Repentance and forgiveness are central throughout the process.
6. Demonic forces are broken off.
7. The counselee is sent home with a record of what Jesus has spoken and told to review it daily for the next 60 days, and to deepen it with corresponding Bible meditations.

See Part Two of this book for an article "Freedom in Sozo by Dawna De Silva." It provides a short introduction to the Sozo healing model.

FREED PARENTS PRAYING FOR THEIR CHILDREN

If parents have received deliverance and broken off generational sins, they will now need to see that their children are ministered to, also. They can examine their children's lives for evidences of things which have been passed on.

They should then gather with their children and as a family go through the prayers for healing. Perhaps the father can speak the prayers and the wife and children can repeat them after him, encouraging all to speak them from their heart. If the children are below a year of age (and thus can't really understand what is happening) I always suggest praying for them quietly when they're asleep.

Note that in Mark 7:24-30, the child was prayed for by proxy, and experienced deliverance and freedom.

PRAYING OVER HOMES AND BUSINESSES

Similar prayers should be prayed over homes, ground and businesses which one may purchase. Pray specifically for generational sins and curses to be broken, soul ties to be cut, the offense of sin committed to be repented of, cleansed and forgiven, and for the Holy Spirit to anoint the land, home or business. Perhaps anoint the building or business with consecrated oil.

THE CONCEPT OF LAND BECOMING CURSED

> *Cursed is the ground because of you; In toil you will eat of it All the days of your life.* (Gen. 3:17)

THE CURSE UPON THE LAND REINFORCED THROUGH SIN

> *What have you done? The voice of your brother's blood is crying to Me from the ground. Now you are cursed from the ground, which has opened its mouth to receive your brother's blood from your hand. When you cultivate the ground, it will no longer yield its strength to you; you will be a vagrant and a wanderer on the earth.* (Gen. 4:10-12)

> *Because of the abominations which you have committed; thus your land has become a ruin, an object of horror and a curse, without an inhabitant, as it is this day.* (Jer. 44:19-23)

> *Therefore the desert creatures will live there along with the jackals; the ostriches also will live in it, and it will never again be inhabited or dwelt in from generation to generation.* (Jer. 50:39)

Note also the curses of Deuteronomy 28 and Leviticus 26. Notice the process used to cleanse an unholy building in 2 Chronicles 29:3-19.

Summary: Objects, land and buildings can be cursed and become demonized through sin.

THE CONCEPT OF LAND BEING HOLY

> *The angel of the LORD appeared to him in a blazing fire from the midst of a bush; and he looked, and behold, the bush was burning with fire, yet the bush was not consumed. He said, "Do not come near here; remove your sandals from your feet, for the place on which you are standing is holy ground."* (Ex. 3:2-5)

THE CONCEPT OF A HOLY BUILDING

> *Then you shall take the anointing oil and anoint the tabernacle and all that is in it, and shall consecrate it and all its furnishings; and it shall be holy. You shall anoint the altar of burnt offering and all its utensils, and consecrate the altar, and the altar shall be most holy. You shall anoint the laver and its stand, and consecrate it.*
> (Ex. 40:9-11)

> *So that the priests could not stand to minister because of the cloud, for the glory of the LORD filled the house of God.*
>
> (2 Chron. 5:14)

Summary: Receiving God's anointing comes as a result of dedication, consecration, and obedience.

SOME INCIDENTALS THAT CAN HELP

Since our body, soul and spirit are so closely linked, taking good care of your body can only assist the healing and growth of your heart and soul.

Provide your body with a healthy diet (Dan. 1:12), plenty of water, exercise, proper rest and regular fasting (Isa. 58:6, 8). Test for chemical imbalances underlying emotional imbalances. Use herbs (Ps. 104:14) and other natural biblical remedies as necessary.

Utilize accountability relationships to make sure you are doing what you are responsible to do.

PART Two

TAKING IT DEEPER

ADDITIONAL WAYS GOD HEALS BY KAY COX

KAY'S TESTIMONIES

Mark has asked me to recall some of the experiences I have had in counseling to demonstrate the validity of the principles he has laid out in this book. Every case and person is unique, so it is very important to follow the direction of the Holy Spirit as you ask questions about their life and minister to their needs. In most cases I will cut generational soul ties, but do not always use all the prayers listed by Mark as a routine. They all have a place in specific cases at different times and represent a good basis from which to work.

I did not want to be a counselor. When my last child Michael went to school four years ago, I stood in the kitchen and said to the Lord, "Here I am, Lord, do with me what You will." One week later, I was working with Pastor Darryl Goodsell, who had spent 23 years counseling according to biblical principles and trusting in God for all his material needs. He is a godly and gentle man who shared his understanding and revelation and experience with me and others unselfishly. Darryl was my mentor for 18 months, until the Lord told us both separately it was time for me to work on my own.

I did not know where the Lord was taking me. While sitting in on sessions with Darryl, I would be given a word of knowledge from the Lord like "jealousy" or "adultery" which was relevant to the person receiving counseling. I began to trust that the Lord wanted these issues dealt with and found that when prayer and submission were applied, great changes began to occur. The Lord led me then to Peter Horrobin's seminar on healing through deliverance and Ellel Ministry, which reinforced and built upon what I had learned with Darryl. I do not see visions as I counsel, but often find it useful to have someone minister with me who does. It frequently helps us focus our prayer on specific areas.

I am a housewife and mother of three doing what the Lord asks. Nothing more. These are some of the ways I have seen the Lord express His power in my life.

One afternoon in May 1998, a 37-year-old lady came to see me complaining of nagging abdominal pain. She had seen several doctors who had done various tests, performed certain procedures and carried out three operations on her, but they had not really come to any conclusion as to why the pain was still there. She had approached yet another surgeon and another operation was looming in the near future. Someone had suggested that she come and see me before going in for surgery again.

After taking quite a detailed history of her family illnesses, etc., I asked if she could tell me when she had first noticed the pain. She could give me the exact month, and when I asked her what she had done that was different to her usual behavior, she said the only thing that she did was to have her Tarot cards read. I asked her if she could forgive the lady who had done the reading, repent of looking to the other side for answers regarding her life, and renounce any future participation in the occult. We then cut any ungodly soul ties to the medium. As I prayed and bound the spirit of witchcraft, she said the pain seemed to rise up in her abdomen in a dragging motion, and then she felt something break and the pain was gone. I asked the Holy Spirit to restore any damage that had been done to her internal organs.

On her return visit to the doctor, she told him that the pain had gone following prayer and that the Lord had healed her. She said he just smiled, and told her to make another appointment when the pain returned. Praise the Lord, that was nearly twenty months ago and there is still no sign of the pain. She came to know Jesus for the first time that day. She received a healing and was baptized in the Spirit and is still following the Lord today.

One night in February 1999, we were working with a group of Christian folk, breaking judgments and inner vows that we had made as children, especially judgments on our parents, teachers, friends, enemies, and anyone else that the Holy Spirit showed us. After we had repented of these judgments and vows and cut any ungodly soul ties to these people, we were praying and forgiving those who had hurt or wounded us in any way. One man came out of the group and told me that, as he was forgiving his mother-in-law, the pain in his knees became almost unbearable and then it was like something popped, and the pain left. He had been in severe knee pain for years and didn't realize that the bitterness and unforgiveness that he had held towards his mother-in-law was manifesting in his bones. How many of us find it difficult to forgive our brothers and sisters, or difficult to not hold grudges? "A merry heart doeth good like a medicine, but a broken spirit drieth the bones" (Proverbs 17:22).

One Sunday morning just before church, a woman approached me and asked if she could have some prayer before the service started. She had been experiencing pain in her right forearm for quite some time and it was really beginning to annoy her. We prayed quietly for a few minutes and asked the Holy Spirit to show us what the root cause of the pain was. After a few moments she opened her eyes and said that the Holy Spirit had shown her that she had been involved in a séance as a child. She repented of this, asked the Lord to forgive her and renounced any further involvement in witchcraft. As I bound the spirit of necromancy, the pain moved up her forearm and came out through her fingers. She was thrilled that once again the Lord had answered her prayers and that she had been healed.

One Saturday afternoon about eighteen months ago, there was a knock on my door and standing in the doorway was a 34-year-old woman named Tracey. Tracey lived a couple of blocks from our house and had known my husband when they attended the same church. I invited her in for a cup of tea, and as she made her way slowly down our long hallway, with the aid of a walking stick, I noticed she grimaced in pain with every step that she took. She told me that in 1996 she had fallen at the local hospital and injured herself, and that she was still experiencing pain in her knee. Then, six months later, she had been involved in a bus accident in which, as she was making her way to the back of the bus, the driver had put his foot on the brake to prevent an accident, sending her flying through the air. She ended up at the front of the bus, down in the stairwell. Her body had not recovered from either of the accidents and she now felt that she needed the walking stick to assist her, making walking a little less painful.

A few months before Tracey arrived on the scene, I had attended one of Peter Horrobin's Ellel conferences where we were taught about the effects of shock and trauma. Peter demonstrated very clearly how, when we are involved in accidents, our physical bodies are attended to, but our souls and our spirits are sadly neglected. As Tracey chose to forgive the people responsible for her accidents and repented of any bitterness and resentment that she felt toward any of them, I prayed and the Holy Spirit ministered to her. She testifies that a warm feeling came over her and she began to feel her body being healed. Her excitement was infectious as she ran out of the room to tell our children of her healing. An hour later my husband arrived home from work and she raced down the hallway to greet him with a big hug and to share her wonderful news. Tracey no longer needed her stick as the pain was totally gone. Jesus had healed her broken body.

Just recently, another person to whom I have been ministering rang to say, "Thank you." She was supposed to have an operation, but since having two sessions breaking soul ties, judgments and inner vows, and experiencing the inner healing that went with it, she no longer needs the operation, and the doctor has given her the all clear. Praise the Lord!

A young girl rang from a coastal town asking if she could come and see me as she had been bleeding for years and, at only 19 years of age, was going to have a hysterectomy. She was having the operation on Friday, so I managed to change some of my booked clients and spent the day counseling her. We dealt with some pretty tragic issues and the Holy Spirit led us to pray about some specific hurts. By the end of the afternoon, as she made her way to the hospital for her anesthetic check, she seemed happy and relieved. The next day, when her gynecologist examined her, she told him that the bleeding had stopped. The operation was canceled at the last minute and she went back to her family. She rang me a few months later to tell me that she was still fine and the bleeding had not returned. It was like a last-minute rescue, and the Lord had answered her prayers.

A 28-year-old woman from Macksville was visiting with her sister, and made an appointment while she was down here. She had difficulty trying to forgive her Dad for abandoning her when she was a baby. As a result, she had not spoken to him for 13 years. As we went through breaking generational soul ties and repenting of bad attitudes and judgments, she felt a huge burden lift from her as she asked the Holy Spirit to help her come to a place where she could forgive him for not being there for her. She cried a lot of tears, and eventually she was able to forgive him. She rang him when she got home and told him that she forgave him and that she loved him very much. A new relationship commenced on that day and she found it much easier to "honor her father" as the Lord would have us all do. Jesus can fill up any hole we have; we just have to ask.

This last healing occurred just a few months ago and the lady, Helen Henderson, has very graciously agreed to share her testimony with you. I thank Helen for her honesty and openness. She has given much of her time and energy to share her testimony with many of the churches and schools in the Newcastle area, and she goes on giving praise and glory to our Almighty God for her wonderful healing. Such faith I have never seen before! Here is Helen's own story.

The story begins 6:00 A.M. September 9, 1999. Told my husband John that I felt unwell—dizzy. 8.00 A.M.—school (I am a schoolteacher)—told a friend that if I didn't feel better soon I was going home, then proceeded to collapse onto the cold floor.

I woke very confused and with left-side weakness. I was taken to the hospital where I was diagnosed as having had a stroke (Cerebrovascular accident, in medical terminology). Transferred to Warners Bay Private Hospital under a medical specialist. I was completely paralyzed on my left side and had difficulty recognizing friends and acquaintances.

Final Diagnosis—My brain had just shut down and was not functioning right. Why? The doctor could not tell me.

The weeks that followed my admission to hospital were the darkest of my life. People would come to visit me and comment on how calm and serene I appeared to be. In truth, I spent most of my waking hours focusing on my sin. Satan had a field day convincing me that I was not worthy of God's love. I had no ability to see the possibility of my ever being restored to physical or, for that matter, spiritual health. I regularly cried myself to sleep and had horrific nightmares when I did sleep. Physically, I was making small steps. I began to sit out of bed for small periods of time that were gradually increased. I had daily physiotherapy and began to use my arm to do small tasks, but I was still unable to use my leg. My foot was floppy and I had to wear a foot-drop splint to hold my foot in place.

The real story, however, begins several months earlier. My dear father died on the 10th of June, 1999. His death caused me to go into deep sorrow bordering on despair. I could not come to grips with the loss of my dad. To top it off, I had an operation one week after Dad's funeral. On my follow-up visit, my surgeon, who is a Christian, said I was physically fine. Then he asked how I really was. I explained that I felt I was in real trouble, because a padded room and a bed looked good to me. He asked what I wanted to do. "See your wife Kay," I replied.

It was a struggle all day, but I finally rang her and arranged a visit, not really knowing what to expect but open to what God was going to do in my life. God in His graciousness blessed me that day. The burdens of a lifetime were lifted from me. I was completely exhausted but elated at what God had done for me. I suppose I expected life to get easier. It didn't! But I was more able to cope with the things that came to me. I believe that I was attacked in not just the physical realm but in the spiritual realm, also. Satan was having a field day with me. I think on the twentieth of September he thought he had won, but God had other plans.

During my time in hospital, friends came to see me—so much love, so much kindness. Total strangers sent me flowers and inquired as to my well-being, but this had no real effect on me. I became darker and darker. I have a very close friend, Margaret. We have been friends for the whole of our lives. She recognized and knew what I was experiencing because her husband Neil had been through a similar experience. She was the only person that I allowed to see what was really happening to me. I vented my frustration, anger and resentment on her and she just sat and let me do it and in great love ministered to me of God's love. It was not that I did not appreciate the love and concern shown to me. I just could not allow others to see my real feelings... FEAR and complete unworthiness of God's love. At this point I had been hospitalized for over nine weeks and things were not looking too good for me.

My medical specialist is a very clever man and very astute. He is not a Christian, but God was not limited by this. He asked my surgeon to arrange for his wife Kay to come and see me, as I was not getting much better. Why hadn't I done this? It goes back to how I felt about myself at the time.

When Kay rang me to arrange an appointment, I knew that God was in control of the situation. I knew and believed God would heal me. Not just the physical healing I obviously needed, but also more importantly the mental, emotional and spiritual problems that had beset me. Believing that I would be healed, I began to tell everyone I came in contact with: nurses, doctors, friends and family, in fact just about everyone, with varying degrees of belief expressed by all. I asked my family to pray and also my KYB group.

Kay arrived on time with Jenny Parkinson, her intercessor, and we seemed to get down to business almost immediately. There were various issues that had to be addressed regarding sin in my life and sin of past generations of my family. The prayer I was asked to pray was very difficult as I had to say aloud those things that I did not really want others to know about. Fortunately, the Lord enabled me to do it.

When Kay began to pray for my physical healing, she did not pray generally, but very specifically, for each part of my body that needed to be healed. She began by praying for my brain—every individual part: the neurons, the blood vessels, the nerves, the gray matter, the white matter, etc. This process was followed for my limbs. When Kay had finished praying for my arm, she told me to raise it up—and I did, right above my head! Previously I could only raise it with great concentration and not above my head. Kay continued down my body, finally praying for my leg and foot. She took the splint off my leg and told me to lift my leg onto her knee. I did this automatically! I was completely amazed! I could not do that before, and yet now I could. Then she told me to walk around my room. I did that, too! Then she flung the door open and I ran down the hallway full pelt. I was overwhelmed with happiness and thanksgiving to God for doing this for me.

News soon spread in the hospital and nursing staff were coming from everywhere to witness the "unbelievable," in human terms. One nurse was so confused by what she saw, she took my arm and carefully walked me back to my room. I rang my husband to tell him what had happened and he thought I'd gone completely demented. He could not comprehend what I was telling him. Finally Kay got on the phone with him to convince him that I was telling the truth. He arrived at the hospital in record time. The joy on his face when he saw me is something that I will never forget.

Most reactions to my healing were positive, except for one nurse. She was very negative and hostile. This reaction had an interesting effect on me. It made me very fearful, so much so that I did not want to leave my room. I rang my friend Margaret, who recognized what was happening. Satan was trying to rob me of the victory and the blessing that the Lord had given me. When I prayed, the problem was gone. When I came out of my room, that particular nurse had just left the nurses' station.

I had to wait twenty-four hours to see my doctor and to be discharged. When he spoke with me, he said that I was one of three miraculous healings he had seen in his time as a doctor and he could not explain any of them. He also did not want to see me for any follow-up—I was cured.

On Tuesday, the 16th of November, God healed me. The most important thing for me in all of this is that I recognized that nothing I did or could do was going to change my situation. In His graciousness, God made me whole. He gave me back my life. I do not know why He chose to do this for me. I definitely do not deserve it. All I know is that the glory belongs to the Lord. Only He is worthy of our praise, and I want to tell others of His greatness and love.

In his subsequent letter to the other doctors involved in Helen's care, her medical specialist described her recovery as... faith healing. Helen had faith and was willing to be healed. The

Lord was glorified and many saw His power that night and received the good news of Jesus as Jenny and I were able to talk to patients and staff who filled the corridors after the commotion.

Throughout my meager three-and-a-half years of doing the Lord's work, I have had the privilege of seeing many wonderful healings—physical healings, emotional healings and spiritual healings—and I never get tired of seeing the amazing power of the Holy Spirit at work. Never get tired of seeing the faces radiating as the Holy Spirit turns God's precious people's mourning into dancing. Some mornings I'll still be awake at 4:00 A.M. wondering, "Did that really happen?" and saying, "Thank You, Jesus, that through the shedding of Your precious blood we are set free. We do have resurrection life! You are real! We do have authority on this earth when we allow You to use us."

TWO-WAY JOURNALING EXERCISE

Lord, what would You like to speak to me concerning the truths in this article?

AVAILABLE TRAINING PACKAGES FOR *PRAYERS THAT HEAL THE HEART*

1. DVD Package—cwgministries.org/Seven_Prayer_Package
2. Online training module with CLU School of the Spirit—CLUSchooloftheSpirit.com/prayers
3. College course with Christian Leadership University—cluonline.com/prayers-course

Resources below are available at: cwgministries.org/Prayer_Worksheets

- Deliverance Pictured
- Deliverance Prayer Ministers Online
- Common Demon Groupings/Names
- Deliverance Cheat Sheet
- Suggested Approach for Counseling
- Counselors which Mark and Patti Virkler Recommend
- Prophetic Prayer Counseling links
- Seven Prayers That Heal the Heart—Adapted for Intercessors Praying for Others
- Bob Lucy's Approach for Dealing With Alters And DID
- Prayers which break the curses of Freemasonry
- Mark Virkler's TV interview with Sid Roth where they discuss the Seven Prayers

AVAILABLE TRAINING PACKAGES

60 Ways to Pray: cwgministries.org/devotionals
- "Teaming Up for Deliverance: A Prophet and Teacher Minister Together"—free audio of this team ministry taking place at cwgministries.org/prophet-teacher-deliverance
- Deliverance from Demons Through a "Revelation-Based Power Encounter" cwgministries.org/deliverance-power-encounter

HOW CAN I FURTHER MY SPIRITUAL TRAINING?

1. **Subscribe** to our free blogs and monthly newsletter: cwgministries.org/subscribe. Each month we offer a Free Worldwide Video Event making valuable training available at no cost for a limited time, as well as provide monthly discounts. Our blogs are teaching and testimonial to encourage you in your walk in the Spirit.
2. **Three educational websites** that offer the training experiences listed below and much more:

    - cwgministries.org
    - cluonline.com
    - cluschoolofthespirit.com

    Training modules listed below can be found on the **above** websites:

    - Hearing God's Voice
    - Counseled by God
    - Hear God Through Your Dreams

- Unleashing Healing Power Through Spirit-Born Emotions
- Overflow of the Spirit
3. Ministry websites listed in the dedication page of this book provide prayer counseling training

BIBLE MEDITATION ON JUDGING

Upon discovering that my tendency to judge was contributing to my increasing anger, I asked the Lord,

"What do You want to show me about judging?"

He replied,

"My child, your anger was not a matter of judging. It was a matter of not forgiving once the judgment was made. A godly judgment is fine. However, to hold a resulting anger in your heart because of a judgment you have made is where you fell into trouble. You may judge with righteous judgment, determine a godly verdict and then commit the matter into My hands after you have done that which I have told you to do. So it is a matter of committing the judgment to Me after your work is done. That is where you have failed, My son. That is where the sin was."

Following is my Scripture meditation on "judging."

VERSES ON JUDGING ORGANIZED INTO CATEGORIES

God is the Judge Over Nations and People

And also that nation, whom they shall serve, will I judge: and afterward shall they come out with great substance.

(Genesis 15:14)

That be far from thee to do after this manner, to slay the righteous with the wicked: and that the righteous should be as the wicked, that be far from thee: Shall not the [Judge] of all the earth do right? (Genesis 18:25)

The adversaries of the LORD shall be broken to pieces; out of heaven shall he thunder upon them: the LORD shall [judge] the ends of the earth; and he shall give strength unto his king, and exalt the horn of his anointed. (1 Samuel 2:10)

The LORD shall judge the people: judge me, O LORD, according to my righteousness, and according to mine integrity that is in me. (Psalm 7:8)

God judgeth the righteous, and God is angry with the wicked every day. (Psalm 7:11)

And he shall judge the world in righteousness, he shall minister judgment to the people in uprightness. (Psalm 9:8)

Arise, O LORD; let not man prevail: let the heathen be judged in thy sight. (Psalm 9:19)

Judge me, O LORD my God, according to thy righteousness; and let them not rejoice over me. (Psalm 35:24)

Judge me, O God, and plead my cause against an ungodly nation: O deliver me from the deceitful and unjust man. (Psalm 43:1)

And the heavens shall declare his righteousness: for God is judge himself. Selah. (Psalm 50:6)

BIBLE MEDITATION ON JUDGING

O let the nations be glad and sing for joy: for thou shalt judge the people righteously, and govern the nations upon earth. Selah.
(Psalm 67:4)

A father of the fatherless, and a judge of the widows, is God in his holy habitation. (Psalm 68:5)

He shall judge thy people with righteousness, and thy poor with judgment. (Psalm 72:2)

He shall judge the poor of the people, he shall save the children of the needy, and shall break in pieces the oppressor. (Psalm 72:4)

But God is the judge: he putteth down one, and setteth up another. (Psalm 75:7).

A Psalm of Asaph. God standeth in the congregation of the mighty; he judgeth among the gods. (Psalm 82:1)

How long will ye judge unjustly, and accept the persons of the wicked? Selah. (Psalm 82:2)

Arise, O God, judge the earth: for thou shalt inherit all nations.
(Psalm 82:8)

Lift up thyself, thou judge of the earth: render a reward to the proud. (Psalm 94:2)

Say among the heathen that the LORD reigneth: the world also shall be established that it shall not be moved: he shall judge the people righteously. (Psalm 96:10)

For the LORD is our judge, the LORD is our lawgiver, the LORD is our king; he will save us (Isaiah 33:22)

Henceforth there is laid up for me a crown of righteousness, which the Lord, the righteous judge, shall give me at that day: and not to me only, but unto all them also that love his appearing. (2 Timothy 4:8)

For we know him that hath said, Vengeance belongeth unto me, I will recompense, saith the Lord. And again, The Lord shall judge his people. (Hebrews 10:30)

And the nations were angry, and thy wrath is come, and the time of the dead, that they should be judged, and that thou shouldest give reward unto thy servants the prophets, and to the saints, and them that fear thy name, small and great; and shouldest destroy them which destroy the earth. (Revelation 11:18)

And I saw heaven opened, and behold a white horse; and he that sat upon him was called Faithful and True, and in righteousness he doth judge and make war. (Revelation 19:11)

And I saw the dead, small and great, stand before God; and the books were opened: and another book was opened, which is the book of life: and the dead were judged out of those things which were written in the books, according to their works. (Revelation 20:12)

And the sea gave up the dead which were in it; and death and hell delivered up the dead which were in them: and they were judged every man according to their works. (Revelation 20:13)

God Delegates Judging to Spiritual Leaders to Perform

And it came to pass on the morrow, that Moses sat to judge the people: and the people stood by Moses from the morning unto the evening. (Exodus 18:13)

BIBLE MEDITATION ON JUDGING

When they have a matter, they come unto me; and I judge between one and another, and I do make them know the statutes of God, and his laws. (Exodus 18:16)

And let them judge the people at all seasons: and it shall be, that every great matter they shall bring unto thee, but every small matter they shall judge: so shall it be easier for thyself, and they shall bear the burden with thee. (Exodus 18:22)

And they judged the people at all seasons: the hard causes they brought unto Moses, but every small matter they judged themselves. (Exodus 18:26)

And thou shalt come unto the priests the Levites, and unto the judge that shall be in those days, and inquire; and they shall show thee the sentence of judgment. (Deuteronomy 17:9)

And the man that will do presumptuously, and will not hearken unto the priest that standeth to minister there before the LORD thy God, or unto the judge, even that man shall die: and thou shalt put away the evil from Israel. (Deuteronomy 17:12)

If there be a controversy between men, and they come unto judgment, that the judges may judge them; then they shall justify the righteous, and condemn the wicked. (Deuteronomy 25:1)

And it shall be, if the wicked man be worthy to be beaten, that the judge shall cause him to lie down, and to be beaten before his face, according to his fault, by a certain number.
(Deuteronomy 25:2)

And Deborah, a prophetess, the wife of Lapidoth, she judged Israel at that time. (Judges 4:4)

And he judged Israel twenty and three years, and died, and was buried in Shamir. (Judges 10:2)

And after him arose Jair, a Gileadite, and judged Israel twenty and two years. (Judges 10:3)

And Samuel judged Israel all the days of his life. (1 Samuel 7:15)

For I verily, as absent in body, but present in spirit, have judged already, as though I were present, concerning him that hath so done this deed. (1 Corinthians 5:3)

Guidelines Concerning How We Are to Judge

Ye shall do no unrighteousness in judgment: thou shalt not respect the person of the poor, nor honour the person of the mighty: but in righteousness shalt thou judge thy neighbour. (Leviticus 19:15)

Judges and officers shalt thou make thee in all thy gates, which the LORD thy God giveth thee, throughout thy tribes: and they shall judge the people with just judgment. (Deuteronomy 16:18)

And the judges shall make diligent inquisition: and, behold, if the witness be a false witness, and hath testified falsely against his brother. (Deuteronomy 19:18)

Give me now wisdom and knowledge, that I may go out and come in before this people: for who can judge this thy people, that is so great? (2 Chronicles 1:10)

And all Israel heard of the judgment which the king had judged; and they feared the king: for they saw that the wisdom of God was in him, to do judgment. (I Kings 3:28)

BIBLE MEDITATION ON JUDGING

Judge not according to the appearance, but judge righteous judgment. (John 7:24)

For what have I to do to judge them also that are without? Do not ye judge them that are within? But them that are without God judgeth. Therefore put away from among yourselves that wicked person. (1 Corinthians 5:12,13)

Do ye not know that the saints shall judge the world? And if the world shall be judged by you, are ye unworthy to judge the smallest matters? (1 Corinthians 6:2)

Know ye not that we shall judge angels? How much more things that pertain to this life? (1 Corinthians 6:3)

I speak to your shame. Is it so, that there is not a wise man among you? No, not one that shall be able to judge between his brethren. (1 Corinthians 6:5)

Let no man therefore judge you in meat, or in drink, or in respect of an holyday, or of the new moon, or of the sabbath days. (Colossians 2:16)

The Way Jesus Judged

And shall make him of quick understanding in the fear of the LORD: and he shall not judge after the sight of his eyes, neither reprove after the hearing of his ears: But with righteousness shall he judge the poor, and reprove with equity for the meek of the earth: and he shall smite the earth with the rod of his mouth, and with the breath of his lips shall he slay the wicked. (Isaiah 11:3-4)

I can of mine own self do nothing: as I hear, I judge: and my judgment is just; because I seek not mine own will, but the will of the Father which hath sent me. (John 5:30)

Ye judge after the flesh; I judge no man. And yet if I judge, my judgment is true: for I am not alone, but I and the Father that sent me. (John 8:15-16)

And if any man hear my words, and believe not, I judge him not: for I came not to judge the world, but to save the world.

(John 12:47)

He that rejecteth me, and receiveth not my words, hath one that judgeth him: the word that I have spoken, the same shall judge him in the last day. (John 12:48)

Guidelines to Avoid Undue Judgment

Agree with thine adversary quickly, while thou art in the way with him; lest at any time the adversary deliver thee to the judge, and the judge deliver thee to the officer, and thou be cast into prison. (Matthew 5:25)

Judge not, that ye be not judged. (Matthew 7:1)

For with what judgment ye judge, ye shall be judged: and with what measure ye mete, it shall be measured to you again.

(Matthew 7:2)

Judge not, and ye shall not be judged: condemn not, and ye shall not be condemned: forgive, and ye shall be forgiven. (Luke 6:37)

Therefore thou art inexcusable, O man, whosoever thou art that judgest: for wherein thou judgest another, thou condemnest thyself; for thou that judgest doest the same things. (Romans 2:1)

And thinkest thou this, O man, that judgest them which do such things, and doest the same, that thou shalt escape the judgment of God? (Romans 2:3)

Let not him that eateth despise him that eateth not; and let not him which eateth not judge him that eateth: for God hath received him. (Romans 14:3)

Therefore judge nothing before the time, until the Lord come, who both will bring to light the hidden things of darkness, and will make manifest the counsels of the hearts: and then shall every man have praise of God. (1 Corinthians 4:5)

For if we would judge ourselves, we should not be judged. But when we are judged, we are chastened of the Lord, that we should not be condemned with the world. (1 Corinthians 11:31-32)

Speak not evil one of another, brethren. He that speaketh evil of his brother, and judgeth his brother, speaketh evil of the law, and judgeth the law: but if thou judge the law, thou art not a doer of the law, but a judge. There is one lawgiver, who is able to save and to destroy: who art thou that judgest another? (James 4:11-12)

God's delegation of judgment to Jesus

For the Father judgeth no man, but hath committed all judgment unto the Son. (John 5:22)

The Principles Underlying Judgment

> *For as many as have sinned without law shall also perish without law: and as many as have sinned in the law shall be judged by the law.* (Romans 2:12)

> *Who art thou that judgest another man's servant? To his own master he standeth or falleth. Yea, he shall be holden up: for God is able to make him stand.* (Romans 14:4)

> *But why dost thou judge thy brother? Or why dost thou set at nought thy brother? For we shall all stand before the judgment seat of Christ.* (Romans 14:10)

> *Let us not therefore judge one another any more: but judge this rather, that no man put a stumblingblock or an occasion to fall in his brother's way.* (Romans 14:13)

> *But he that is spiritual judgeth all things, yet he himself is judged of no man.* (1 Corinthians 2:15)

> *Let the prophets speak two or three, and let the others judge.* (1 Corinthians 14:29)

A SUMMARY ON JUDGING

God is the Ruler and ultimate Judge over the world (Revelation 19:11, 20:12-13; Hebrews 10:30; Isaiah 33:22). God has delegated judgment to Jesus (John 5:22) and to spiritual leaders (Exodus 18:13, 16, 22, 26; Deuteronomy 17:9; 25:1-2; 1 Corinthians 5:3).

God gives us numerous guidelines for how we are to judge. They include: not giving special respect to the rich or to the poor (Leviticus 19:15; James 2:2-4); judging justly (Deuteronomy

16:18); making diligent inquisition (Deuteronomy 19:18); praying for divine wisdom (2 Chronicles 1:10); not judging according to appearance but with righteous judgment (John 7:24); judging those within the Church, not without (1 Corinthians 5:12); and not judging concerning meat or drink or in respect to a holiday, a new moon or the Sabbath (Colossians 2:16).

Jesus judged not by sight, but with righteous judgment (Isaiah 11:3-4). He only judged according to what the Father was showing Him (John 5:30). The words of Jesus will be used to judge people at the last day (John 12:48).

It is best to minimize judgment. Ways of minimizing judgment include: not judging unless absolutely necessary (Matthew 7:1); agreeing with your adversary quickly so you are not taken before a judge (Matthew 5:25); knowing that you will be judged with the same harshness that you judge others (Matthew 7:2); not judging others for the same things that you yourself are doing (Romans 2:1); not judging others for what they eat (Romans 14:3); waiting and letting God judge the hearts of man at the final judgment (1 Corinthians 4:5); judging ourselves so God doesn't have to judge us (1 Corinthians 11:31-32); and not speaking evil of our brother (James 4:11-12).

Principles which underlie judgment include: determining whether a person had access to the law or not (Romans 2:12); letting God judge His servants (Romans 14:4); and not judging our brothers (Romans 14:10, 13). Prophets/prophecies are to be judged (1 Corinthians 14:29). The spiritual judge the carnal; the carnal cannot judge the spiritual (1 Corinthians 2:15)

MY PERSONAL SUMMARY CONCERNING JUDGING

It is wisest to minimize judging in my life as excessive judgment can easily lead to sin, which brings with it much negative repercussion in one's life.

Any judgments I make must flow out of my journaling time with the Lord. If God issues a judgment, I am to perform what He tells me to do and then set aside any and all personal anger concerning the judgment before the sun goes down, or else the judgment has moved into sin on my part. "Let not the sun go down on your wrath" (Ephesians 4:26).

This is an important distinction I had not made in the past. I would carry the anger of the judgment for days, weeks, months and years. I also felt that living in judgment and anger against an institution was acceptable. These are the places where I have sinned. These are the reasons why judgment within me was feeding a spirit of anger. Thank You, Lord, for showing me this.

BIBLE MEDITATION ON SEX

Following are insights from Proverbs 5 and 7 and the Song of Solomon on healing lust and growing into pure, vibrant marital love. Read this aloud to yourself whenever you are tempted.

- Keep this teaching as the apple of your eye (look at it)
- Bind it on your fingers (let it guide your actions)
- Write it on your heart (memorize it)
- Make it your intimate friend (keep it close to you)

So you may be kept from an adulteress. (Proverbs 7:2-5)

PROVERBS CHAPTER FIVE (NASB) —THE PITFALLS OF IMMORALITY

The adulteress:
- Her lips are smooth, enticing and drip honey.
- She does not ponder the path of life.
- Her ways are unstable and she does not know it.
- The end of an encounter with an adulteress is bitter as wormwood.
- She cuts sharp as a two-edged sword.
- Her path leads to death.
- She goes to Sheol.

Avoiding relationships with an adulteress:
- I keep far away from her.
- I do not go near the door of her house.

What an encounter with an adulteress will do to me:
- I give my vigor to her.
- I give over years of my life to a cruel taskmaster.
- She is filled with my strength.
- My hard-earned goods go to her house.
- I will groan in the latter end when my flesh is consumed.

Enjoying your wife's love instead of an adulteress:
- Drink from her love.
- Don't let her love go to another; let it be yours alone.
- Be blessed with her love.
- Rejoice in her.
- Let her breasts satisfy you at all times.
- Be exhilarated always with her love.

God is watching my actions:
- God sees all my paths.
- My iniquities will capture me.
- I will be held with the cords of my sin.
- I will die for not listening to instruction.

PROVERBS CHAPTER SEVEN (NASB)—THE WILES OF THE HARLOT

How to be led astray by an adulteress:

- Be simple and lack sense.
- Go near her place.

- Have darkness cover your dark actions.
- See the seductive way she dresses.
- You are an ox being led to the slaughter.
- You are in bondage to a fool.
- Your liver is pierced.
- This will cost you your life.

How an adulteress leads you astray:
- She is cunning as she reels you in.
- She is boisterous and rebellious and brazen.
- She goes out to meet her prey.
- She initiates physical contact.
- She claims to be good and godly.
- She flatters you.
- She offers you a full night of lovemaking.
- She continues until you are seduced and follow.

LISTEN:
- Do not let your heart turn aside to her ways.
- Do not stray into her paths.
- She has many she has killed.
- She will take you to Sheol and to death.

TRANSITIONAL THOUGHTS

But if they do not have self-control, let them marry; for it is better to marry than to burn with passion. (1 Corinthians 7:9)

- If you are not married and are having trouble handling your sexual desires, then seek God to lead you to a marriage partner as you also seek Him for grace to handle your

sexuality while waiting for marriage to occur.
- While seeking God in faith for a marriage partner, follow His Spirit's leading. You may be led to go to a certain place and/or to look for a certain sign to find your marriage partner, as Isaac's servant was (Genesis 24:114). Or you may be led to simply continue in your everyday work, and your marriage partner will come to you, as Rebekah did (Genesis 24:15-67). Follow the Lord's leading as you pray for God to bring you and your partner together.
- A spouse should be someone who will assist in fulfilling God's destiny for your life.
- While deepening a relationship with a potential spouse, stay in public places, and use discretion in your actions (especially as they relate to touching) so as to not fall into fornication.
- In marriage, one's physical needs can be met, however one still must watch over his/her mind and not allow lust to reign.
- The safeguard of not going near a harlot's house, and thus being enticed by her and having your liver pierced through, should be obeyed whether married or single (Proverbs 7:8-23). In today's world, that would mean creating fences such as the following:
    - Do not go into adult sections of video rental stores.
    - Do not go in a store which sells adult magazines.
    - Do not go to "R" or "X" rated movies.
    - Do not have cable or satellite television, or, if you do, purchase a television with a chip that blocks out "R" and "X" rated movies.
    - Obtain a service that blocks out all sexually-oriented materials on the internet.

- Do not go near sections of town which have adult services.
- Do not go near a person's home to whom you are drawn sexually, or, if you must, never go alone.

SONG OF SOLOMON (NASB)—THE JOY AND ECSTASY OF MARITAL LOVE

Chapter 1:
- The desire is there for kisses on the mouth.
- Fragrant oils are used.
- They are together.
- The husband may invite his wife into a time of sexual encounter.
- The wife acknowledges the beauty of her body.
- The husband acknowledges the beauty of his wife's body.
- Ornaments and beads of gold and silver are placed on the wife.
- The husband may lay all night between his wife's breasts.
- The wife acknowledges her husband as handsome.

Chapter 2:
- The husband acknowledges that his wife is the most beautiful woman of all.
- Embracing and fondling are part of the lovemaking.
- The husband requests to see his wife's nude form.
- The husband requests to hear his wife's sweet voice.

Chapter 3:
- The wife seeks her husband.
- The wife holds on to her husband and will not let go.
- The wedding is a joyous occasion.

Chapter 4:
- The husband describes the beauty of each part of his wife's body starting at the head and working down to the breasts.
- The passion of love makes the husband's heart beat faster.
- The wife's love is better than wine.
- The wife's lips drip honey.
- Honey and milk are under the wife's tongue.
- The wife invites her husband to eat choice fruits from her.

Chapter 5:
- The husband eats and drinks deeply from his wife.
- When one wants to make love, the other should not make excuses.

Chapter 6:
- There is a mutual delight in each other.

Chapter 7:
- The husband describes his wife's beauty starting with her feet, then her hips, her navel, her belly, her breasts, her neck, and her head.
- The husband touches each part, especially enjoying his wife's breasts and her mouth.

Chapter 8:
- They enjoy fondling and caressing and loving one another.

COMMON DEMON GROUPINGS

You can easily cast out three or so closely related demons, at one time. So in preparing for deliverance, I suggest you create a list of the demons you have become aware of as you completed the first six prayers in *Prayers That Heal the Heart*. Make an attempt to group related issues into the most appropriate cluster. For example, doubt, fear, and unbelief may constitute one cluster; rejection, inferiority, and abandonment may constitute another cluster. In each cluster put the word "strongest" next to what you sense is the strongest force in the cluster, and the word "feeder" next to what you sense is the primary feeder of this force.

You are likely to have more than one heart wound, so you would repeat these steps for each heart wound. When deliverance is complete these lists will serve as a review reminder and pictorial overview of the demonic strongholds and issues from which Christ has set you free. Once a cluster is identified, you can do self-deliverance, although my recommendation is that you invite a couple of people trained in deliverance to minister deliverance to you.

BELOW IS A SAMPLING OF COMMON DEMON GROUPS

These are examples only, designed to spur your thinking and reflection as you ask the Lord to show you what's in *your* heart which needs healing and deliverance.

ANGER is the strongest demon—primary feeder is judgment
- hatred
- malice
- violence
- murder
- temper
- vengeance
- retaliation
- unforgiveness
- bitterness

FEAR is the strongest demon—primary feeder is doubt
- fear of authority
- fear of men
- unbelief
- spirit of rush
- spirit of false responsibility
- dread, worry, anxiety
- fear of cancer

FINANCIAL LACK is the strongest demon—primary feeder is covetousness
- belief in poverty
- robbing God by not tithing

COMMON DEMON GROUPINGS

- not believing in covenant blessings
- greed
- debt
- dishonesty
- idolatry of possessions
- failure

SENSUALITY is the strongest demon—primary feeder is lust & fantasy
- pornography
- premarital sex
- sexual abuse
- fornication/adultery
- demonic sex
- rape
- bondage/control
- incest

DEPRESSION is the strongest demon—primary feeder is self-pity
- rejection
- despair
- helplessness
- hopelessness
- sadness
- withdrawal
- suicide

GRIEF is the strongest demon—primary feeder is loss
- despair

- heartbreak
- pain
- sorrow
- torment
- weeping
- anguish
- agony

SHAME is the strongest demon—primary feeder is guilt
- anger
- condemnation
- disgrace
- embarrassment
- hatred
- self-hate
- self-pity
- inferiority

ABANDONMENT is the strongest demon—primary feeder is isolation
- desertion
- divorce
- loneliness
- neglect
- rejection
- self-pity
- victimization
- blocked intimacy

DECEPTION is the strongest demon—primary feeder is infidelity
- cheating
- confusion
- denial
- lying
- secretiveness
- trickery
- untrustworthiness
- self-deception

MENTAL INSTABILITY is the strongest demon—primary feeder is hysteria
- craziness
- compulsions
- confusion
- insanity
- paranoia
- schizophrenia

CONTRIBUTIONS FROM JOHN SANDFORD AND ELIJAH HOUSE MINISTRIES

One way to discover the unbiblical beliefs I am holding is to look at the fruit in my life and ask, what is the root belief that I am holding that is producing this "bad" fruit?

For example, the seed of judgment or negative expectation sown in my spirit obediently sends out a message to all within its reach. My spirit might say, "I am programmed to fail; please respond to me in that light." In this case, everyone else's spirits hear and receive that message and respond in kind. Their spirits say, "Let's do everything we can to ensure that this message is fulfilled." And so I continue to attract events, people, and situations to my life which ensure my failure over and over again. I draw to myself that which I believe to be true. I create my own lifestyle based on the beliefs I hold within.

JOHN SANDFORD TAUGHT US THAT NEGATIVE EXPECTATION ACTIVATES FOUR LAWS

1. **The law of faith**—"It shall be done to you according to your faith" (Matt. 9:29). It works regardless of whether I am believing for God's destiny for me or satan's lies.

2. **The law of judgment is to be replaced with the law of honor**—"Do not judge so that you will not be judged. For in the way you judge, you will be judged; and by your standard of measure, it will be measured to you" (Matt. 7:1-2).

   "Honor your father and your mother, that your days may be prolonged in the land which the LORD your God gives you."
   (Ex. 20:12)

3. **The law of sowing and reaping**—"Whatever a man sows, this he will also reap" (Gal. 6:7).
4. **The law of multiplication**—"For they sow the wind, And they reap the whirlwind" (Hos 8:7).

ROCHELLE HOLBEN, THE CURRENT EXECUTIVE DIRECTOR OF ELIJAH HOUSE, SHARES THE FOLLOWING:

Elijah House® prayer ministry was developed through the pioneering work of John and Paula Sandford. It is pastoral in nature, based on scriptural principles and led by the Holy Spirit. Inner healing at Elijah House® looks for the root causes that lie beneath the surface of most problems. Bitter roots, as we call them, feed patterns in us that lead to broken relationships, habitual sin, and many other kinds of bad fruit. Once bitter roots are discovered, the prayer minister leads the seeker in prayer to the foot of the Cross, to forgive those who wounded him/her, and to receive forgiveness for judgments and other strongholds the heart has formed.

Elijah House® is an inner healing ministry that equips and empowers individual hearts to be healed and changed through sanctification and transformation. Truly, fully, and completely. We facilitate inner healing via prophetic prayer ministry and pastoral counseling to people all over the world. Find us here Elijahhouse.org

EXTENDED JOURNALING QUICKENS THE HEALING PROCESS

EXAMPLES OF SOME OF THE JOURNALING WHICH I DID AS PART OF MY HEALING

One big issue in my life has been anger. I got angry at almost everything. As I was healing the wound of anger, the Lord spoke the following in my journaling, granting me another way of looking at things that made me angry. I encourage you to do extended journaling on the issues you are seeking healing from. He is the Wonderful Counselor.

EXTENDED DIVINE VISION AND REVELATION CONCERNING ANGER AGAINST INSTITUTIONS

My child, you see institutions as negative and bad and dead. They are not all that. Some may be partially dead, but many still have much life within them. And the finest institutions are always reinventing themselves into that which is new and vital and relevant to the people whom they serve. The best churches are doing that. The best businesses are doing that, and the best governments are doing that. So do not see all institutions as being dead, for all are not.

You are to come alongside institutions and not against them. You are to offer life to them and find ways to integrate that which

I have given to you to them. They are not your enemy. They are to be viewed as your friend. You are to see My hand upon them and My grace upon them. You are to see them as Mine and not the enemy's. Thus you will be able to offer My life unto them.

If you close off your spirit to them, you will not be able to give My gift of life through you to them. Receive them as part of My handiwork, for all of history has been filled with institutions, and you will see in My Word that it was I who created governments and rule over them. It is I who created the Tabernacle in the wilderness with all the patterns and ceremonies that went with it. That all became an institution. A living institution. An institution created by Me and reflecting Me. That is what a true institution is to do. That which you create is to do that. That which others create is to do that.

So reject not institutions but come alongside them and see them as the work of My hand. Those that need to be reinvented into My life stream will do so or they will die. That is the pattern of the universe. That which falls out of My life stream dies. That which remains in My river bears much fruit for the healing of the nations. Remain in My life stream. Do not let anger and bitterness overcome you. For thus you would fall out of My life stream.

EXTENDED VISION AND REVELATION CONCERNING ANGER AGAINST PHARISEEISM AND THE NEED FOR OPPOSITES

My child, you think Phariseeism is wicked and should be destroyed. Did I destroy all Pharisees when I walked the earth? No, I think not. I let them walk and perform their deeds and I even let them do their best to destroy Me. However, what they thought would bring My destruction—My death on the Cross—actually brought forth My victory and My ministry unto all the ages.

Do you think that is any less true in your life than it was in Mine? Do you think I do not work all things out for good to those who love Me and are called according to My purpose? Of course I do, and of course, I am in your life. If I choose to raise your ministry up higher and it is attacked by Pharisees, (something you fear and which angers you) can they destroy what I have purposed to do? No, and again I say unto you, no! Not Pharisees, and not satan. They can only do that which I give them the strength and the breath to do. I am Lord of all. Satan's handiwork is only used to highlight the advance of My purposes in My universe.

Who are you to set your attention upon the wicked ones? Have I told you to do that? Have I taught you to do that? No and again I say unto you, no! I have told you to set your attention upon Me and upon My purposes in your life and in My world. So why are your eyes set upon the heathen or upon the Pharisees? If I choose to use them to advance My purposes, what is that to you? You set your eyes upon your Lord and your Master, and all will go well in your life. Behold, I have spoken, and behold, it is to be done.

FREEDOM IN SOZO
BY DAWNA DE SILVA

"Where the Spirit of the Lord is, there is freedom" (2 Cor. 3:17).

Achieving freedom doesn't have to take years. When we follow the Holy Spirit's leading and connect to His presence, freedom is the by-product.

When we first started the Sozo ministry in 2003, Teresa and I quickly realized that people's relationships with their earthly fathers, mothers, and siblings closely mirrored their relationships with Father God, Jesus, and Holy Spirit.

For example, if someone had an earthly father who did not protect them in the home, then they usually had a difficult time believing Father God would come through and protect them in their daily life. This orphan lens of abandonment they wore affected their ability to see God's true nature as Protector. Once a person could identify this mindset and replace it with God's truth, freedom was received.

In over twenty years of running Sozos, I have learned that many Christians have deep relationships with Jesus or Father God or even Holy Spirit, but not all three. They may feel comfortable with the idea of Father God or Holy Spirit, but have never actually pursued a meaningful relationship with all three.

This is why I teach often on the subject "Stepping through the Door of Jesus." My desire is for every Christian to know all aspects of God's being. Yes, Jesus is Lord. Holy Spirit is Lord. And Father God is Lord too. Father God, Jesus, and the Holy Spirit are combined in a tri-dimensional partnership that exists in one supreme King—one from which we receive truth and get to relationally experience.

Whenever we do Sozos, our number one priority is getting our clients to experience the truth of the Trinity: Father God, Jesus, and Holy Spirit.

THE FATHER LADDER

When I sit down to do a Sozo session, I have two primary Sozo tools: The Father Ladder and The Four Doors. (There are many more Sozo tools, but for the purposes of this introduction, I will only go over these two.)

The Father Ladder is a tool that helps people identify lies they believe about themselves, others, and/or God. Once they discover the lies they believe and hand them over to God, the person is able to walk through forgiveness, renounce the lies, and receive God's truth.

Applying the Father Ladder tool is simple. You can start by saying to the client (the person receiving the Sozo), "Repeat after me. Father God, are there any lies I'm believing about You?"

If the person hears, feels, or senses, "yes," and responds so, then the next question can be, "Father God, what is the lie I am believing?"

People will usually then get a picture, word, or an impression. God communicates to each of us differently, so it's important to not force someone to hear or experience God in a specific way.

I have found that asking clients, "What do you hear, sense, or see?" is a safe way of allowing people to process and hear however God speaks to them.

Once you identify the lie that the person believes, you can move on to the next step of the Sozo process—forgiveness.

The forgiveness process usually starts like this, "Repeat after me. Father God, who do I need to forgive that taught me this lie?"

Usually God will show the person a picture of a parent or sibling, a picture of their boss or friend—anyone in their life that they need to forgive. In some cases, people might need to forgive themselves.

It really is incredible how much forgiveness helps get rid of the lies we believe (Matthew 18:21-35). Once God reveals who we need to forgive (a parent, a sibling, our nation, the world), we can release our unforgiveness to God, renounce partnership with the lie we are believing, and replace our faulty mindset with His truth.

This discovery and renunciation process reminds me of a man I once Sozoed in Minnesota named Chuck. At the end of our conference, I stayed to pray individually for attendees. Coming up to me in tears, Chuck confessed he was an ex-addict who had come to our conference as part of his recovery program, and he was desperate for change.

Chuck was a tough biker, dressed in all leather, and had huge tattoos covering his arms. I asked Chuck what he needed prayer for and he said, "I got this Jesus guy down and after this weekend

I even understand the Holy Spirit, but I just don't get this Father God guy."

I asked Chuck to close his eyes and asked him if he could see Jesus. "Yes, I can see Jesus." He said.

I had him then pray, "Jesus, will you please take me to Your Father?"

As soon as Chuck repeated the prayer, he jerked his head back as if he was being slapped. I leaned in and whispered, "Father God will never strike you."

Chuck instantly fell to the floor, curled up in a fetal position, and started sobbing violently. I wasn't quite sure if his outburst was a "Jesus" sob or a demonic sob, so I knelt down and asked, "Is this a good cry or a bad cry?"

"Good!" Chuck exclaimed, sobbing. "Father God is holding me!"

Chuck stood on that day on the prayer line an orphan, but hit the ground an adopted son. From that day on, his relationship with Father God was changed. Because of Chuck's years of physical abuse from his earthly father, he was unable even as a Christian to step through the door of Jesus and meet His loving Heavenly Father. That is, until his fear of God's abuse was addressed and healed.

It is interesting how I have found over the years how many followers of Jesus still struggle with their connection to the Father. But to these obstacles I say, "Jesus came to show us the Father!" He came to bridge the orphan gap between man and God so we could "boldly go before the throne of grace" (Hebrews 4:15-16). Jesus came as a direct representation of His Father and yet, even His disciples did not make this connection:

Philip said to Him, "Lord, show us the Father, and it is enough for us." Jesus said to him, "Have I been so long with you, and yet you have not come to know Me, Philip? He who has seen Me has seen the Father; how can you say, 'Show us the Father'? Do you not believe that I am in the Father, and the Father is in Me? The words that I say to you I do not speak on My own initiative, but the Father abiding in Me does His works. Believe Me that I am in the Father and the Father is in Me; otherwise believe because of the works themselves" (John 14:8-11, NASB).

This verse caught my attention a few years ago and made me wonder, "Is it possible for Christians to know Jesus and still not know the Father?" Yes, I believe it is possible and sadly very common. I call this condition "stopping at the door of Jesus."

Over the years, I have found that many believers stop at the door of Jesus and fail to step through to the Father and/or the Holy Spirit. Yes, Jesus is God and yes, we are saved when we accept Him as our Lord. We may even be filled with the Holy Spirit and walk in great displays of power, but if we stop at the door of Jesus and fail to go through to Father God, then we will continue to partner with an orphan spirit that distances us from Father God's truth.

I believe that identity comes from our fathers. This is why the enemy has worked hard to break down the traditional family model. Fathers speak identity over us. Mothers provide nurturing and comfort. Siblings serve as our friends/companions.

In Scripture, Father God spoke identity over Jesus (see Matthew 17). The Holy Spirit served as His comforter and teacher. All throughout the New Testament, the Bible shows us that Jesus is our eternal friend and sibling.

To this day Jesus serves as our ultimate companion who brings us before the Father and leads us into relationship with the Holy Spirit.

THE FOUR DOORS

The other Sozo tool that I use regularly is called The Four Doors. The Four Doors helps people identify the access areas of sin in their life. These doors, classified by Argentinian deliverance minister Pablo Bottari, are fear, anger, sexual sin, and the occult.

Scripture tells us to leave no footholds to the enemy. This tool is simply a way of identifying these footholds or hooks and closing them so we can have complete freedom in God. Sozoers prioritize processing through each of these doors with their clients to make sure they have no open access points to the enemy.

Using The Four Doors is simple. To start the tool, I simply ask the person receiving prayer, "Repeat after me. Jesus, is there a door to "fear/anger/sexual sin/occult" (one door at a time) open in my life?"

If the person hears, "yes", then I walk them through repentance of sin, forgiveness of others, and then asking forgiveness from God. Once the sin is renounced, God's forgiveness is received, and the door is shut to the enemy, sin no longer has a foothold in that area of their life.

One of my favorite testimonies with The Four Doors comes from years ago when a man named Jeff came in for a Sozo session. He was a pastor who, for the last forty years, had been struggling with an addiction to pornography. As a pastor, he was facing termination, but no matter how hard he tried to give it up, he would cycle back into it.

Feeling hopeless, Jeff said, "I'm giving God one more chance to set me free. If this doesn't work, I'm going to resign."

Using The Four Doors tool, I had him repeat, "Father God, would You show me where I first opened a door to sexual sin?"

Instantly, God took Jeff to a memory where he was twelve. In the memory, his father had just passed away and he had become the "man" of the house by taking over his father's chores. Jesus showed Jeff a picture of him as a small boy lifting twenty-pound sacks of feed for the farm's animals.

When I asked Jesus to show Jeff where He was during this time, Jeff began to weep. Collecting himself, he said Jesus was there putting His own shoulder under the sacks of feed for Jeff to carry the food out to the animals.

As this memory played out, Jeff continued to cry, tears in his eyes. "What's God showing you? I asked.

"God is showing me that it was during this season I believed the lie that I was 'too little for the job'. Later that year, I found pornography in the barn. When I felt too small for the job, pornography made me feel like a man."

In just a few minutes, God helped Jeff identify the root (his need to self-comfort). This root caused his bad fruit (pornography) to appear, which was being used in order to help him feel more like a man. Once Jeff was able to renounce partnership with this lie of "I am inadequate for the job," he was able to repent and replace it with God's truth—"Jesus is always with me and helping me."

By the end of our session together, Jeff felt relaxed and hopeful. Bouncing in his seat, he exclaimed, "It's finally going to be a fair fight!"

Because Jeff's struggle with pornography was not based solely in his flesh (his physical desires), it seemed impossible for him to stay free. But as we discovered, his addiction was anchored in a belief system that was telling him "I am too little for the job." Whenever someone in church leadership would question him, or if his wife would doubt an important decision he had made, Jeff would spiral back to feeling like that small boy struggling with his chores, and pornography would be there waiting to comfort him.

Five years later, Jeff called me to celebrate. He said he had never struggled with pornography since our Sozo session together. Why? Because where the spirit of the Lord is there is freedom.

CONCLUSION

These are just a few highlights of some of the Sozo tools we use in our inner healing/deliverance sessions. Freedom comes from building a connection to the Trinity, forgiving offenders, and repenting for the sin in our lives.

It is never our intention to control or move the conversation toward a particular goal or destination. We make sure our clients see and hear what God is saying to them for themselves. Our lasting desire is to help them realize that they can hear God for themselves and work through their own issues with God in their lives.

After receiving a Sozo, clients are sent home with a paper filled with the notes the Sozo minister took during the session. These notes remind the client of the truths God spoke to them during their session. To stay free, I encourage those ministered to to take these notes and meditate on them for the next sixty days. Usually, I recommend reading the truths over daily and studying God's Word so His truths begin to function in their minds automatically.

DAWNA DE SILVA IS FOUNDER AND CO-LEADER OF THE INTERNATIONAL BETHEL SOZO MINISTRY

For any more information on Sozo, or if you would like to schedule a Sozo for yourself, please visit our website at www.bethel.com/ministries/transformation-center. You can also check out my books *Sozo: Saved, Healed, and Delivered and Shifting Atmospheres* at Bethel's online store https://shop.bethel.com/

Sozo training courses are available at desilvaministries.com and Dawna can be reached at dawnadesilva.com.

HOW OFTEN DID JESUS MINISTER DELIVERANCE?

The following table lists forty-one different times when it is recorded in the Gospels that Jesus prayed for people to be healed. Of these forty-one, twelve incorporated prayers for deliverance. That means that in one-fourth to one-third of Jesus' prayers for healing, the Gospel writers specifically mention the fact that they involved the casting out of demons. Obviously, additional healing prayers of Jesus may have involved deliverance which was just not specifically mentioned, so the proportion could actually be higher.

Therefore, if I am praying for people to be healed, I would assume that between one-fourth and one-third of my prayers would involve deliverance. After all, if I am not going to pattern my healing prayer ministry after Jesus, who am I going to pattern it after? Jesus is the greatest healer the world has ever known.

Evaluate your own prayer ministry approach to see if you are minimizing or over-doing deliverance prayer.

THE HEALING MINISTRY OF JESUS

- **(D)** means **D**eliverance was mentioned /
- **(NDM)** means **N**o **D**eliverance **M**entioned

Description, Reference, and Parallel Passages
1. Man with unclean spirit. Mark 1:23-25 **(D)**, Luke 4:3335 **(D)**
2. Peter's mother-in-law. Matthew 8:14-15 (NDM), Mark 1:30-31 (NDM), Luke 4:38-39 (NDM?—"He rebuked the fever and it left her")
3. Multitudes. Matthew 8:16-17 **(D)**, Mark 1:32-34 **(D)**, Luke 4:40-41 **(D)**
4. Many demons. Mark 1:39 **(D)**
5. Leper. Matthew 8:2-4 (NDM), Mark 1:40-42 (NDM), Luke 5:12-13 (NDM)
6. Paralytic. Matthew 9:2-7 (NDM), Mark 2:3-13 (NDM), Luke 5:17-25 (NDM)
7. Man with withered hand. Matthew 12:9-13 (NDM), Mark 3:1-5 (NDM), Luke 6:6-10 (NDM)
8. Multitudes. Matthew 12:15-16 (NDM), Mark 3:10-11 (NDM)
9. Gadarene demoniac. Matthew 8:28-32 **(D)**, Mark 5:113 **(D)**, Luke 8:26-33 **(D)**
10. Jairus' daughter. Matthew 9:23-25 (NDM), Mark 5:3543 (NDM), Luke 8:49-56 (NDM)
11. Woman with issue of blood. Matthew 9:20-22 (NDM), Mark 5:25-34 (NDM), Luke 8:43-48 (NDM)
12. A few sick people. Matthew 13:58 (NDM), Mark 6:56 (NDM)
13. Multitudes. Matthew 14:34-36 (NDM), Mark 6:55-56 (NDM)

HOW OFTEN DID JESUS MINISTER DELIVERANCE?

14. Syro-phoenician's daughter. Matthew 15:22-28 **(D)**, Mark 7:24-30 **(D)**
15. Deaf and mute man. Mark 7:32-35 (NDM)
16. Blind man. Mark 8:22-26 (NDM)
17. Child with evil spirit. Matthew 17:14-18 **(D)**, Mark 9:14-27 **(D)**, Luke 9:38-43 **(D)**
18. Blind Bartimaeus. Matthew 20:30-34 (NDM), Mark 10:46-52 (NDM), Luke 18:35-43 (NDM)
19. Centurion's servant Matthew. 8:5-13 (NDM), Luke 7:210 (NDM)
20. Two blind men. Matthew 9:27-30 (NDM)
21. Mute demoniac. Matthew 9:32-33 **(D)**
22. Blind and mute demoniac. Matthew 12:22 **(D)**, Luke 11:14 **(D)**
23. Multitudes. Matthew 4:23 **(D)**, Luke 6:17-19 **(D)**
24. Multitudes. Matthew 9:35 (NDM)
25. Multitudes. Luke 7:21 **(D)**
26. Multitudes. Matthew 14:14 (NDM), Luke 9:11 (NDM), John 6:2 (NDM)
27. Great multitudes. Matthew 15:30 (NDM)
28. Great multitudes. Matthew 19:2 (NDM)
29. Blind and lame in temple. Matthew 21:14 (NDM)
30. Widow's son. Luke 7:11-15 (NDM)
31. Mary Magdalene and others. Luke 8:2 **(D)**
32. Crippled woman. Luke 13:10-13 **(D)**
33. Man with dropsy. Luke 14:1-4 (NDM)
34. Ten lepers. Luke 17:11-19 (NDM)
35. Servant's ear. Luke 22:49-51 (NDM)
36. Multitudes. Luke 5:15 (NDM)

37. Various persons. Luke 13:32 **(D)**
38. Nobleman's son. John 4:46-53 (NDM)
39. Invalid. John 5:2-9 (NDM)
40. Man born blind. John 9:1-7 (NDM)
41. Lazarus. John 11:1-44 (NDM)

Note: The following occurrence is worthy of special mention for it specifically states that this woman's infirmity was caused by a spirit.

> *And He was teaching in one of the synagogues on the Sabbath. And behold, there was a woman who for eighteen years had a sickness caused by a spirit; and she was bent double, and could not straighten up at all. And when Jesus saw her, He called her over and said to her, "Woman, you are freed from your sickness." And He laid His hands upon her; and immediately she was made erect again, and began glorifying God.* (Luke 13:1013, NASB)

THE HEALING MINISTRY OF THE DISCIPLES

The following references will assist those who want to explore the ongoing healing ministry of the disciples.

1. Jesus' ministry described. Matthew 11:2-6, Luke 7:1823
2. The twelve sent. Matthew 10:1-11:1, Mark 3:13-19, Luke 9:1-11
3. The seventy-two sent. Luke 10:1-24
4. Disciples attempt to cast out demons. Matthew 17:1421, Mark 9:14-29, Luke 9:37-45
5. Power to bind and loose. Matthew 16:13-20
6. Great Commission. Matthew 28:16-20, Mark 16:1420, Luke 24:44-53, Acts 1:1-11

7. Signs and wonders at Apostles' hands. Acts 2:22, 4247
8. Healing of lame beggar. Acts 3:1-4
9. Prayer for confidence and healing signs. Acts 4:23-31
10. Signs and wonders at Apostles' hands. Acts 5:12-16
11. Ministry of Stephen. Acts 6:8-15
12. Ministry of Philip. Acts 8:4-13
13. Ananias and Saul. Acts 9:10-19
14. Peter heals Aeneas (Lydda). Acts 9:32-35
15. Peter heals Dorcas (Joppa). Acts 9:36-43
16. The ministry of Jesus. Acts 10:34-41
17. Magician struck blind by Paul. Acts 13:4-12
18. Paul and Barnabas in Iconium. Acts 14:1-7
19. Lame man at Lystra. Acts 14:8-18
20. Paul raised at Lystra. Acts 14:19-20
21. Slave girl at Philippi. Acts 16:16-40
22. Paul at Ephesus. Acts 19:8-20
23. Eutychus raised from the dead. Acts 20:7-12
24. Paul recalls Ananias. Acts 22:12-21
25. Paul on Malta. Acts 28:1-10
26. Galatians 3:5
27. Hebrews 2:4

HOW TO HEAR GOD'S VOICE

HOW CAN WE RECEIVE COUNSEL FROM OUR WONDERFUL COUNSELOR IF WE CANNOT HEAR HIS VOICE?

We see then why it is *crucial* to master the skill of hearing God's voice. In this book we have only scratched the surface of the greatest skill you will ever learn, which is how to commune with God. We have said that hearing God's voice is as simple as 1) quieting yourself down, 2) fixing your eyes on Jesus, 3) tuning to flow and 4) writing.

The river of the Holy Spirit within provides flowing thoughts (His voice), flowing pictures (His visions) and flowing emotions (His heart).

Mastering this skill of communion with God is 1) foundational to the way God intended life to be lived, beginning with the example in the Garden of Eden where He walked and talked with Adam and Eve in the cool of the day. Jesus, our perfect example, demonstrated this lifestyle by doing nothing on His own initiative but only what He heard and saw His father doing (Jn. 5:19,20,30; 8:26,38). Of course the entire book of Revelation demonstrates John using these same 4 keys (Rev. 1:9-11—stillness, vision, spontaneity, journaling) and journaling out 22 chapters of divine encounter. **So from Genesis to Revelation, this is God's intended lifestyle.**

HOW WIDELY USED ARE THESE FOUR KEYS?

Over half of the Bible was written by men who used these four keys. See article at: cwgministries.org/million

The universal acceptance and affirmation of these four keys is evidenced in that they have been translated and are freely available in 54+ languages at cwgministries.org/translations.

As you can see, there is much more to learn than the brief introduction we have provided in Chapter One. Insights such as the principle that "the flow comes from the vision being held before your eyes" and "how to avoid praying with an idol in your heart and getting a messed up journal entry" are so helpful to understand. We also teach how to enter His courts properly by using "the Tabernacle Experience," and how to break off the blockages so you can hear and see as God initially intended.

All this and much more is taught in our 10-hour training on hearing God's voice, which we consider foundational to the Christian lifestyle and to healing the heart. We are convinced **heart healing occurs through divine encounter**. To assist you in developing a daily lifestyle of divine encounter through an intimate and conversational relationship with Jesus, we make the following resources available:

- Communion With God Ministries: CWGMinistries.org (See the book *4 Keys to Hearing God's Voice*.)
- Christian Leadership for You School of the Spirit: CLUSchooloftheSpirit.com (See the e-learning module Hearing God's Voice.)
- Christian Leadership University: CLUonline.com (See the course REN103 Communion With God.)

IMMANUEL APPROACH TO HEART HEALING BY KENT LARSON

The Immanuel Approach is based on one of the names of God we usually associate with Christmas. Immanuel, which means "God is with us" (Isa. 7:14 and Matt. 1:23).

BASIC DEFINITION

Simply defined, the Immanuel Approach is a guided, interactive prayer model (and lifestyle) that begins with connecting with Jesus in a positive memory so that you can then interact with Him from a place of peaceful, secure attachment in all of life, including both negative or positive past, present and future moments. Since Jesus is outside of time, He is in every moment of your life, whether you perceived Him there or not. In this beautiful, gentle process, you are now able to see everything as He sees it. This "re-framing" of your life from His presence, love and perspective changes everything and produces lasting transformation.

FOUNDERS

The Immanuel Approach was developed by Christian psychiatrist, Dr. Karl Lehman M.D. and Dr. Jim Wilder, PhD (Neuro-theologian). As these two brilliant, godly men collaborated and sought the Lord for a solution to helping highly traumatized people find lasting recovery, the revelation of beginning each healing prayer session in a positive memory became evident to them both. Combining breakthrough brain science research with Biblical understanding, the Immanuel Approach was born!

BEGINNING IN A POSITIVE MEMORY

What makes the Immanuel Approach unique is that every healing session begins with connecting with the living, interactive presence of Jesus in a positive memory rather than in a painful one. Positive memories can be either one in which you felt a strong connection with God or a simple appreciation memory. Examples of God connection memories could be moments like a beautiful worship service, or an experience when you knew the Lord was with you, or a time a scripture verse personally spoke to you, or perhaps a meaningful prayer time. Examples of simple appreciations could be a beautiful sunset, an unexpected gift, a favorite vacation or family gathering, a moment with a child or grandchild, a pet, a garden, a stunning view, etc. It's important to find a memory that has no pain attached to it. We then coach the recipient to amplify the feeling of appreciation by describing the details of the memory, including feeling words and even body sensations. This activates the right brain and helps you re-experience the memory as much as possible. You are encouraged to imagine yourself in the memory rather than looking at it like you were watching a video. We recognize that these moments are all gifts from God and that He was with us in them.....Immanuel.

WHY IS GRATITUDE IMPORTANT?

Gratitude is clearly an important value in all of Scripture. Psalm 100:4 is the clearest example of this, "Enter His gates with thanksgiving and His courts with praise; give thanks to Him and praise His name" (NIV). The Message translation says it like this: "Gratitude is the password into the presence of God." The brain science correlates with this truth as it has revealed that even the act of looking for something to be grateful for shifts the chemicals in our brain-mind-spirit system and causes the relational dynamics in our brains to be more open and receptive to receive what the Lord has for healing, restoration and transformation. Dr. Wilder has said that "Gratitude reminds our brains what it feels like to be connected to God." (*Joyful Journey* p.16)

LOCATING JESUS

After amplifying appreciation in the positive memory, you are then coached to locate Jesus in the memory, using the eyes of your heart, your godly imagination. It's important to notice everything about seeing Jesus there with you. This begins a beautiful dialogue with Him. The prayer recipient is continually coached to maintain the connection with Jesus and pay close attention to every spontaneous thought, image, feeling or even body sensation that comes into their awareness and to simply report whatever is going on. This typically results in a beautiful experience of feeling loved, seen, heard and understood by the God who is near, attentive and so tender in His love. This powerful face to face encounter and interaction with Jesus often accomplishes deep heart healing without ever needing to address specific painful memories.

ADDRESSING PAIN

However, the prayer coach may be led by Holy Spirit to suggest the recipient ask Jesus if He has anything today for their healing today. Often Holy Spirit will spontaneously bring to mind a memory. As the prayer coach we are trusting that if He brings up an issue or memory, He has a good plan to bring healing and resolution. The recipient is coached to stay connected to and focused on Jesus and to ask Him if He wants to take them to that memory. This is another unique aspect of the Immanuel Approach as we only go to painful memories if Jesus brings them up. At this point, the recipient is encouraged to simply notice and report everything, even if it feels random or unimportant. It's important not to edit out anything as we are depending on Holy Spirit to access memories that might have been buried.

JESUS, THE BRILLIANT THERAPIST

We have seen over and over the brilliance of how Jesus leads people through significant healing as He stays close and walks with them through pain and trauma, re-framing everything! People feel safe with Jesus after interacting with Him in the positive memory and can more easily receive what He wants to give them to heal past trauma. The painful memory can then become wisdom, maturity, character, deepened intimacy with Jesus and peace that truly passes human understanding.

LEARN MORE

If you would like to learn more about the Immanuel Approach please visit MercyTransformation.com.

IMMANUEL JOURNALING TO HEAL PAINFUL FEELINGS/MEMORIES BY KENT LARSON

Sometimes in the process of journaling, the Lord will lead you to dialogue with Him about painful feelings or memories. He wants to be with you in a gentle and intimate way as He "attunes" to you. He wants you to feel seen, heard, understood and comforted in ways that only He can do as you interact with His living, loving presence. As Dr. Karl Lehman M.D. says, "Stop trying to stop the pain and talk to Jesus about it." (*Outsmarting Yourself* p.157)

At the burning bush encounter, Moses hears God say, I see you….., I hear you.….. I understand how hard this is for you..….., I am with you in this..…., and I have what you need..…. (See Exodus 3).

This kind of encounter with God is available to all of us through a simple process called Immanuel Journaling. Following is a summary of what this journaling model can look like.

As you quiet yourself down, spend a few minutes expressing gratitude to the Lord for who He is and for a specific gift of love, joy, peace, grace or beauty He has given you. ("Gratitude is like a password into the presence of God." Ps. 100:4 The Message) As you then focus on Jesus, tune to spontaneity and begin to write, ask the Lord if there's anything He wants to talk about today.

Or you could ask more specific questions that would lead you to a painful memory, "Jesus, when did I lose my peace recently?" Or, "Jesus, what good plans do You have for my healing today?"

Then continue to write in response to these five questions:

1. Jesus, how do You see me?
2. Jesus, how do You hear me?
3. Jesus, how do You understand how big or hard this is for me?
4. Jesus, how are You with me in this, and how do You treat my weaknesses tenderly?
5. Jesus, what do You have for me to restore me to peace?

These five questions correlate with what is called the "pain processing pathway" that Dr. Karl Lehman M.D. explains in his book, *Outsmarting Yourself*. This process is an important way to metabolize painful experiences in our lives so that instead of becoming trauma, they become wisdom, insight, maturity, skills and empathy. Hope begins to grow for true and lasting transformation into Christlikeness and our true, redeemed selves. We begin to live from the hearts Jesus gave us.

SIMPLE EXAMPLE OF THE IMMANUEL JOURNALING PROCESS

1. Quiet yourself down (listen to quiet worship music, breathe) and stir up gratitude.

   Gratitude

   "Jesus, thank You for that moment in worship when I felt like I was in the eye of a tornado....surrounded in white, brilliant light and perfectly quiet and still. I couldn't sing any longer, but just

entered the stillness of Your presence....caught up in the moment. I saw myself surrounded by You, Father, Jesus, Holy Spirit; right in the center of Trinity. I felt joy but also intense peace. My body was perfectly quiet and still. My face turned upward, basking in the light. I felt held in Your love. Chosen. Seen."

2. Focus on Jesus
3. Tune to spontaneity
4. Write

Jesus' response to my gratitude

"Beloved, in that moment of worship I gave you a glimpse of heavenly, kingdom reality because you are already in Me. Remember John 14:20. I am in My Father and you are in Me and I am in you. This is where you belong forever. Chosen, seen, and held in the center of My love and nothing can ever separate you from this place. Every time you worship, and many times in between, step into this visual reality and feel the joy and peace rest upon you, deeper and deeper; quieting you, reminding you who you really are and where you really are! And keep looking for Me. There is so much more than you've ever imagined!"

Jesus, what do You want to talk about today?

"Your anxiety about Thanksgiving."

Jesus, how do You see me?

"Beloved, I see you sitting at the table writing out the menu and shopping list. Your shoulders are tense."

Jesus, how do You hear me?

"I hear you wondering if this will be good enough. Will your family like it? Will it all turn out ok?"

Jesus, how do You understand how big this for me?

"I know that big family gatherings and holidays are hard for you because of how much you want it to be good; for everyone to feel celebrated and experience joy together. I know you feel a sense of responsibility to make it all happen; as if it depends on you"

Jesus, are You with me in this and how are You tender towards my weakness?

"I'm right here, even as you prepare. And I'll be with you through the whole process. Stop and breathe for a moment. Can you see Me with you right now? I love being with you in every moment of your life."

Jesus, what do You have for me to restore me to peace?"

"Beloved, I will help you stay in peace. Just take a moment to listen. I can help you love and bless your family as you stay connected to Me in the process. Just lean back in My arms even now and feel the peace wash over you. Can you see Me at the table with your family? Can you see Me smiling and in perfect peace? I love each one and as you look in their eyes around the table, they will see My love for them in your eyes."

IMPASSIONED REPENTANCE REMOVES BLOCKAGES

If you have prayed through the seven prayers and you are still falling back into the same sin, then you need to impassion your repentance with some detailed pictures of the end result of both sinfulness and righteousness as it relates to the issue you are struggling with.

Complete the following questions on paper or on computer. Use as much detail and vividness as you possibly can. The more graphic and lifelike the picture, the more power and passion it will generate within you. Your desire to sin in any specific area should be dealt a death-blow by your completing the exercise on the following pages.

IMPASSIONED REPENTANCE WORKSHEET (PAGE 1)

A detailed picture of the devastation and destruction resulting from the sin of _____.

"Lord, show me the destruction it will bring into my life if I continue in the sin of _____."

Tune to Holy Spirit flow and pictures as you write:

- Biblical (and other) principles which relate to this sin.
- A detailed picture of the sin and the way it grows in one's life.
- A detailed picture of what it will do to my physical health.
- A detailed picture of what it will do to my soul's health.
- A detailed picture of what it will do to my spiritual health.
- A detailed picture of what it will do to my relationship with God.
- A detailed picture of what it will do to my acquaintances.
- A detailed picture of what it will do to my spouse.
- A detailed picture of what it will do to my children.
- A detailed picture of what it will do to my ministry.
- A detailed picture of what it will do to my job/finances.
- A detailed picture of what it will do to my eternal life.

"As a result of this meditation, here is my confession of what I will do: _____." (Speak this aloud several times.)

IMPASSIONED REPENTANCE WORKSHEET (PAGE 2)

A detailed picture of the blessing of the righteous act of _____.

"Lord, show me the blessing it will bring into my life if I continue in the righteousness of _____."

Tune to Holy Spirit flow and pictures as you write:

- Biblical (and other) principles which relate to this act.
- A detailed picture of this act of righteousness and the way

IMPASSIONED REPENTANCE REMOVES BLOCKAGES

it grows in one's life.
- A detailed picture of what it will do to my physical health.
- A detailed picture of what it will do to my soul's health.
- A detailed picture of what it will do to my spiritual health.
- A detailed picture of what it will do to my relationship with God.
- A detailed picture of what it will do to my acquaintances.
- A detailed picture of what it will do to my spouse.
- A detailed picture of what it will do to my children.
- A detailed picture of what it will do to my ministry.
- A detailed picture of what it will do to my job/finances.
- A detailed picture of what it will do to my eternal life.

"As a result of this meditation, here is my confession of what I will do: _____*."* (Speak this aloud several times.)

Concluding instructions: Meditate upon this completed "Impassioned Repentance Worksheet" for the next two weeks in your daily devotional time, asking God to deepen, broaden, and internalize these truths in your life. Read it aloud, for speaking is part of meditating and speaking it aloud deepens the truths within you.

IMPASSIONED REPENTANCE WORKSHEET ON LUST

Lust is an issue that nearly all men encounter and probably 95% of women. Following is a completed sample of an "Impassioned Repentance Worksheet" on the topic of lust, pornography, and adultery/fornication. Obviously, greater detail can be added in answering each of the questions below.

A DETAILED PICTURE OF THE DEVASTATION AND DESTRUCTION OF THE SIN OF LUST, PORNOGRAPHY, AND ADULTERY/FORNICATION

"Lord, show me the destruction it will bring into my life if I continue in the sin of lust/pornography."

Tune to Holy Spirit flow and pictures as you write.

A Detailed Picture of the Sin and the Way It Grows in One's Life

Lust is an appetite of the flesh which has become perverted and grown quickly out of control. It is the twisting of love, which focuses on giving to others, into lust, which focuses on demanding from others. It believes that greater satisfaction is achieved by grasping from others to meet one's needs rather than experiencing the joy of giving to others. This is a lie.

IMPASSIONED REPENTANCE WORKSHEET ON LUST

As with all appetites of the flesh (eating, sleeping, sex), when indulged, it continues to grow until it is out of balance and disruptive to one's life. It believes that if it can just have more, it will be satisfied. This is a lie. It will never be satisfied by more. Its appetite will just continue to grow, becoming larger and larger with its passions becoming more and more perverted and demonic as it goes along, incorporating many unspeakable images and acts. It provides pleasure for the moment, but leaves destruction in its wake. It leads from lust to pornography to sexual immorality and adultery/fornication. Pornography is a lie. It does not depict life as it really is.

Every sexual union causes you to join your life force with the prostitute you are with and with the other hundreds or thousands with whom that prostitute has joined herself. Your life force becomes scattered, and you pick up the life force of many others, many of which are demonic and destructive and negatively impact your life.

Biblical (and Other) Principles Which Relate to This Sin

- Whatever I fix my eyes upon grows within me. If I fix them on lust and perversion, then lust and perversion grow within me. If I fix my eyes upon God and a wholesome love toward my spouse, then that grows within me. Watch over your eyes with all diligence.
- Sexuality is a constant inner God-given drive. However, this appetite can get out of control and become one's master.
- Pornography involves lust, which is forbidden in Scriptures.
- At times, the "call for sexuality" should be transformed into other creative energy releases. The river of the life force within

a person can be expressed through many channels, including sex, companionship, creative expression, expressing one's heart motivation, etc. The urge toward sexuality may actually be an inner call for intimacy, physical sensation, or sex. The call for intimacy can also be met by an intimate conservation and/or companionship (either in person, or by phone or letter, or by journaling with the Lord). The call for physical sensation and release can be met through exercise.

- Meditate upon Proverbs chapter five, "the pitfalls of immorality," and chapter seven, "the wiles of the harlot." Perhaps memorize these chapters. At a minimum, make a list of the important truths God gives you from these chapters.

A Detailed Picture of What It Will Do to My Physical Health

Assuming that lust eventually leads to sexual immorality, my body will be consumed with various sexual diseases such as venereal disease and AIDS. This leads to a pain-ridden life and a painful death, as well as public humiliation.

A Detailed Picture of What It Will Do to My Soul's Health

My soul will become twisted as it views people of the opposite sex as sex objects rather than people. I will not see straight. I will not enjoy the pleasures of life. I will see only one thing, perverted sex, everywhere I look.

A Detailed Picture of What It Will Do to My Spiritual Health

I will experience guilt and sinfulness, and be cut off from spiritual growth and development. A person's morality determines his theology. Since I will feel separated from God, I will lose my spiritual passion. I will become lukewarm and spiritually rebellious. I will be hardened inside, rather than tender.

A Detailed Picture of What It Will Do to My Relationship With God

My guilt over my sexual sin will cause me to hide from God, to fear God, to be angry at God. I will seek to steer clear of spiritual things, or I will turn into a hypocrite. I will no longer be honest within. I will be dishonest, evil and vile. I will likely become a mocker of religious things.

A Detailed Picture of What It Will Do to My Acquaintances

All people of the opposite sex will become objects rather than friends. People will not trust me, for if I break my marriage vows, I will break any and every vow I ever make. Wholesome people will shy away from me. Perverts will be drawn to me.

A Detailed Picture of What It Will Do to My Spouse

My marriage will lose its passion as I find sexual satisfaction elsewhere. I will begin to disdain my spouse and my marriage. Adultery will probably cause the break-up of my marriage. I will lose my spouse, my happiness, and my joy of being married. I will be left alone in life. I will come home to an empty house, day after day. If I didn't maintain my vow to my spouse, I probably will not maintain any vow to anyone. I will drift from relationship to relationship, eventually being left alone.

A Detailed Picture of What It Will Do to My Children

I will probably lose my children's love, honor and respect. They will have anger at me for violating my marriage vow, and for harming and humiliating their father/mother and themselves. They will be damaged as they grow up in a single-parent household, and will have a distorted view of God, life and family. They will be unhappy and tend to pass my sins on to their families and children. I will probably lose a close relationship with my grandchildren. My chance to pass on a godly heritage will be gone.

A Detailed Picture of What It Will Do to My Ministry
I will likely lose my ministry position. I will cut off my service to God and to the building of the kingdom of God. Many people will judge me, will not trust me, and will reject me. Any joy I have found in ministering to others will be a thing of the past.

A Detailed Picture of What It Will Do to My Job/Finances
If I am employed in the ministry, I will likely lose my employment. I will have two homes to support rather than one, so I will be reduced financially. Paying prostitutes for sex will cause a great financial drain on my life. The curse of God will be upon my finances. Proverbs says I will be reduced to a loaf of bread.

A Detailed Picture of What It Will Do to My Eternal Life
Because of the hardening of my heart toward the things of God, I am likely to not repent, but to begin a life of ongoing rebellion toward God. Thus I would fall from God's grace through Christ and spend eternity in torment in hell (Galatians 5:4; Hebrews 6:4-6; Matthew 7:21-23; Colossians 2:19).

As a Result of This Meditation, Here Is My Confession as to What I Will Do (Speak This Aloud Several Times, and Whenever Tempted)
I will establish the following fences in my life: I will cut off all potential sources of pornography. I will not shop in stores

which sell it. I will only use internet web services which screen out all pornography. I will not maintain any pornography in my possession. I will not go near any location where I could be tempted. When tempted to lust, I will picture Jesus instead. I will commune with Him and worship before His throne. I will also exercise, and have honest conversations with friends and family so that the desire for intimacy can be met through this means. When tired or discouraged, and thus more susceptible to temptation, I will be extra careful. Sleep will be the best remedy.

When I feel attraction toward a person of the opposite sex, I will put in place the extra safeguard of never being alone with him/her. I will seek to avoid a relationship with him/her to protect both him/her and me.

I will meditate upon Proverbs 5 and 7, and record what God shows me.

If I am still unable to overcome this temptation, I will seek counseling and/or establish an accountability relationship in this area. Lust should respond well to the seven prayers in this book. I will pray through these prayers as they relate to the problem of lust.

A PICTURE OF THE BLESSING OF THE RIGHTEOUS ACT OF PURE SEXUAL LOVE

"Lord, show me the blessing it will bring into my life if I continue in the righteousness of pure sexual love." Tune to Holy Spirit flow and pictures as you write.

A Detailed Picture of This Act of Righteousness and the Way It Grows in One's Life

Since pure sexual love is an activity between a husband and a wife, both the husband and the wife should explore this topic of the deepening of pure marital sexual love. It will take two to make this happen. So agree to both work through the following process.

Pure sexual love which is expressed within marriage is intended to produce an ongoing bond and union between the marriage partners, bringing joy and passion throughout the entire marriage. The physical union of the two marriage partners makes them one, and this joining causes a sharing of the gifts and life flow of one to the other. Eventually, they will begin to look alike, think alike, and respond alike.

Studies show that married people have sex more often than non-married people, therefore you will have greater sexual fulfillment than the immoral unmarried person.

A married couple is to grow together sexually throughout their marriage, as well as in every other way.

Biblical (and Other) Principles Which Relate to This Act

- But if they do not have self-control, let them marry; for it is better to marry than to burn with passion (1 Corinthians 7:9).
- Being together with your spouse provides sexual safety. This should be sought. Traveling alone should be avoided.
- Having a warm, loving relationship with your spouse enhances sexuality. This should be sought. Pursuing deeper intimacy and companionship with your marriage partner is one of the best things you can do to enhance one's sexuality.
- Give and it will be given back to you. Give love in the way which represents love to your partner. Women want companionship, love and relationship. Men tend to want more the act of sex.

IMPASSIONED REPENTANCE WORKSHEET ON LUST

- Read a good book on sexuality in marriage. Read Song of Solomon to gain an understanding of sexual fulfillment in marriage. Make a list of key things God shows you from the Song of Solomon.
- Sexuality is richest when it is an expression of love.
- God recognizes our weaknesses and the mistakes we make in life, and meets the repentant sinner with His mercy and grace. The blood of Jesus washes away all sexual sin. Seek God's perfect will in sex, rather than His permissive will.
- Flee youthful lusts or you will be ensnared. Put up fences which protect yourself from sexual temptation. No pornography, no sexual movies, television, or books. No going to places where sexual temptation abounds. No doing any activity which leads you to sexual temptation.
- If necessary, get capable, spiritual counseling to overcome sexual problems. Inner healing and deliverance can help deal with sexual problems.
- No demanding of sexual exploits from one's marriage partner which violates his/her heart, soul or mind.
- One is drawn to that on which he fixes his eyes. Fix your eyes upon a strong, healthy, passionate, fulfilling marriage, and that is what you will get. Receive pleasure and fulfillment from this vision.

A Detailed Picture of What It Will Do to My Physical Health

Sex within marriage will be a blessing to my physical health. It will produce love, joy, and peace, which all produce positive health responses physiologically. The receiving of my partner's life force through this sexual union will complete and deepen and enlarge me.

A Detailed Picture of What It Will Do to My Soul's Health

It will produce love, joy, and peace, which will heal and restore my soul. I will feel satisfied and fulfilled and blessed to be given such a gift from my Maker and from my spouse.

A Detailed Picture of What It Will Do to My Spiritual Health

The growth in all levels of intimacy with my spouse will encourage a continuing growth of intimacy with the Lord. My marriage will be a picture of the spiritual intimacy the Lord and I are to have, and thus a constant encouragement toward that intimacy. I will continue to seek the Lord.

A Detailed Picture of What It Will Do to My Relationship With God

I will be at peace with God, and thankful for the love He has given me through my spouse. I will have a clear conscience, and thus be able to maintain a passionate desire to grow and to go on with God. My zeal will increase. God's revelation will increase within me. My knowledge and wisdom will increase.

A Detailed Picture of What It Will Do to My Acquaintances

I will maintain the trust and companionship of my friends, as they will sense that I am a moral and trustworthy person. My number of acquaintances shall continue to grow, and they will be moral and trustworthy people.

A Detailed Picture of What It Will Do to My Spouse

My spouse will continue to grow and to bloom, because he/she will know that he/she is loved, honored, and respected. Our marriage will continue to grow in love and intimacy and closeness. It will remain warm throughout our marriage, as we each seek to express love to the other in ways that are meaningful to them.

A Detailed Picture of What It Will Do to My Children

My children will continue to grow in their respect, love, and honor of me. We will maintain a close relationship throughout our lives. I will enjoy the friendship of my grandchildren, and I will pass on a godly anointing through several generations.

A Detailed Picture of What It Will Do to My Ministry

It will enhance my ministry. People will be able to look upon me with trust and respect. God's grace, knowledge, wisdom, and anointing will be able to flow unrestricted through me. I will be able to help others in the areas of sexual purity because I have discovered God's grace in this area myself. My ministry will continue to grow and expand.

A Detailed Picture of What It Will Do to My Job/Finances

God's blessing will continue to flow upon my job and my finances. He will bless everything I put my hand to. My barns will overflow. God's blessing and prosperity will be drawn to me.

A Detailed Picture of What It Will Do to My Eternal Life

My heart will remain strong, pure, and fervent. I will go on to heaven, and spend eternity in the presence of my Father. I will enjoy an everlasting life of joy, blessing, and rest.

As a Result of This Meditation, Here Is My Confession as to What I Will Do (Speak This Aloud Several Times, and Whenever You Need to Reinforce These Truths in Your Life)

I will build intimacy and friendship with my spouse by loving him/her in the ways that are most meaningful to him/her.

For the husband: This will include taking her out on dates, eating meals out, purchasing flowers, writing love notes, holding hands, touching in non-sexual ways, caring, and daily expressing love, appreciation, and approval verbally. I will also avoid criticizing my wife or trying to remake her into my image or the image of what I think she should be. I will accept her for who God has made her to be. I will not seek to dominate, manipulate, or pressure her. I will respect her.

For the wife: This can include making his favorite meal, honoring and respecting him, letting him see and enjoy me naked, dressing in enticing lingerie, letting him regularly enjoy a sexual love feast with me, including much touch and caressing and intercourse and sexual variations.

For both: I will not close off my spirit from my spouse. I will remain open and loving and kind and compassionate. I will repent of any negative judgments, bitter root expectations, and inner vows I have toward them. I will believe the best—that they do love and cherish me and that they want to satisfy me sexually and can and will and do satisfy me sexually, and that I can satisfy them sexually. I renounce any belief or inner vows to the contrary—that they don't love me, don't want to satisfy me sexually, or that they can't and don't satisfy me sexually, or that I will never be able to satisfy them sexually. These are lies from the pit of hell. I reject them as feeders to demonic activity within me. I will only feed on the truth of the Holy Spirit, not the lies of the enemy.

I also renounce any inner vows I have made that I will not or cannot fully give myself sexually to my spouse. I purpose through the Holy Spirit to fully give myself sexually to my spouse.

I will meditate upon Song of Solomon and record what God shows me.

If I am still unable to overcome this temptation, I will seek counseling and/or establish an accountability relationship in this area. Most sexual problems should respond well to the seven prayers in this book. I will pray through these prayers as they relate to my sexual problem.

CONCLUDING INSTRUCTIONS

Meditate upon this completed "Impassioned Repentance Worksheet" daily in your devotional time for the next two weeks, asking God to deepen, expand, and internalize the truths given above. Read it aloud, for speaking is part of meditating and speaking it aloud deepens the truths within you. Whenever tempted, come back and read this meditation aloud again.

INNER HEALING FOR AN ORGAN PRAYER WORKSHEET

In addition to healing prayer, great nutrition, and exercise, you can restore a damaged organ in your body by removing any emotions which contributed to the organ's malfunction and any false identification you may have made with this infirmity by saying, "This is who I am." For example, "I am a heart attack victim." This worksheet guides you through the steps.

SEVEN REMINDERS TO HELP YOU MAXIMIZE THE TRANSFORMING POWER OF THIS PRAYER

1. **Music:** Have soft soaking music playing in the background (keep it very soft).
2. **Emotions:** Identify and replace emotions which contributed to the damage of the organ, and take the time to feel emotional responses throughout the entire prayer.
3. **Picture everything as you pray it:** Especially picture the organ you are praying for. When possible, lay your hands on the organ you are praying for as that will help focus your attention and God's healing power directly on that organ. If the infirmity is throughout your body, lay your hands wherever the Holy Spirit leads you to lay your hands.

INNER HEALING FOR AN ORGAN PRAYER WORKSHEET

4. **Flow:** Tune to flowing thoughts, flowing pictures and flowing emotions.
5. **Review** this prayer and expand your journaling on following days to deepen its impact.
6. **Speak aloud:** Read this prayer aloud. Once you have journaled what the Lord is speaking to you and your response to Him, go back and read that aloud also. This will deepen its impact. Life is in the power of your tongue (Prov. 18:21).
7. **Pause** after each phrase letting it soak in. I plan for 30–45 minutes for this prayer encounter.

INTERACTIVE PRAYER FOR HEALING AN ORGAN

"Lord Jesus, I come to You concerning (name organ or infirmity) and the emotions and beliefs within me which have contributed to its malfunction. I speak to (name organ or infirmity): I am sorry that you have suffered and been damaged. I never intended to harm you. Please accept my apology for what you have had to experience. From this day forward I choose to protect and restore you. I choose to love and care for you.

"Lord, what do You want to speak to me on this organ's behalf? What beliefs and emotions contributed to this malfunction?" (Tune to flowing thoughts which light upon your mind. Allow emotions to flow freely as you dialogue with Jesus about this organ. Let this be a powerful healing encounter with deep emotions.)

- Record what God says.
- Record your response to God and to this damaged organ (repent as necessary).
- Record any response you receive back.

Cleansing self and cells from false identification: "I release these unhealthy emotions to You (name each). Jesus, please cleanse from my memory and all my cells any identification I have made with these unhealthy emotions, where I have said, 'This is who I am.'" (Watch Jesus as He cleanses your cells, sweeping them clean, filling them with His divine light.)

"Lord, cleanse me from any false identification that I have made with the damaged organ saying, 'This is who I am and I must now live with this condition for the rest of my life.' I release this false identification to You, Jesus. I do not identify myself as a victim. This is **not** who I am. This was simply something I have experienced.

"Jesus, I ask You to remove this false identity and restore to me my true identity of who I am in You. My identity is that I am Your loved, protected and cared-for child. I receive Your healing, transforming touch. I lay down my barriers of unbelief, self-effort and self-protection, and acknowledge I am healed by the mighty hand of God."

- Journaling: See, feel and record what you are experiencing as you stay tuned to flow (perhaps shaking, restoration, peace…)

Deliverance—"Thank You, Jesus. I command all demons connected with this trauma, emotion and infirmity to leave now in Jesus' name. (Address, renounce and command each one to leave, naming them by using a description of what they have caused.) Be gone! You are dismissed. I no longer have need of you." (Breathe out heavily a few times—Pause—See and feel Jesus performing this deliverance and the release it brings. *Spirit* and *breath* are the same word in the Greek New Testament.)

Healing—"Lord, pour Your healing oil into my being. (If you can, lay your hands near the organ that you are praying for to focus your attention and God's healing power.) Renew and restore me (see Him doing this). Thank You, Lord, for setting me free!"

Comment—You normally will feel a release, and very likely shaking, as the Spirit moves upon you—unless you are like I was for many years—one of those people who locked feelings and emotional responses out of your life.

Vision of my new reality and my future—"Lord, is there anything You would like to speak to me or show me which would seal this new identity into my being?" Tune to His flowing thoughts and flowing pictures and flowing emotions and journal out what He reveals. Reread it several times over the next few days.

- Record what Jesus says…

DEFINITION OF WHEN A HURT IS HEALED

"A hurt is healed when you can see the gift God has produced in your life through it."

- Lord, what is the gift You have produced in my life through this situation?
- I now live in God's Kingdom emotions of love, joy, peace, compassion, gratitude and thankfulness (Rom. 14:17).

A FOLLOW-UP PRAYER

I often go back and review the prayer and healing experience from the previous day, letting the Holy Spirit deepen and expand it. I might even do this for a couple of days.

Then I move on: "Holy Spirit, please bring to my mind other events throughout my lifetime which have fueled this condition so identification with these events can also be renounced." Take the list of events the Holy Spirit gives you and pray the above prayer for each of them. Birth is a traumatic event which may go on this list.

The more thorough the prayer, the more complete the healing and the greater your freedom from fear and its resulting negative impact upon your being.

FREE RESOURCES AVAILABLE AT: CWGMINISTRIES.ORG/PRAYER_WORKSHEETS

- Sea of Galilee soft soaking music and visionary meditation for two-way journaling
- Download this "Inner Healing for an Organ" Prayer Worksheet and complete it; or you can do your journaling in your journaling notebook.
- Download the slightly revised version of the above worksheet which is titled "Removing a Besetting Sin" and complete it.
- Does Heart Surgery Cause the Heart to Pick Up a Spirit of Fear?
- Clearing Cellular Memories Worksheet.PDF
- Clearing Cellular Memories Worksheet MSWord

INNER HEALING FOR HELLISH SITUATIONS

Our culture says, "A picture is worth a thousand words." Is that true? I believe it is. Life is made up of individual scenes. Some scenes are positive and some are negative. Pictures carry great power with them. One picture is as strong as a thousand confessions. If a picture were combined with a thousand confessions, think how strong that would be!

Let us say a woman has a negative picture of men in her mind because a man raped her. She may know that she is supposed to forgive everything against everyone (Mark 11:25), and that she is not to let the sun go down on her wrath (Ephesians 4:26). So she may say a thousand times, "I forgive him." But if she still maintains a picture in her mind of the man raping her, then that picture will create more energy within than her confession of forgiveness, and she will find that in her heart she still hates the man (if not all men).

What this woman needs is a new picture to replace the old one. She needs a picture of how Jesus was responding to the situation, because surely Jesus was there. David said, "Even if I go to Hades, you are there" (Psalm 139:8). So what was Jesus doing in that hellish situation? What did Jesus do when He was in a similar hellish situation, when men had mocked Him and tore off His clothes, and spit on Him, and plucked out His beard and smashed thorns into His head and hung Him up to die the most painful of all deaths?

He looked down upon his tormentors and said, "Father, forgive them, for they know not what they do" (Luke 23:34).

Can this woman who was raped invite Jesus to come and stand beside her and show how He was responding to the situation she was in and what He is asking her to do? If she can, she will then have a new picture of herself with Jesus in the scene, doing with Jesus the supernatural, the impossible, ministering deep forgiveness in a situation which in the natural would be totally unforgivable. If she can, she will be healed of the negative spiritual energies polluting her heart and soul which were birthed by this traumatic event and fed by her holding these negative pictures in her heart for months or years. She will have a new energy rooted in forgiveness which now permeates her inner being.

Note: Generally we go back to just *after* the rape scene happened rather than back to the middle of it, so as to not have trauma overwhelm the client and cut off the ability of Jesus to minister grace.

You may suspect that in this scenario the woman not only has a negative picture she must get rid of, but she most likely also has a negative expectation and inner vow which also must be renounced and removed. The negative expectation is probably something like, "All men are pigs." The inner vow may be, "I will never trust a man again." So now we have three things producing sin energies within the woman. In addition, she is determining her future fate because her spirit is sending out a strong message of expectation to every man who can hear, saying, "I expect you to treat me badly, and I don't trust you." The man's spirit hears the two messages which are saying to him, "I am supposed to act like an unfeeling animal around her. I am not to be trusted when in her presence." Therefore, she will be drawing more molestation and abuse toward herself.

This woman will need healing on several levels. If generational curses are part of this, she will also need to break them. If demons of fear and mistrust have entered, she will need to get rid of them, not to mention all the demons of sexual perversion which will likely need to be dealt with.

UNGODLY BELIEFS REPLACEMENT WORKSHEET—COMPLETED SAMPLE

UNGODLY BELIEFS/WORD CURSES AND CORRESPONDING VOWS

	LORD, WHAT NEGATIVE EXPECTATIONS ARE CONTRIBUTING CONTRIBUTING TO (STATE HEART WOUND)? **I expect/believe that ...**	LORD, WHAT INNER VOWS ARE CONTRIBUTING TO (STATE HEART WOUND)? **Therefore I vow to do this (an action) ...**
1.	I'll probably fail	give up and die
2.	I will not have financial freedom—never enough	equate poverty with godliness
3.	my sin is unforgivable	hide from God
4.	I don't deserve God's blessing	make it on my own
5.	my children will rebel	seek to control them
6.	life is unfair & God doesn't intervene	distrust and withdraw
7.	people won't accept me	put up a protective wall
8.	I must be perfect.	try hard
9.	men don't cry	stuff my feelings
10.	I'm no good	act out my evil impulses
11.	I'm not very gifted so I can't succeed	not try to accomplish great things
12.	the forces around me are too powerful	stay invisible so I am not squashed
13.		
14.		
15.		
16.		
	I repent for the ungodly belief that ...	**I repent for the inner vow that I will ...**

UNGODLY BELIEFS WORKSHEET—COMPLETED SAMPLE

REPLACE WITH GODLY BELIEFS AND GODLY PURPOSES

	LORD, WHAT WOULD YOU SAY TO REMOVE THIS LIE? However, God says ...	I CHOOSE OBEDIENCE TO WHAT YOU, LORD, HAVE SPOKEN TO ME. So I purpose by the power of the Spirit to...
1.	"I make your way prosperous"	step out in faith
2.	"I give you the power to make wealth"	believe God for financial prosperity
3.	"I have offered you a land of milk and honey"	possess my promised land
4.	"My blood washes away all your sin"	repent and be cleansed
5.	"...will not depart from the way he should go"	train my children, not provoke them
6.	"I work all things out for good"	trust that God rules over all
7.	"Give My love away to others"	stay open and loving
8.	"I am the perfect One"	trust in God's perfection, not my own
9.	"Jesus wept"	be responsive to my heart's emotions
10.	"You are righteous through Christ"	put on Christ's righteousness
11.	"You can do all things through Christ"	see Christ within empowering me
12.	"You are seated with Christ in heavenly places"	rule with Christ over the forces of evil
13.		
14.		
15.		
16.		
	I accept what God has spoken that ...	**I purpose by the power of the Holy Spirit to ...**

UNGODLY BELIEFS REPLACEMENT WORKSHEET—TO COMPLETE

UNGODLY BELIEFS/WORD CURSES AND CORRESPONDING VOWS

	LORD, WHAT NEGATIVE EXPECTATIONS ARE CONTRIBUTING TO _____? **I expect/believe that ...**	LORD, WHAT INNER VOWS ARE CONTRIBUTING TO _____? **Therefore I vow to do this (an action) ...**
1.		
2.		
3.		
4.		
5.		
6.		
7.		
8.		
9.		
10.		
11.		
12.		
13.		
14.		
15.		
16.		
17.		
18.		
19.		
20.		
	I repent for the ungodly belief that ...	**I repent for the inner vow that I will ...**

UNGODLY BELIEFS WORKSHEET—TO COMPLETE

REPLACE WITH GODLY BELIEFS AND GODLY PURPOSES

	LORD, WHAT WOULD YOU SAY TO REMOVE THIS LIE? **However, God says ...**	I CHOOSE OBEDIENCE TO WHAT YOU, LORD, HAVE SPOKEN TO ME. **So I purpose by the power of the Spirit to...**
1.		
2.		
3.		
4.		
5.		
6.		
7.		
8.		
9.		
10.		
11.		
12.		
13.		
14.		
15.		
16.		
17.		
18.		
19.		
20.		
	I accept what God has spoken that ...	**I purpose by the power of the Holy Spirit to ...**

WHAT IF I GET STUCK?

Underlying principle: Ensure that the basic avenues for receiving God's grace are open and being used!

When you (or your client) are not experiencing healing as you know you should be, determine which avenues for receiving God's grace are being used and which aren't.

YES OR NO
I...
1. Am hearing God's voice and receiving divine vision concerning this problem, journaling it out and doing what God is instructing me to do.
2. Bind demons when attacked with negatives. (e.g., "Satan, I bind you in Jesus' name." "Jesus, I release Your power to handle this situation.")
3. Seek, receive and interpret revelation from God through my dreams concerning this problem.
4. Am healing this heart problem by addressing it using the language of the heart (i.e., emotion, flow, pictures).
5. Have completed a "Contributing Strands Worksheet" concerning this problem.
6. Have prayed through the seven prayers concerning this problem (i.e., "Prayers That Heal the Heart").

7. Have completed a "Biblical Meditation Worksheet" concerning this problem.
8. Have completed an "Impassioned Repentance Worksheet" concerning this problem.
9. Have established divinely-ordained fences of protection in the area of this problem.
10. Have received counsel from those to whom I submit concerning this problem, and am acting upon it.
11. Have confessed this sin to my spiritual counselor and made myself accountable in this area.
12. Am functioning in my divinely-ordained ministry, and am ministering God's life to others.

If you have applied these 12 foundational experiences of Christianity, and are still struggling with unresolved heart issues, then you should seek out a spiritual counselor for additional help.

ALSO AVAILABLE FROM BRIDGE-LOGOS

DIALOGUE WITH GOD
Mark and Patti Virkler

Find out how prayer—our link to God—is the most powerful and vital activity of our life. This book will lead you into a life-changing dimension of two-way communication with our loving GOD.

> *"Dialogue With God has dramatically changed my prayer life. I have found I can dialogue with Christ on a daily basis. I believe this inspired approach to be absolutely essential to the growth of every serious Christian."*
>
> — DR. RICHARD WATSON,
> Dean of the School of Education,
> Oral Roberts University

ISBN: 978-0-88270-620-7

ALSO AVAILABLE FROM BRIDGE-LOGOS

AM I BEING DECEIVED?
Mark and Patti Virkler

Am I Being Deceived? answers questions like:

How can I be spiritual without becoming "New Age"? What does the Bible teach concerning visualization? How do Pharisees react to the move of the Holy Spirit? What does the Bible say about dreams, visions, and imagination? What does the Bible say about faith versus a positive mental attitude?

Learn the answers to these questions and many more. Get rid of the shackles that may be holding you back from true freedom and worship.

ISBN: 978-0-88270-866-9

ALSO AVAILABLE FROM BRIDGE-LOGOS

BEAUTY FROM ASHES
Donna Sparks

In a transparent and powerful manner, the author reveals how the Lord took her from the ashes of a life devastated by failed relationships and destructive behavior to bring her into a beautiful and powerful relationship with Him. The author encourages others to allow the Lord to do the same for them.

Donna Sparks is an Assemblies of God evangelist who travels widely to speak at women's conferences and retreats. She lives in Tennessee.

www.story-of-grace.com

www.facebook.com/
donnasparksministries/

www.facebook.com/
AuthorDonnaSparks/

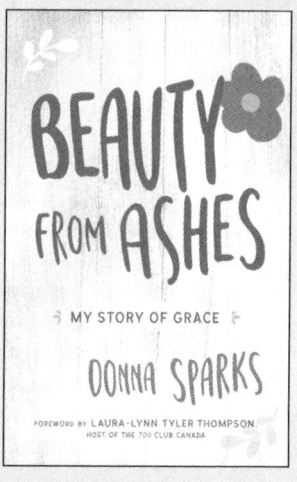

ISBN: 978-1-61036-252-8

BRIDGE LOGOS